TIME·LINE
HISTORY
OF THE
WORLD

TIME·LINE
HISTORY OF THE WORLD

Gordon Kerr

Futura

A Futura Book

First published by Futura in 2007

ISBN: 978-0-7088-0674-6

Produced by Omnipress, UK

Printed in UAE

Futura
An imprint of
Little, Brown Book Group
Brettenham House
Lancaster Place
LondonWC2E 7EN

Photo credits: Getty Images

Contents

Introduction

Time line: History of the World attempts to chronicle all major events from the very beginning of the universe right up to the present day. This was an extremely ambitious undertaking, as everything that has ever happened can be seen as being important in some way. The universal law of cause and effect means that a lone butterfly flapping its wings in Brazil can potentially cause a tornado in Texas. Nothing occurs in isolation, everything is a consequence of something else. In fact a universe in which events are allowed to happen in a vacuum is as inconceivable to the majority of people as the sound of one hand clapping.

Most people's knowledge of the history of the world in which we live is pretty episodic. We piece together fragments learned in school with those we have read in newspapers, books or taken from the internet and television in order to form a jigsaw of the past. This jigsaw is almost completely personal to the individual, and inevitably inaccurate – sometimes drastically so. Many very young children believe that their grandparents grew up in a world of black and white simply because they believe that TV represents the world exactly as it is. They are unable to allow for poetic licence, just as a lot of adults are unable to tolerate the notion that the 25 December was not assigned as Jesus' birthday until 320 years after his birth. No matter what facts they are presented with to prove it.

If we were all born with an awareness of history, and therefore an innate sense of how small our own lives really are, humankind might not have prevailed as it has. Our relationships, jobs and the minutiae of ordinary life might suddenly seem superfluous, or simply not worth bothering about, and if that happened to the population *en masse*, it could spell disaster for our species.

When an unexpected world-altering event happens during our lifetime – such as Chernobyl, the assassination of JFK, or the 9/11 bombings – many of us experience a sudden sharpening of perspective. On the day that Islamic extremists hijacked and crashed two commercial passenger planes into the twin towers of the World Trade Center in New York, many people, including those completely unaffected by the attacks themselves, were suddenly confronted by the reality of their mortality and felt instinctively driven to re-evaluate their lives. It is through major events like these that ordinary people are able to catch a glimpse of the bigger picture – the thread that holds time together.

Time line: History of the World attempts to chronologically document world events. Patterns inevitably evolve and develop over the centuries. One cannot help but notice the same rivalries, jealousies and brutal conflicts appearing again and again throughout the passage of time. The conflicts of Christian versus Muslim, white versus black, Protestant versus Catholic and slave versus oppressor recur with depressing frequency, but alongside the violence and bloodshed astonishing people also appear. What kind of man must Alexander the Great have been? Dead at 33, but emperor of much of the known world. Or Timur, also known as Tamberlane, the great 14th century Mongol warlord, a fascinating and contradictory figure. How much did events in his life coincide with those of other great leaders such as Ghengis Khan, Mahatma Gandhi or Malcolm X?

To know where one is, one must know where one has been. *Time line: History of the World* will help readers to make a little more sense of the confusing world in which we live.

the Ancient World

Big Bang – AD 527

13.7 billion years BC
The Universe begins with the Big Bang.

Big Bang plus 1 second
Hydrogen nuclei begin to form.

Big Bang plus 3 minutes
Nuclear fusion ceases.

Big Bang plus 379,000 years
The first atoms are formed.

4.6 billion
The Sun and planets begin to form.

4.5 billion
A large body crashes into the Earth; debris from it becomes the Moon.

4 billion
An atmosphere consisting of water vapour, carbon dioxide and nitrogen is created on Earth; clouds form.

3.5 billion
Bacteria and algae begin to appear; the first signs of primeval life.

2.5 billion
Oxygen-breathing organisms thrive.

600,000,000
The first animals appear including algae, flatworms and jellyfish.

570,000,000
Complex life forms begin to appear in the oceans.

438,000,000
A probable meteor impact wipes out 85% of the world's marine species.

400,000,000
Marine creatures adapt to living on land, evolving into amphibians and insects.

245,000,000
An unknown event kills around 95% of creatures.

210,000,000
Seventy-five per cent of the Earth's species are rendered extinct, possibly by a meteorite impact.

200,000,000
The first mammals evolve.

65,000,000
A comet or asteroid strikes Mexico's Yucutan Peninsula, wiping out many species, including the dinosaurs, and allowing the mammals to thrive.

4,000,000
Australopityhecines, the earliest hominids, evolve in Africa.

2,500,000
Homo habilis ('skilful man'), the earliest human species, is using stone tools.

1,800,000
Homo erectus has a brain twice the size of earlier species.

1,700,000
Homo erectus leaves Africa.

200,000
The first modern humans (*Homo sapiens*) appear in Africa.

100,000
Modern humans migrate to the Middle East.

75,000 Modern humans arrive in South East Asia and China.

70,000 Neanderthal man is using fire and advanced tools.

60,000 Modern humans arrive by boat in New Guinea and Australia.

45,000 In Africa, the oldest known instrument, the flute, is being played.

40,000 The last Ice Age; *Homo sapiens* arrives in Europe, in the form of Cro-Magnon Man, living alongside Neanderthals.

26,000 In Central Europe, houses are being built with clay roofs.

18,000 The first sculptures are made in Asia.

16,000 Humans cross the Bering Strait to Alaska. On the Russian Steppes, mammoth bones are used to construct dwellings.

14,000 Humans arrive in South America.

12,000 Ceramic arts begin to appear in Japan.

11,500 Clovis culture begins in North America.

10,000 Agricultural development begins in the Yellow River Valley and elsewhere in China.

8400 Dogs are being domesticated.

8000 The population of the world is 5 million. Sheep and cattle are being domesticated.

7250 Catal Hüyük in Anatolia has a population of 6,000; copper smelting and textile manufacture is beginning.

7000 Farming tribes from Anatolia spread into Greece and northwards. There is evidence of a walled settlement at Jericho. Pottery develops and man begins to use metals.

5400 The Badkeramic culture of farmers and potters develops in Europe.

5000 The rising sea level destroys the last land bridge between Britain and Europe.

4400 Horses are domesticated and used for transport and warfare.

4300 The first megalithic tombs are built in western Europe.

4236 The first date in the ancient Egyptian calendar.

4000 The Egyptians use boats with sails. Pottery is being made in Ghana. The rice-farming Yang-shao culture flourishes in China.

3760 The first date in the Jewish calendar.

3750 Fishing villages are beginning to be established in Peru.

3500 The Sumerians use a form of writing and numbering known as cuneiform. The potter's wheel and the kiln are invented in Mesopotamia. The Haida culture begins in Canada. Copper is combined with tin to make bronze.

3200 The emergence of the first civilization in Sumer, in present-day Iraq; a collection of city states along the Euphrates and Tigris rivers.

3100 Menes unites Upper and Lower Egypt, founding the 1st dynasty. Hieroglyphics begin to be used to communicate in Egypt.

3050 The oldest known medical text, known as the Edwin Smith Papyrus, is written.

3000 Around this time, the wheel is invented; Danubian cultures begin to flourish; lake dwellers appear in Europe; Phoenicians settle the Syrian coast; the Egyptians invent papyrus; bricks are first used in Assyrian and Egyptian cultures; the Hittites migrate into Anatolia; the Windmill Hill culture is established in Britain; neolithic villages along the Indus begin to develop into large cities; village life is established in China; settlements form in Louisiana and around the Great Lakes in North America; agriculture is being practised in Mexico, Honduras and El Salvador; the camel is domesticated; the abacus is in use; chariots are being used.

2900
The Deluge, or Great Flood of the Bible, may have occurred around this date. Work begins on constructing Stonehenge in England.

2800 Farming villages are appearing in the Amazon region.
2780 The first pyramid, the Step Pyramid, is constructed at Saqqara.
2750 The legendary Gilgamesh rules Uruk, Sumeria.
2700 Cheops, ruler of Egypt, builds the Great Pyramid at Giza. In China, tea is being drunk and silk is being woven.
2697 The 'Yellow Emperor', Huang-ti comes to power in China.
2660 The beginning of Egypt's Old Kingdom.
2540 The Great Sphinx of Giza is built by King Khafre.
2500 The Beaker culture stretches from the Netherlands to France. Trade routes develop overland between Spain and the Balkans. Egyptians begin to mummify dead royals. The Indus Valley civilization of India emerges. Bronze technology spreads from the East into Europe. Ziggurats, multi-tiered temples, are built in Mesopotamia. The earliest skiers are depicted on a rock carving in Norway. The Chinese invent acupuncture.

Stone tools are being used in Scandinavia. Along the Danube in Europe, the soil is being tilled.
2350 Sargon the Great of Akkad conquers Sumeria and founds the first great empire.The Yao dynasty in China.
2300 The earliest sighting of a comet is recorded in China.
2200 The founding of the Hsia dynasty, in China.
2193 The Akkadian Empire falls.
2180 Egypt's Old Kingdom ends in chaos.
2134 The earliest recorded observation of a solar eclipse.
2100 The Empire of Ur is founded.
2080 Mentuhotep founds Egypt's Middle Kingdom period, until around 1640 BC.
2000 The Bronze Age is under way in northern Europe. Minoan civilization begins on Crete. The earliest recorded observation of a lunar eclipse, at Ur in Mesopotamia. Intensive farming begins in Mesoamerica. The *Epic of Gilgamesh* is written around this time, one of the earliest literary works. Austronesians settle the Pacific islands.
1960 Egypt invades Nubia.

1950 The end of the Empire of Ur.

1925 The Hittites conquer Babylon.

1830 The first dynasty of Babylonian kings is founded.

1800 3,000 standing stones are erected at Carnac in France.

1760 In China, the Shang Dynasty is founded.

1730 The Hyksos found the XVth dynasty in Egypt.

1728 Hammurabi the Great comes to power in Babylon, expanding the Babylonian Empire.

1700 The Chinese of the Shang dynasty develop a writing script.

1600 Stonehenge is completed around this date. Mycenaean civilization emerges in southern Greece. The Minoans use an alphabetic script called Linear A. The Egyptians write a medical book showing the correct workings of the heart.

1570 The New Kingdom in Egypt; the Hyksos are driven out. The Temple of Amun is built at Karnak.

1505 Queen Hatshepsut comes to power in Egypt; she commissions a sculpture of herself as a sphinx.

1500 The Egyptians invent glassmaking and build the earliest known sundial; a 24 letter alphabet is being used by the Egyptians around this time. Aryan-speaking Indo-Europeans are settling in India. Harappan civilization in modern-day Pakistan declines. Olmec culture develops in Mexico. The Jomon period in Japan is at its peak.

1490 The beginning of the expansion of the Egyptian empire, under Tutmosis III, to include Palestine, Syria and Nubia.

1450 Mycenaeans from Greece settle in Anatolia, Sicily and southern Italy; they conquer Crete, ending Minoan civilization.

1420 Egypt enjoys a golden age under Amenhotep.

1400 Knossos, capital of the Minoan civilization on Crete, is destroyed by fire. The cities of Tyre, Sidon and Byblos are thriving centres of trade. The Iron Age has begun in India and western Asia. The Vedas, the earliest Hindu sacred writings, are created in India. Salt is a precious commodity, exchanged for wine, pottery, glass, tin and gold.

1375 The Hittite Empire in Asia Minor becomes powerful, with Suppiluliumas as king.

1366 The Assyrian Empire becomes powerful.

1361 An eclipse of the moon is recorded by Chinese astronomers.

1353 Amenhotep IV introduces sun worship and adopts the name Aknehaton.

1319 Ramases I founds the XIXth dynasty in Egypt.

1313 Ramases' son, Seti, reconquers lost Egyptian lands in Palestine and Syria.

1304 Ramases II, the Great, comes to power in Egypt.

1300 Moses leads the Hebrews out of Egypt to Palestine to establish the kingdom of Israel. Work begins on the rock temples of Abu Simbel.

1298 Ramases II and the Hittites fight the Battle of Qadesh; both claim victory.

1283 Peace is declared between Ramases and the Hittites.

1275 Shalmaneser becomes ruler of Assyria and extends its territory.

1232 Ramases II's son defeats the Israelites.

1200 Proto-Celtic people of Indo-European origin start to settle in Central Europe.The Period of the Judges begins in Israel. There is turmoil in Shang Dynasty China. The Olmec civilization is at its peak in Central America – a complex of pyramids, temples and palaces is built at San Lorenzo.
  Dorian-speaking Greeks are settling on the Peloponnese in Greece. King Tukulti-Ninurta of Assyria defeats the Babylonians. The Olmec sculpt massive stone heads. The Shang dynasty in China is in turmoil.

1190	Troy is destroyed by the Mycenaeans after a long siege.
1188	Ramases III becomes ruler of Egypt.
1180	The Hittite Empire ends around this time.
1175	The Philistines, Greeks, Sardinians and Sicilians join together to invade Egypt; they are defeated by Ramases III.
1174	The Twelve Tribes of Israel agree to support each other.
1173	Babylon is sacked by the Elamites.
1170	Phoenician cities, Tyre in particular, become powerful.
1150	Mycenaean civilization begins to decline.
1140	The first Phoenician colony in North Africa is founded at Utica, in modern-day Tunisia.
1125	Nebuchedrazzar I is king of Babylon.
1116	Tiglathpileser I comes to power in Assyria and conquers Babylon.
1111	Emperor Wu Wang founds the Chou Dynasty in China, establishing a feudal system.
1100	Indo-Europeans – among them the Latin, Sabine and Samnite tribes – are arriving in Italy from the north. Aramaeans from central Syria invade Assyria and Babylon, destroying both. The Olmec in the Americas are manufacturing rubber balls for ball games. The Andean Chavín de Huántar people of South America construct a large temple. Austronesians settle in Tonga and Samoa.
1072	The death of Ramases XI in Egypt brings the New Kingdom to an end. Smendes becomes Pharaoh, founding the XXIst Dynasty.
1050	Samuel becomes king of Israel; Israel is conquered by the Philistines.
1045	The Shang dynasty is replaced by the Zhou dynasty.
1025	Saul becomes king of Israel and leads a successful rebellion against the Philistines.
1000	The population of the world is 50 million. Around this date: In Italy, Proto-Etruscans build city states between the rivers Arno and Tiber; Greeks colonize parts of Asia Minor and start to use iron; Indo-Europeans migrate from Central Asia to Iran; Saul dies in the Battle of Gilboa and is succeeded by David as king of Israel, who captures Jerusalem and makes it his capital; the religious text, the *Rig Veda* is compiled in India; in northern India, regional kingdoms are being created; Zhou kings rule the Central Kingdom in China; Pinto Indians establish settlements in California; Cochise culture flourishes in the modern-day area of New Mexico and Arizona.
961	David dies and is succeeded by his son, Solomon. The Olmec invent the tortilla.
935	Assudan II revives Assyria, re-establishing its ancient boundaries.
922	Solomon is succeeded by his son Rehoboam but Jeroboam rebels against him; the kingdom is split into Judah and Israel.
900	In Italy, Etruscan culture spreads to modern-day Tuscany, Latium and Umbria. The Euboeans, Greek traders, settle on the west coast of southern Italy. The Olmec capital in Mexico is destroyed and a new complex at La Venta takes over.
885	Lycurgus of Sparta creates laws and institutions.
876	Assyria, under Ashurnasipal II, once again becomes a great power in Mesopotamia.
850	Around this time, Homer writes his epic poems, the *Iliad* and the *Odyssey*.
842	An Israelite soldier, Jehu, founds a new dynasty in Israel.
814	The city of Carthage is founded by the Phoenicians in North Africa.
800	The Celts arrive in England. Apollo is worshipped at Delphi in Greece.
783	Jeroboam II presides over a period of prosperity in Israel.
776	The first recorded date for the Olympic Games in Greece.

770 In China, nomads attack the Zhou; China is divided into the Eastern Zhou and Western Zhou kingdoms.

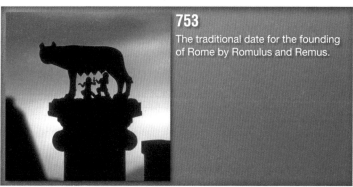

753
The traditional date for the founding of Rome by Romulus and Remus.

750 Carthage is a trade hub for the western Mediterranean. Scythian horsemen sweep into the Crimea, the Dnieper and the Danube regions. The Nubian kingdom of Kush conquers Egypt, ruling for 100 years.

732 The city state of Damascus is conquered by the Assyrians.

721 Israel falls to Assyria; the Jews are exiled. Ethiopian kings rule Egypt in the XXVth Dynasty.

710 The Assyrians destroy the kingdom of Chaldea, situated around the estuaries of the Tigris and Euphrates rivers.

700 Mayan civilization develops. Around this time, China is torn by a power struggle between the Spring and Autumn states. Iron swords become more common in Europe.

689 The Assyrian army destroys Babylon and floods the site.

683 Athens ends its hereditary monarchy.

682 Judah falls to the Assyrians.

663 Assurbanipal's Assyrian army sacks Thebes in Egypt and drives out the Nubians.

650 Sparta defeats Messina in the Second Messenian war.

647 The Assyrians defeat the Elamites in Iran.

626 The Chaldean general, Nabopolassar, becomes king of Babylon and declares independence from Assyria, founding the Chaldean or Neo-Babylonian Empire.

621 Athens' first written laws are introduced by Dracon.

616 The Etruscan, Tarquinus Priscus, becomes king of Rome.

609 The end of the Assyrian Empire.

608 In the Battle of Megiddo, Necho of Egypt defeats and kills Josiah, king of Judah.

605 Nebuchadrezzar II, the Great, becomes king of Babylon and beats Necho at Carchemish in Syria. Judah comes under Babylonian rule.

600 Olmec culture goes into decline. Chinese astronomers create a star map showing 1,460 stars.

594 Solon, the 'father of democracy' becomes sole ruler of Athens, reforming the laws.

587 The Babylonian king, Nebuchadrezzar II, sacks Jerusalem and takes the people of Judah prisoner in Babylon.

580 Nebuchadrezzar begins the construction of the Hanging Gardens of Babylon, one of the Seven Wonders of the World.

563 Prince Siddharta Gautama, the Buddha, is born.

559 Cyrus the Great founds the Persian Empire.

551 K'ung Fu-tzu – Confucius – the Chinese philosopher is born.

546 In the Battle of Sardis, Croesus, the last king of Lydia, is defeated by Cyrus; the Persians overrun Asia Minor.

539	The Greeks defeat the Carthaginians. Cyrus conquers Babylon; Judah and Phoenicia become Persian provinces.
534	Tarquinius Superbus becomes the last king of Rome.
530	Cambyses becomes ruler of Persia.
525	Cambyses conquers Egypt.
522	Darius I becomes ruler of Persia; the Persian Empire is divided into 20 satrapies, or provinces.
520	North-western India is conquered by Persia.
510	In Rome, Tarquinius Superbus is overthrown.
509	The Romans drive the Etruscans out of Rome and establish the Roman Republic.
508	Cleisthenes introduces democracy to Athens. The Etruscan ruler, Lars Porsena, attacks Rome. Rome signs a treaty with Carthage.
500	The population of the world is 100 million. Around this time: Bantu-speaking peoples are spreading in East Africa; the Adena society is creating earthen burial mounds in the eastern part of North America.
499	The Ionians, supported by Athens, rise up against their Persian rulers.
496	The Romans defeat the Latins in battle at Lake Regillus.
494	In Rome the plebeians revolt and gain political rights from the patricians. Darius sacks Miletus, ending the Ionian revolt.
493	Rome signs a treaty with the other countries of the Latin League confederation; they guarantee each other support against the Etruscans.
492	Mardonius leads the first Persian expedition against Athens but a storm destroys his fleet.
490	The second Persian expedition is defeated by the Athenians at the Battle of Marathon.
486	Xerxes I of Persia launches the third Persian expedition, and the Greeks are defeated at Thermopylae; the Greek fleet defeats the Persians at the Battle of Salamis.
480	European Celts begin to migrate to Britain. The Greek natural philosopher, Oenopides measures the tilt of the Earth's axis of rotation.
479	In the Battle of Plataea, the Greek army defeats the Persian army; the Persian fleet is destroyed at Mycale and the invasion ends.
470	Hanno, ruler of Carthage, sails down the African coast as far as Cameroon.
460	The 'Age of Pericles' begins in Athens; a golden age including the promotion of arts and literature and the construction of important buildings. The First Peloponnesian War between Athens and Sparta breaks out (until 451).The Egyptians rebel against Persian rule.
450	Herodotus, the first historian, visits Egypt. The Twelve Tables – wooden tables on which the laws of Rome are written – are created. Confucianism gains popularity among Chinese scholars.
449	Sparta and Athens wage war over who should control the Oracle at Delphi.
447	Work starts on the construction of the Parthenon, completed 432.
446	Sparta and Athens conclude the Thirty Years' Peace.
445	Nehemiah rebuilds the walls of Jerusalem.
440	In Rome, plebeians win the right to marry patricians.
431	The Second Peloponnesian War (until 421).
430	Plague breaks out in Athens. Herodiotus completes *The Histories*.
429	Pericles dies of plague. The Acropolis is completed. Plato is born.
424	Xerxes II of Persia is assassinated; he is succeeded by Darius II.
421	The Peace of Nicias ends fighting between Athens and Sparta.
415	Athens and Sparta go to war again.

411   In Athens, the 'Government of the 5,000' seizes power, but democracy is quickly re-established.

409   Carthage invades Sicily.

407   Athenian general, Alcibiades, subdues a revolt in subject states.

406   The Athenian fleet defeats the Spartans in the Battle of Arginusae.

405   Lysander of Sparta defeats the Athenian fleet off Aegospotami.

404   The Spartans take Athens. The Government of the Thirty Tyrants in Athens.

403   Pausanius restores democracy in Athens. The collapse of the Zhou dynasty in China leads to the Warring States period.

400   The Greeks, under Xenophon, are beaten at Cunaxa; the fighting 'Retreat of the Ten Thousand' follows. Around this time, Zapotec society is developing in the Oaxaca Valley in Mexico.

399   Socrates is condemned to death for heretical teaching.

395   Athens, Thebes, Corinth and Argos form a coalition against Sparta. Lysander of Sparta dies in battle.

394   Sparta defeats the coalition at the Battle of Coronae.

391   The Romans, under the dictator Marcus Furius, conquer the Etruscans.

390   The Gauls sack Rome but fail to capture the Capitol.

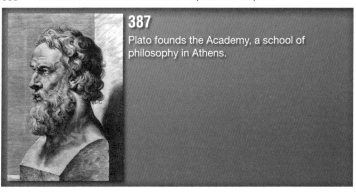

387

Plato founds the Academy, a school of philosophy in Athens.

386   The Spartan ruler, Antalcidas, makes peace with Persia.

385   Greek philosopher, Democritus, claims that the indistinct band of light in the sky at night is a cluster of small stars.

384   The birth of the Greek philosopher Aristotle.

380   The beginning of the last native Egyptian dynasty, the XXXth.

371   The Athenian League is formed by Thebes to combat Sparta.

370   The Athenian League and Sparta make peace.

366   The first plebeian council is elected in Rome.

359   Philip II becomes king of Macedonia.

355   The Third Sacred War begins when the Phocians seize Delphi. Macedonia goes to war with Athens. Alexander the Great is born.

346   The Athenian statesman, Philocrates, sues for peace from Macedonia.

343   Artaxerxes III of Persia conquers Egypt.

339   The start of the Fourth Sacred War. Philip of Macedonia conquers Greece.

336   Philip of Macedonia is assassinated; he is succeeded by his son, Alexander III, the Great.

334   The launch by Alexander of a campaign against Persia; he defeats Darius III at the River Granicus.

333   Alexander defeats Darius at the Battle of Issus and captures Tyre, bringing the Phoenician Empire to a close.

332   Alexander conquers Egypt and founds the city of Alexandria.

331   Alexander defeats Darius at the Battle of Gaugamela, effectively bringing the Persian Empire to an end.

330   Darius III is murdered; Alexander takes control of Persia.

327   Alexander invades India.

326   Alexander wins the Battle of Hydaspes but when his army refuses to advance, he retreats.

323   The death of Alexander; his empire is divided among his generals. Ptolemy becomes satrap of Egypt. The birth of Euclid.

321   The Maurya Dynasty is founded in northern India by Chandragupta.

320   Ptolemy takes Jerusalem; Lybia becomes a province of Egypt.

312   Construction begins of the Appian Way from Rome to Capua.

310   The Etruscans and Samnites attack Rome, but are defeated.

307   Alexander's generals in Greece, among them Antigonus and Demetrius, become kings of their individual territories.

306   A trade treaty is signed between Rome and Carthage.

305   Ptolemy becomes king of Egypt; he is then proclaimed Pharaoh. Seleucis becomes king of Babylon, founding the Seleucid dynasty.

304   Rome makes peace with its enemies and gains territory around Naples. Seleucis gives up his claim on India to Chandragupta in exchange for 500 elephants.

301   Antigonus I dies in battle against Seleucis and his allies; Seleucis rules Syria and Ptolemy rules Palestine.

300   Rome and Carthage sign a treaty. Around this date, the Maya are constructing monumental pyramids; the state of Choson is founded in northern Korea; the first kite is made in China.

290   The Third Samnite War ends in victory for Rome.

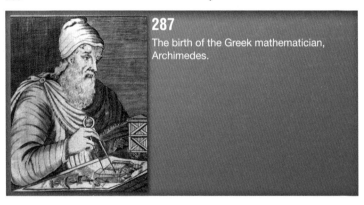

287

The birth of the Greek mathematician, Archimedes.

285   Ptolemy II Philadelphus becomes ruler in Egypt.

280   The library at Alexandria is founded.

276   Antigonus II Gonatus becomes king of Greece.

272   Antigonus defeats an invasion by Pyrrhus of Epirus.

264   The First Punic War between Rome and Carthage ends. Rome holds its first gladiatorial games.

254   Rome captures Panormus in Sicily from Carthage.

250   The Hebrew scriptures are translated into Greek. Around this time, Moche and Nazca societies are developing in Peru.

247   Ptolemy III comes to power in Egypt. Ashoka rules the Maurya Empire in India; he becomes a Buddhist. Devanampiya Tissa, in power in Sri Lanka, also converts to Buddhism.

241   Peace between Rome and Carthage; Sicily, surrendered by Carthage, becomes the first Roman province.

240   Greek scholar, Eratosthenes, accurately measures the Earth's circumference.

238 Carthage begins the conquest of Spain.

225 Rome defeats the Celts at Telamon, in Italy.

223 Antiochus III, the Great, becomes Emperor of Babylonia.

221 Philip V comes to power in Macedonia. Ptolemy IV Philopater becomes ruler of Egypt. In China, the Ch'in Dynasty, from which the country takes its name, is founded.

218 The Second Punic War begins and Carthaginian general, Hannibal, leads his army over the Alps from Spain to invade Italy.

217 Hannibal destroys the Roman army at Lake Trasimene.

216 Hannibal wins at Cannae.

215 Philip of Macedonia attacks Rome in support of Carthage, beginning the First Macedonian War. The Roman general, Marcus Claudius Marcellus, defeats Hannibal at Nola.

214 Marcellus begins the recapture of Sicily from the Carthaginians. Construction of the Great Wall of China begins.

206 Publius Cornelius Scipio the Younger defeats the Carthaginians in Spain. The Han Dynasty is founded in China.

205 The Peace of Phoenice ends the First Macedonian War.

203 Ptolemy V Epiphanes becomes ruler of Egypt; the Rosetta Stone is carved, recording his accession.

200 The Second Macedonian War in which the Greeks, with Roman support, rebel against Macedonian rule; Philip of Macedonia is forced to surrender Greece. Around this date: The Romans invent concrete; the Nazca lines begin to appear in Peru; the Hohokam people of modern-day Arizona begin work on a system of canals.

192 Antiochus III loses the Syrian War to Rome.

185 Around this time, the Mauryan Empire loses central authority in India.

184 The Sunga Dynasty is founded in India by Pushayanitra.

183 Hannibal commits suicide rather than be captured by the Romans.

181 Ptolemy VI becomes ruler of Egypt.

175 Antiochus IV Epiphanes becomes ruler of the Seleucid Empire.

171 The Macedonians under Perseus attack Rome, beginning the Third Macedonian War.

170 Antichus IV invades Egypt and captures Ptolemy IV; Egyptians proclaim his brother Ptolemy VIII Euergetes king; Antiochus withdraws and the brothers rule jointly.

168 The Romans defeat and capture King Perseus of Macedonia at the battle of Pydna, bringing an end to the Antigonid line of Macedonian kings.

167 The Seleucid ruler, Antichus, begins the persecution of the Jews who rebel under Judas Maccabaeus; Jewish worship is restored.

160 Judas Maccabaeus is killed in battle against Syria; his younger brother, Jonathan Maccabaeus, becomes leader of the Jews.

157 Judaea becomes an independent principality.

149 Following the Fourth Macedonian War, Macedonia becomes a Roman province.

146 In the Third Punic War Rome destroys Carthage.

145 Ptolemy VIII Neos Philopater rules Egypt under the regency of his mother, Cleopatra II; the throne is seized by Ptolemy VIII Euergetes who marries Cleopatra II and then her daughter, Cleopatra III.

143 Simon Maccabaeus becomes leader of the Jews.

141 Jersualem is liberated by the Jews and Judaea is declared an independent kingdom.

140 Wu Ti becomes Martial Emperor of China.

135 In the First Servile War, the revolt of Roman slaves in Sicily is crushed.

134 John Hyrcanus, son of Simon Maccabaeus, becomes ruler of Judaea.

116 The Ptolomeic Empire is split, resulting in years of turmoil.

111 War breaks out between Rome and Jugurtha, king of Numidia, in northern Africa.

108 The Celtic Cimbri ravage Gaul. Emperor Wu Ti of China conquers Choson.

106 Gaius Marius is elected consul and is sent to Africa to fight Numidia.

105 The Romans defeat Jugurtha, and bring him to Rome in chains.

104 Aristobulus I becomes king of Judaea. Jugurtha is executed by the Romans.

103 The Second Servile War begins in Rome, lasting until 99 BC. Alexander Jannaeus becomes King of Judaea on the death of Aristobulus.

100 Around this time: Pyramid temples appear in Teotihuacan and elsewhere in Mesoamerica; Sima Qian writes *Records of the Historian*, a history of China; Chinese mathematicians begin to use negative numbers; ice is first used for refrigeration in China.

91 War between Rome and the Italian cities. Civil war breaks out in Rome; Sulla defeats Marius.

89 Under Sulla, Rome gains control of Italy. All Italians are granted Roman citizenship.

88 In the First Mithridatic War, Rome fights against Mithridates IV Eupator, king of Pontus.

87 Sulla defeats Mithridates and conquers Athens.

83 The Second Mithridatic War; Rome invades and conquers Pontus. The death of Emperor Wu Ti in China leads to a period of disorder.

82 Sulla becomes dictator of Rome.

78 The death of Sulla.

76 Salome Alexandra becomes ruler of Judaea.

74 In the Third Mithridatic War, Mithridates annexes Bithnya which is claimed by Rome.

73 Roman general, Lucius Licinius Lucullus, occupies Pontus. Spartacus leads an unsuccessful revolt of slaves and gladiators in the Third Servile War.

67 Hyrcanus II comes to power in Judaea and a civil war starts with his brother, Aristobulus II.

65 Roman general, Pompey the Great, invades Syria and takes Palestine. The birth of the Roman poet, Horace.

63 Pompey captures Jerusalem and annexes Syria and Judaea. Mithridates VI of Syria commits suicide.

61 Gaius Julius Caesar, Governor of Spain, wins his first important victories.

60 The First Triumvirate consisting of Pompey, Crassus and Caesar rules Rome.

58 Caesar is appointed Governor of Gaul.

55 Caesar conquers northern Gaul and stages a failed attempt to invade Britain.

54 Caesar invades Britain for a second time and with more success; Cassivellaunus, a powerful British ruler, agrees to pay tribute to Rome.

53 Crassus dies in battle against the Parthians.

52 Pompey becomes sole Consul of Rome.
Vercingetorix leads a revolt in Gaul which is crushed by Caesar.

51 Caesar completes his conquest of Gaul and writes *De Bello Gallico* about it. Cleopatra VII and her brother Ptolemy XIII jointly rule Egypt.

50 Pompey's supporters try to block Caesar's return to take up the consulship.

49 The Senate forces Caesar to give up his command in Gaul. Caesar crosses the Rubicon into Italy, starting a civil war; Pompey flees to Greece.

48 Caesar defeats Pompey at Pharsalia in Greece; Pompey flees to Egypt and is murdered.

47 Caesar conquers Cleopatra's enemies and she becomes his mistress. Antipater becomes procurator of Judaea and his son, Herod, Governor of Galilee.

46 Caesar returns to Rome with Cleopatra. He defeats Pompey's son, Sextus, in Africa which becomes a Roman province. Caesar becomes Dictator-for-Life of Rome; he introduces the Julian calendar, defeats Sextus in Spain and names his nephew Octavius (Octavian) as his heir.

44 Caesar is assassinated; Marcus Antonius (Mark Anthony) seizes power.

43 The Second Triumvirate is formed by Octavian, Mark Anthony and Marcus Lepidus. Anthony orders the murder of Cicero, the orator.

42 A temple is erected to Caesar in the Forum. In the Battle of Philippi, the Triumvirate defeats Brutus and Cassius who commit suicide.

37 The Triumvirate is renewed for five years. Anthony, already married to Octavian's sister, Octavia, marries Cleopatra in Egypt. Herod the Great becomes king of Judaea.

32 Anthony divorces Octavia; Octavian declares war on Anthony and Cleopatra.

31 Octavian defeats Anthony and Cleopatra in the naval Battle of Actium.

30 Anthony and Cleopatra commit suicide; Octavian proclaims Egypt a Roman province.

27 Octavian, under the title Augustus, is given supreme power by the Senate, although Rome is still nominally a republic. Augustus begins a two-year campaign in Spain to quell rebellion.

23 Augustus adopts the unofficial title of princeps, chief of the republic.

15 The Roman Empire is extended to the Upper Danube.

12 Augustus's stepson, Tiberius Claudius Nero Caesar, crushes revolt in Pannonia.

10 Around this time, the Dead Sea Scrolls are produced.

8 The deaths of the Roman poets Virgil and Horace.

5 The probable year of birth of Jesus of Nazareth at Bethlehem.

4 The death of Herod the Great. His kingdom is split between his sons.

AD 1

The population of the world is 200 million. Jesus is born, according to the Anno Domini era created by Dionysius Exiguus in 525. Ovid writes the poem *Metamorphoses*. Around this date: The great early Mayan city El Mirador, in northern Guatemala, is at its height. Teotihuacan in the Valley of Mexico has a population of more than 40,000.

2 The first census in China shows a population of 57 million.

4 Caesar Augustus summons Tiberius to Rome, and names him his heir and future emperor. The Lex Aelia Sentia regulates the manumission, or liberation, of slaves in the Roman Empire. Nicholas of Damascus writes a 14-volume *History of the World*.

5   Rome acknowledges Cymbeline, king of the Catuvellauni, as king of Britain.

6   The latest possible year of birth of Jesus of Nazareth, based on the Quirinius census in that year. The Zealot movement develops in Judaea, the members of which regard God as their only master.

7   Strabo writes *Geographia* (some claim around AD 18), a work covering the world known to the Romans and Greeks at the time of Emperor Augustus; the only such book to survive from the ancient world.

8   The Roman poet, Ovid, is banished from Rome and exiled to the Black Sea. The invention of paper in China; it is first used by the army.

9   Wang Mang becomes Emperor of China, ending the Han dynasty and founding the Hsin dynasty.

10   The birth of St Peter, one of Jesus' disciples and the first pope.

14   The death of the Roman Emperor, Augustus; Tiberius becomes emperor.

17   The death of Livy, Roman historian. Tacfarinas, the Numidian leader, leads a revolt against Roman government in North Africa.

18   The death of Ovid. Caiaphas becomes high priest in Jerusalem.

25   The baptism of Jesus by John the Baptist. The Han dynasty is restored in China.

26   Pontius Pilate is appointed Prefect of Judaea.

29   John the Baptist is beheaded by King Herod Antipas, perhaps at the whim of Salomé, but more likely for political reasons.

30   The Sermon on the Mount (according to some, although 27 or 28 are also thought possible). The Triumphal Entry of Jesus into Jerusalem on Sunday, March 29 (Palm Sunday). Judas Iscariot, disciple of Jesus, reportedly commits suicide. The crucifixion of Jesus (suggested date, but it is also suggested that he died on April 3, 33). The probable beginning of the pontificate of St Peter (until 64).

32   The conversion to Christianity of Saul (Paul) of Tarsus.

33   A financial crisis hits Rome; many aristocratic families are ruined.

37   Caligula becomes Emperor of Rome.

39   The Trung sisters establish a short-lived autonomous state in Vietnam.

40   Mauretania – modern-day Morocco and north-western Algeria – is annexed by Rome.

41   Caligula is assassinated by his Praetorian Guards. Claudius becomes emperor. The disciples of Jesus are called Christians for the first time.

43

Roman Emperor Claudius invades Britain; Romans found the cities of London, then known as Londinium, and Peterborough, and begin to construct a road that later becomes Ermine Street. Mark the Evangelist becomes the first Orthodox Patriarch of Alexandria, thus establishing the Christian Church in Africa. Vietnam becomes a province of China.

46   A census shows that there are more than 6,000,000 Roman citizens. The Romans build the first London Bridge.

48   The 300-year-old Central Asian Hsiung-nu Empire dissolves.

50   Roman Emperor Claudius adopts Nero Claudius Caesar Drusus as his son. Londinium takes over from Colchester as capital of the local Roman province. Hero of Alexandria invents a steam turbine. The

kingdom of Axum is founded in Ethiopia. The Kushan Empire controls the north of India. Around this date, Buddhism arrives in China. Nazca culture flourishes along the coast of Peru.

51 Caractacus, a British resistance leader, is captured and taken to Rome.

54 The death of Claudius; Nero succeeds him as Emperor of Rome.

55 The apostle Paul writes his First Epistle to the Corinthians.

56 War between Rome and Parthia. Paul writes his Second Epistle to the Colossians (probable date).

57 Accession of the Chinese Emperor, Han Ming-Ti.

58 Paul, imprisoned in Caesarea, revokes his Roman citizenship and is sent to Rome to be judged; he writes his Epistle to the Romans. Ming-Ti, new Emperor of China, introduces Buddhism to China and the West Indus Valley.

59 Petronius pokes fun at Roman immorality in the *Satyricon*.

60 Boudicca, Queen of the Iceni, leads a rebellion against the Romans in Britain.

61 Boudicca is defeated in the Battle of Watling Street and killed by the Roman governor, Suetonius Paulinus. A Roman force explores the Nile Valley as far as Sudan.

62 An earthquake damages cities in Calabria, including Pompeii.

64 The Great Fire of Rome destroys half the city; Emperor Nero allegedly plays his lyre and sings while watching the blaze from a safe distance.

66 Halley's Comet is visible. The Great Jewish Revolt against the Romans ends with the destruction of the Temple in Jerusalem.

67 Pope Linus succeeds St Peter as the second pope. The apostles, Saints Peter and Paul are possibly martyred in the same year.

68 Nero commits suicide.

69 Civil war in the Roman Empire; the 'Year of the Four Emperors' ends with Vespasian in power. A bridge suspended by iron chains is built in China.

The building of the White Horse Temple signals the official arrival of Buddhism in China.

72 Work begins on the Colosseum in Rome.

76 Wales is annexed by Rome.

77 Agricola, Governor of England, extends Roman influence to the mouth of the Clyde. A Roman squadron explores the north of Scotland, as far as the Orkney and Shetland Islands. The Romans develop a simple method of distillation.

78 The base year (year zero) of the Saka era used by some Hindu calendars, the Indian national calendar, and the Cambodian Buddhist calendar. The philosopher Wang Chong (Wang-Tchoung) claims all phenomena have material causes.

79 Titus succeeds his father, Vespasian, as Roman Emperor. The eruption of Mount Vesuvius destroys Pompeii and Herculaneum, killing many, including author and philosopher, Pliny the Elder. Gnaeus Julius Agricola enters Scotland but is resisted by the Caledonians. In China, a commission of scholars compiles the text of works by Confucius and his school.

80 The Colosseum amphitheatre in Rome is completed. The original Pantheon in Rome is destroyed by fire. Around this date, the Gospel of Luke and Acts are written.

81 Domitian succeeds his brother Titus as Roman Emperor.

90 The Gospel of John is written.

96 The Book of Revelation is written (traditional date). A schism in Buddhism creates a new, popular religion in India, Mahâyâna (Grand Vehicle).

97 Chinese troops reach the Caspian Sea.

98 Trajan, a brilliant soldier and administrator, becomes the first emperor from a Roman province, Italica, near Seville in Spain.

99 Mirrors made of glass, backed with a tin sheet, replace previous efforts made entirely of metal.

100 Lions are extinct in Europe by this date. Bricks become the primary building material in the Roman Empire. The compilation of the *Kama Sutra* begins in India. In China, paper becomes the main medium for written communication and the wheelbarrow makes its first appearance. Teotihuacan, in what is now Mexico, has a population of 50,000. Around this date: The beginnings of the Moche civilization in Peru; Hopewell culture flourishes on the upper Mississippi, around what is now Ohio; the development of Mogollon culture in the south-western United States; the first magnetic compass is used in China.

104 The death of the Roman poet, Martial.

109 The Christian Church proclaims itself to be universal (catholic).

110 The Gospel of John is written in Asia Minor.

113 The death of Pliny the Younger, Roman lawyer and scientist.

115 The Jewish community in Cyrenaica (north-eastern Libya) revolts against the Roman administration. Alexandria in Egypt is destroyed during the Jewish–Greek civil wars.

117 Emperor Trajan is succeeded by Hadrian, another Spaniard.

118 The Roman Forum, commissioned by Trajan, is finished.

120 Emperor Hadrian visits Britain where the Foss Dyke is being constructed. The Greek historian Plutarch dies. Kushan king, Kanishka, takes control of large areas of northern India and Pakistan. The invention of the seismograph by Zhang Heng, in China.

121 Hadrian fixes the border between Roman Britain and Caledonia on a line running from the River Tyne to the Solway Firth.

122
Work begins on the construction of Hadrian's Wall to defend the Roman province of Britain from invasion from the north.

123 In Ireland, Mug Nuadat defeats the Irish king, Conn of the Hundred Battles. Chinese scientist, Zhang Heng, corrects the calendar to bring it into line with the seasons.

125 Reconstruction work begins on the Pantheon in Rome.

130 The death of the satirist, Juvenal. Basra becomes the capital of Arabia.

134 The opening of the Athenaeum, a university of rhetoric, law and philosophy in Rome.

138 The death of the Roman Emperor, Hadrian; Antoninus Pius succeeds him.

142 Construction of the Antonine Wall begins in Scotland.

150	The construction of the Great Pyramid of the Sun in Teotihuacan, the tallest pre-Colombian building in the Americas. Around this time, the earliest atlas, Ptolemy's *Geography*, is compiled.
151	Mytilene and Smyrna are destroyed by an earthquake.
155	The Romans begin to abandon Hadrian's Wall.
160	In Rome, soap containing grease, lime and ashes is manufactured. The first Buddhist monks appear in China.
161	Marcus Aurelius succeeds Antoninus Pius as Emperor.
166	The end of the war between Rome and Parthia. Plague lays waste to the Roman Empire.
168	The death of Ptolemy, Greek astronomer and astrologer.
170	Marcus Aurelius orders humane treatment for Christians and slaves throughout the Empire.
180	The death of Marcus Aurelius brings an end to the long period of peace known as the Pax Romana. The Goths reach the banks of the Black Sea. A long smallpox epidemic sharply decreases the population of Rome.
181	The Lake Taupo Volcano in New Zealand erupts; the effects are seen as far away as Rome and China.
184	In China, a rebellion by the Yellow Turban sect, a peasant movement, weakens the Han dynasty.
185	In India, Vasudeva becomes Kushan Emperor. Chinese astronomers make the earliest identification of a supernova.
190	A Roman road crosses the Alps by the Simplon Pass. Cleomedes teaches that the moon reflects sunlight and does not glow on its own. The rise of the Hindu Chola kingdom near Tanjore in southern India.
193	Pertinax becomes Roman Emperor but is assassinated by the Praetorian Guard, who then sell the throne in an auction to Didius Julianus. When he, too, is assassinated, a Lybian, Septimus Severus, takes over.
195	In China, the Xiongnu federation crosses the Great Wall and establishes itself in Shanxi province.
197	Roman troops capture and sack Byzantium and retake Mesopotamia.
200	The population of the world is 257 million. Roman Emperor Septimius Severus builds a chain of forts and trenches in order to strengthen frontier defences in North Africa. Around this date, major construction begins at the city of Tiahuanaco, close to Lake Titicaca in Bolivia.
202	A Roman law bans female gladiators.
210	The Romans make peace with the Scots after suffering heavy losses invading Scotland.
211	Roman Emperor Septimus Severus dies in York; he is succeeded by his sons, Caracalla and Geta.
212	All free-born people within the Roman Empire are granted Roman citizenship.
220	The Goths invade Asia Minor and the Balkans. The end of the Han dynasty in China, followed by the Three Kingdoms (Wei, Wu and Shu) and the Jin dynasty.
221	Liu Bei, a Chinese warlord and a descendant of the royal family of the Han Dynasty, proclaims himself Emperor. The Shu Han Kingdom is established.
222	The kingdom of Wu is established in China.
224	Around this date, Parthian power comes to an end in the Persian Empire.
225	The first Christian paintings appear in Rome, decorating the Catacombs. Ardashir I is crowned 'King of Kings' of Persia, beginning the 400-year reign of the Sassanid Empire.
226	In Ireland the rule of High King Cormac mac Airt begins.

230	Ardashir I of Persia invades the Roman province of Mesopotamia and Roman Emperor Alexander travels east to fight him.
235	Civil war and chaos cripple the Roman Empire until 284 as 26 claimants to the imperial throne vie for power.
238	Origenes publishes The Old Testament in five languages. Revolt in Africa against Roman rule begins a half-century of unrest.
239	In the Chinese kingdom of Wei, Wei Qi Wang succeeds Wei Ming Di.
241	Shapur I succeeds Ardashir I as king of Persia.
242	The Roman Emperor Gordian III evacuates the Cimmerian cities in the Bosphorus; the territory is now controlled by the Ostrogoths.
243	Gordian III defeats Shapur I of Persia in the battle of Resaena. Sun Liang becomes emperor of the Chinese kingdom of Wu.
247	The first Gothic invasion of the Roman Empire takes place. Civil War begins in Japan.
249	Decius, proclaimed emperor by the army, defeats and kills incumbent Emperor Philip the Arab at Verona.
250	The Goths invade Moesia in the areas of present-day Serbia and Bulgaria. The classic period of Mayan civilization begins in Guatemala, Honduras and eastern Mexico.
251	In the Battle of Abrittus, the Goths defeat the Romans; joint-emperors Decius and Herennius Etruscus are killed. A 15-year plague begins in the Roman Empire.
253	The period of the Thirty Tyrants in the Roman Empire; generals in the border regions are declared emperors by their troops. The Goths invade Asia Minor and appear at the walls of Thessalonica.
256	The Franks cross the Rhine; the Alamanni reach Milan; cities in the Roman Empire begin to build walls as the defence of its frontiers begins to crumble.
258	Gaul, Britain and Spain separate from the Roman Empire; they form the Gallic empire.
260	Roman Emperor Valerian is defeated and captured by Shapur I of Persia. Nanjing University is founded in Nanjing, China.
262	The Goths burn down the original Temple of Artemis at Ephesus.
263	The Wei kingdom conquers the kingdom of Shu Han, one of the Chinese Three kingdoms.
264	Sun Hao succeeds Sun Xiu as ruler of the Chinese kingdom of Wu.
265	Gallienus, Roman co-emperor with his father Valerian, repels the invasion of the Goths in the Balkans. Emperor Wu of Jin becomes the Jin dynasty's first emperor.
267	The Goths launch one of the first major barbarian invasions of the Roman Empire.
268	Gallienus defeats the Goths at the Battle of Naissus.
269	The library at Alexandria is burned down during a raid by Zabdas, a general of Zenobia, queen of the Palmyrene Empire in Syria.
270	A serious economic crisis strikes the Roman Empire; inflation soars to 1,000% in some areas.
271	The Aurelian walls around Rome are built (finished in 276). The first use of a magnetic compass in China.
272	Saint Denis, the first bishop of Paris, and two of his disciples are beheaded near a hill later called Montmartre, the Mountain of the Martyrs.
274	The Gallic empire is reconquered by Roman Emperor Aurelian. The Roman Empire is united again. The Jin dynasty conquers the Eastern Wu dynasty in China.
280	The Germanic tribe, the Thuringii, appears. The kingdom of Wu is dissolved by Jin, finally ending the Three Kingdoms period of China.
284	Diocletian, Emperor of Rome introduces major reforms including a tetrarchy; four emperors ruling the Empire together.

290   Jin Hui Di succeeds Jin Wu Di as Emperor of China.

300   Around this date: The Franks penetrate northern Belgium; the elephant becomes extinct in North Africa; the Bantu in south-east Africa begin to herd cattle, having been cereal farmers; the Mayans create a system of writing and develop a calendar.

301   Armenia becomes the first nation to accept Christianity as its state religion.

304   The Hun Liu Yuan establish the Han kingdom, beginning the Sixteen Kingdoms era in China.

305   The Council of Illiberis decrees that priests must be celibate.

306   Christianity is established in Britain. The Civil War of the Eight Princes, started in 291 ends.

307   Jin Huai Di becomes Emperor of China.

311   Luoyang, capital of China, is sacked by barbarians under the leadership of the Huns; the emperor is captured.

312   The Roman Emperor Constantine acknowledges Christianity as the Roman religion.

313   Constantine issues the Edict of Milan, ending all persecution of Christians in the Roman Empire.

315   Crucifixion is abolished as a punishment in the Roman Empire. The Arch of Constantine is completed in Rome.

316   The Xiongnu sack Chang'an, capital of the Chinese Western Jin Dynasty. Jin Mindi, the emperor, surrenders, bringing the dynasty to an end.

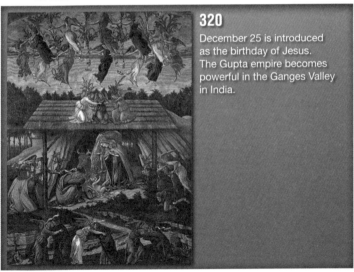

320
December 25 is introduced as the birthday of Jesus. The Gupta empire becomes powerful in the Ganges Valley in India.

324   Constantine defeats Licinius at the Battle of Chrysopolis, and becomes sole Emperor of Rome, thus ending the Tetrarchy. St Peter's Church in Rome is founded.

326   Constantine I founds Constantinople and incorporates Byzantium into the new city.

330   Constantine I moves the capital of the Roman Empire from Rome to Byzantium, later known as Constantinople. Bishop Frumentius begins his conversion of the kingdom of Axum in Ethiopia-Eritrea to Christianity.

332   Emperor Constantine I defeats the Visigoths in battle; they become Roman allies.

337   The death of Constantine I.

340   Constantine's sons, Constans and Constantius II, split the Roman Empire between them.

349   The Mou-jong (proto-Mongols) take control of the north of China.

350   Emperor Constans is killed by Magnentius, who is proclaimed emperor. Kushite civilization is brought down by invasion from the kingdom of Axum.

351   In India, a new process makes it possible to extract sugar from sugar cane.

352   The Germanic tribes, the Alamanni and the Franks, defeat the Roman army, taking control of 40 towns between the Moselle and the Rhine.

353   Constantius II defeats Magnentius and becomes sole Roman Emperor.

356   The worship of non-Christian images is banned in the Roman Empire and Constantius II orders the closure of all pagan temples. Work begins on the first basilica of St Peter in Rome.

360   Around this time: Early invasions of Europe by Huns from Central Asia; the first invasions of Britain by the Saxons.

361   Julian becomes Roman Emperor and tries to restore paganism. Emperor Ai succeeds Emperor Mu in China.

362   Emperor Julian invades Persia, but is forced to retreat.

363   Julian attacks Persia with an army of 90,000 men and is killed in the fighting. Jovian is declared Emperor. The Huns reach the Caspian Sea.

364   Jovian surrenders Mesopotamia to the Persians and dies shortly after; Valentinian I becomes Emperor, with co-emperor Valens. The Council of Laodicea decides the doctirine of the Christian Church and the contents of the Bible.

365   Emperor Fei succeeds Emperor Ai in China.

366   The Alamanni invade the Roman Empire.

367   The Great Conspiracy: an assault featuring Saxons, Irish and Attacotti combines with a revolt of the garrison on Hadrian's Wall to devastate Roman Britain. St Athanasius of Alexandria is the first person to list the 27 books of the New Testament.

368   Count Theodosius quashes the Great Conspiracy in Britain. Valentinian defeats the Alemanni along the Empire's border, at the Rhine.

369   Shapur II, the Persian king, occupies the pro-Roman kingdom of Armenia.

370   The Ostrogoths are conquered by the Huns. The Huns destroy the empire of the Alans and cross the Volga and the Don.

372   Valentinian I defeats the small Germanic tribe, the Quadi, and the Sarmates and crushes the Moors in Africa. Emperor Fei of China is dethroned and replaced by Jianwen. Emperor Xiaowu, in turn, succeeds Jianwen.

374   Spearthrower Owl becomes Emperor of Teotihuacan.

375   The death of Valentinian I. Gratian and Valentinian II become Roman Emperors. The *Talmud of Babylon* – approximately 2.5 million words on 5,894 pages – is written by Rav Ashi. The first two Korean Buddhist temples are built.

376   The Huns arrive on the Roman frontier. The beginning of the reign of Chandragupta II, king of India.

377   Persian King Shapur II pushes the Huns back across the Caucasus. The Chinese painter Gu Kaizhi paints his work *The Goddess of the Lo River*.

378   The Visigoths defeat the Romans at Adrianople; Emperor Valens is killed in the battle.

379   Niall becomes king of Ireland. Theodosius I becomes Roman Emperor at Sirmium; Gratianus refuses the title of Eastern Emperor. Ardeshir II becomes king of Persia.

380 Theodosius I declares Christianity to be the official religion of the Roman Empire. The invasion of the Roman Empire by the Vandals. The annexation of the western provinces by Indian King Gupta gives him control over commerce with Europe and Egypt. The Vulgate, a translation in Latin of the Bible by St Jerome, is published.

382 Theodosius I concludes a peace treaty with the Visigoths, allowing them to settle south of the Danube. Alaric I becomes king of the Visigoths.

383 Arcadius becomes Emperor of Rome; Roman troops in Britain declare Magnus Maximus to be their emperor, as do Gaul, the Italian provinces and Hispania. Shapur III becomes king of Persia. In Mexico, the Toltecs are constructing the tallest pyramids on earth. In China, in the Battle of Feishui, the Jin dynasty defeats the former Qin dynasty.

384 King Chimnyu becomes king of Baekje in Korea and declares Buddhism the official religion.

385 Copper extraction and casting begins in Kansanshi, on the border of Zaire and Zambia in southern Africa.

386 Theodosius I of Rome makes peace with Persia; they divide Armenia between them. Magnus Maximus invades Italy, driving out Valentinian II, who takes refuge with Theodosius. The conversion of St Augustine. The beginning of the Northern Wei Dynasty in China. A period of division between the north and the south of China (until 589).

387
The birth of St Patrick, patron saint of Ireland.

388 Magnus Maximus is defeated at the Battle of the Save, and Valentinian II is restored as Western Roman Emperor. Bahram IV becomes king of Persia.

389 Pagan buildings in Alexandria, including the library, are destroyed on the order of Theodosius.

390 Rudrasena becomes emperor of Vakataka in the Deccan Plateau of India. The *Kama Sutra* is revised by Vatsyayana.

391 Theodosius establishes Christianity as the official state religion of the Roman Empire, making the worship of other gods illegal.

392 Arbogast, a Frankish general, nominates Eugenius as Emperor of the Western Roman Empire, after assassinating Valentinian II.

393 Emperor Theodosius I outlaws the Olympic Games; they have been held for 1,000 years. Gao Zu succeeds Tai Zu as Emperor of the Later Qin Empire in China.

394 Emperor Theodosius I defeats and kills Eugenius and Arbogast at the Battle of the Frigidus.

395	The death of Theodosius I; the empire is divided into East and West. Arcadius becomes Eastern Emperor; Honorius becomes Western Emperor. Alaric, the Visigoth king, goes to war against the Roman Empire. St Augustine becomes Bishop of Hippo Regius.
396	The Romans enlist the Franks and the Alemanni to defend the Rhine border. The Huns occupy the Romanian plains of Pannonia. The Eleusinian Mysteries come to an end, as Alaric I destroys the ancient sites in Greece. Emperor An succeeds Emperor Xiaowu as ruler of the Chinese Jin Dynasty.
397	The Berber prince, Gildo, foments a rebellion against the Roman Emperor Honorius
399	Yazdegerd I becomes king of Persia. Chinese Buddhist historian, Fa-Hien, begins his journey through India and Sri Lanka, written about in his work, *A Record of Buddhistic Kingdoms, Being an Account by the Chinese Monk Fa-Hien of his Travels in India and Ceylon in Search of the Buddhist Books of Discipline*.
400	The population of the world reaches 206 million. The first invasion of Italy by Alaric. Around this date: The Franks establish themselves in northern Holland; the Vandals start to move westward from Dacia and Hungary; the use of iron spreads through eastern Africa; construction begins at Great Zimbabwe, an ancient South African city; the Gupta empire grows until it controls all of India; Buddhist scriptures are translated into Chinese; the Zapotec state with its capital at Monte Alban flourishes in southern Mexico; chrysanthemums are introduced to Japan. Persian astronomers invent the astrolabe.
401	The Visigoths attack northern Italy. *The Mahabharata*, one of the two major Sanskrit epics of ancient India, is completed. The Visigoths are defeated at the Battle of Pollentia.
402	The Avars, led by Shelun, establish a nomadic empire that ranges from Mongolia to the Irtysh.
404	The last gladiatorial competition takes place in Rome.
405	The Armenian alphabet is invented by Mesrob Mashdots, an Armenian monk.
406	Roman legions in Britain mutiny against Honorius and select Marcus as their new Emperor; he is assassinated and replaced by Gratianus. Stained glass is used for the first time in churches in Rome.
407	Gratianus is assassinated, and Constantine III takes over the Roman garrison in Britain; he leads the Roman military units from Britain to Gaul, occupying Arles, generally seen as Rome's withdrawal from Britain. The Vandals invade Gaul.
408	Constantine III captures Hispania. Theodosius II succeeds his father, Arcadius, as Emperor of the Eastern Roman Empire; the Huns attack the Eastern Empire, but are repulsed.
409	The Vandals, Alans and Suevi break through Constantine III's garrisons and take Hispania. The Visigothic king, Alaric I, lays siege to Rome for a second time; he sets up Priscus Attalus as Western Emperor. There is famine in Hispania, Gaul and the Italian Peninsula.
410	The Visigoths sack Rome.
412	The Visigoths move into the south of Gaul, led by Ataulf, successor to Alaric.
413	Kumara Gupta I succeeds his father Chandragupta as ruler of the Gupta Empire.
415	The Visigoths leave Gallia Narbonensis and invade Hispania. The Jews are expelled from Alexandria. Krakatoa erupts.
419	Emperor Gong succeeds Emperor An as ruler of the Chinese Jin dynasty.

420 Bahram V succeeds Yazdegerd as king of Persia. The Jin Dynasty ends in China; Liu Yu (Emperor Wu of Liu Song) is the first ruler of the Song Dynasty.

421 Constantius III becomes joint-emperor of the Western Empire.

423 On the death of Honorius, Joannes, a senior civil servant, seizes the throne of the Western Roman Empire, and is declared Emperor.

424 Song Wen Di succeeds Song Shao Di as ruler of the Chinese Song Dynasty.

425 Valentinian III becomes Western Roman Emperor.

426 King Gunderic of the Vandals also becomes king of the Alans.

428 Geiseric becomes king of the Vandals and Alans.

430 St Patrick reaches Ireland on his missionary expedition. Feng Ba is succeeded by Feng Hong as emperor of the Northern Yan, one of the states vying for control of China.

434 Aëtius, a general in the service of Emperor Valentinian III, takes power in Rome, holding it for 20 years. Attila the Hun, with his brother Bleda, gains control over the Hun tribes.

436
Attila the Hun attacks Burgundy, wiping out the royal family.

438 Yazdegerd II becomes king of Persia.

439 Carthage falls to the Vandals. North China is united under the Northern Wei Dynasty; the era of the Northern Dynasties begins.

440 Geiseric, king of the Vandals, captures Sicily. Bodhidharma, the founder of Zen Buddhism, is born.

443 The Burgundians create a kingdom on the banks of the Rhône.

445 Attila the Hun attacks Western Europe.

447 The first English kingdom is created when Thanet is granted by Vortigern, the ruler of the Britons, to the Saxon leader Hengist. Attila the Hun meets the Romans in the indecisive Battle of the Utus. The Huns invade the Balkans as far as Thermopylae.

450 Saxons, Angles and Jutes invade Britain. Marcian is proclaimed Eastern Emperor by Aspar and Pulcheria. Around this date, the Huaca del Sol, the largest adobe structure in the Americas, is built.

451 Attila is defeated at Chalons by Western Roman general, Aëtius. The Council of Chalcedon formalizes Christian orthodoxy. At the Battle of Vartanantz, the Armenian army is defeated by the Persians.

452 Attila invades Italy but dies. Tai Wu Di is succeeded by Nan An Wang, and then by Wen Cheng Di as ruler of the Northern Wei Dynasty in China.

453 Theodoric II succeeds his brother, Thorismund, as king of the Visigoths.

454 Emperor Valentinian III assassinates Aëtius in Ravenna.

455 Valentinian III is murdered by former soldiers of Aëtius, in revenge for Valentinian's killing of Aëtius the previous year. Petronius Maximus becomes Emperor but is later killed by an angry mob; Roman military commander Avitus is proclaimed Emperor. Rome is plundered by the Vandals. The Ostrogoths conquer Pannonia and Dalmatia. Skandagupta succeeds Kumaragupta as ruler of the Gupta Empire.

456 St Patrick returns to Ireland as a missionary bishop.

457 Four thousand Britons are slain at Crayford in battle against Hengist and his son Oisc. Majorian is declared Western Roman Emperor, while Leo I becomes emperor in the east. Childeric I succeeds Merovech as king of the Franks. Hormizd III becomes king of Persia.

460 Emperor Majorian is defeated by the Visigoths. The Coptic Church splits from the Orthodox Church of Alexandria. The Hepthalites conquer the Kushans and enter India.

461 Majorian resigns and Libius Severus becomes Emperor.

462 The Statue of Zeus, one of the Seven Wonders of the Ancient World, is destroyed by fire after being moved to Constantinople.

465 Song Qian Fei Di and then Song Ming Di become rulers of the Song Dynasty in China.

466 Emperor Leo I repels the Hun invasion of Dacia. Euric succeeds his brother Theodoric II as king of the Visigoths.

467 Anthemius becomes Western Roman Emperor.

471 Xiao Wen Di succeeds Xian Wen Di as ruler of the Chinese Northern Wei Dynasty.

472 General Ricimer proclaims Olybrius Emperor, and places Rome, where Western Emperor Anthemius is located, under siege; Anthemius is slain fleeing the city.

473 Glycerius is named Western Emperor. Gundobad becomes king of the Burgundians.

474 Julius Nepos becomes Western Roman Emperor, deposing Glycerius. Leo II briefly becomes Eastern Emperor and on his death Zeno takes over, concluding a treaty with the Vandals that ends 45 years of war.

475 Emperor Zeno is forced to flee Constantinople. Basiliscus is acclaimed Eastern Emperor in Constantinople. The Talmud, the source of the majority of Jewish religious law, is completed. Bodhidharma travels to China.

476
The date regarded as representing the fall of the Roman Empire; the last Western Emperor, Romulus Augustus, is expelled by the Germanic invader Odoacer who occupies the city. Zeno is restored as the Eastern Roman Emperor.

477 Huneric becomes king of the Vandals. Song Shun Di succeeds Song Hou Fei Di as ruler of the Chinese Song Dynasty.

478
The first Shinto shrines are built in Japan.

479 The end of the Song Dynasty and beginning of the Southern Qi Dynasty in southern China; Qi Gao Di is the first ruler of the Qi Dynasty.

480 Odoacer defeats an attempt by Julius Nepos to recapture Italy; Julius is killed. Narasimhagupta Baladitya succeeds his father Skandagupta as ruler of the Gupta Empire.

481 Clovis I becomes king of the Franks upon the death of Childeric I.

482 Qi Gao Di becomes ruler of the Chinese Southern Qi Dynasty.

484 Alaric II succeeds Euric as king of the Visigoths. Gunthamund becomes king of the Vandals.

486 Roman rule in Gaul ends with the defeat at Soissons of the Roman governor Syagrius by the Franks under Clovis I.

488 Hengist dies and is succeeded by his son Oisc as king of Kent. Theodoric the Great becomes king of the Ostrogoths and invades Italy. The Gothic tribe, the Gepids, capture Belgrade. Kavadh I succeeds Balash in Persia.

489 Theodoric defeats Odoacer at the battles of Isonzo and Verona, forcing his way into Italy. Large Buddhist temples are built in China; the first Confucian temple is constructed in northern China.

490 Odoacer's army surrenders to Theodoric the Great in Milan.

491 Ælle, the first king of the south Saxons, besieges and conquers the fortified town of Anderitum in southern Britain. Anastasius I becomes ruler of the Byzantine Empire.

493 St Patrick dies; the Battle for the Body of St. Patrick is fought. Odoacer makes peace with Theodoric the Great, but is later killed by him.

494 Pope Gelasius canonizes St George. An earthquake devastates Latakia in Syria.

495 Cerdic of Wessex raids Hampshire.

496 Clovis I defeats the Alamanni in the Battle of Tolbiac and accepts Catholic baptism at Rheims. Thrasamund becomes king of the Vandals. Kavadh I of Persia is deposed and exiled by his brother Djamasp. The ruling Tuoba family in the Chinese Northern Wei Dynasty change their family name to Yuan.

497 The Alemanni are defeated by the Franks under Clovis I near Bonn. Aryabhata, an Indian astronomer and mathematician, calculates pi (ϖ) to be: 62832/20000 = 3.1416, correct to four rounded-off decimal places.

499 Kavadh I of Persia deposes his brother Djamasp and regains the throne of Persia. Indian astronomer, Aryabhatra, invents the number zero.

500 Ostrogoth Theodoric becomes ruler of what remains of the Roman Empire in Italy. The Visigoths rule Spain. Emperor Xuanwu of Northern Wei China becomes sovereign of the Northern Wei Dynasty. Around this date: The Battle of Mons Badonicus in which Romano-British and Celts defeat an Anglo-Saxon army; the beginning of the Heptarchy (seven kingdoms) period in England; the Kingdom of Wessex is founded; the legendary king of Dál Riata, Fergus Mór, begins his reign in Scotland; the monument of Ale's Stones is built in Sweden; the Ghanaian Empire becomes the most important power in West Africa; the Huns, a nomadic Central Asian people, destroy the powerful Gupta Empire of India; instability in China; the Thule people move into Alaska; Hopewell culture in northern America builds elaborate burial mounds, makes pottery, and uses iron weapons; Polynesians, originating in South-East Asia, settle in the Hawaiian Islands and on Easter Island, and continue to travel eastwards.

501 Qi He Di succeeds Qi Dong Hun Hou as the ruler of the Chinese Southern Qi Dynasty.

502 The Southern Qi Dynasty in southern China ends and the Liang Dynasty is founded; Liang Wu Di succeeds Qi He Di.

503 War breaks out between the Byzantine Empire and Persia, lasting until 557.

504 Theodoric the Great defeats the Gepids.

506 The Breviary of Alaric, a collection of Roman law, is compiled by order of Alaric II, king of the Visigoths.

507 The West Saxons invade Dumnonia, a Brythonic kingdom in south-west England and defeat the West Welsh at Llongborth. They also slay a powerful British king named Natanleod at the Battle of Netley. Clovis I defeats the Visigoths near Poitiers, ending Visigothic power in Gaul. Gesalec succeeds his father Alaric II as king of the Visigoths.

508 Clovis I establishes Paris, known as Lutetia, as his capital

511 The Frankish kingdom is split in four after the death of Clovis I. Childebert I becomes king of Paris; Clotaire I king of Soissons; Chlodomer king of Orléans, and Theuderic I king of Rheims and Austrasia.

512

The birth of St David, patron saint of Wales. The earliest known dated text in the Arabic alphabet, is written at Zebed in Syria. The island nation of Usanguk is conquered by the Korean Silla Dynasty general, Lee Sabu.

516 Sigismund becomes king of Burgundy.

518 Justin becomes Byzantine Emperor.

519 Cerdic becomes king of Wessex.

520 The kingdom of East Anglia is created. Bodhidharma arrives in China.

522 Amalaric becomes king of the Visigoths. Yusuf dhu-Nuwas captures power in Yemen.

523 Hilderic becomes king of the Vandals. The death of St Brigid of Ireland.

524 The Franks defeat the Burgundians in the Battle of Vézeronce. Childebert

I annexes Orléans and Chartres after the death of Chlodomer, king of the Franks. Roman Christian philosopher, Boethius, publishes the *Consolations of Philosophy*.

525 Bernicia in north-east England is settled by the Angles. The southern Arabian country of Yemen is conquered by King Kaleb of Axum; he builds churches.

526 Athalaric succeeds Theodoric as king of the Ostrogoths. An earthquake in Syria and Antioch kills approximately 300,000.

527 Cerdic of Wessex and his son Cynric defeat the Britons at Chearsley. The Kingdom of Essex is founded when the Saxons land north of the Thames and take control of the land between what is now London and St Albans. Justinian becomes Emperor of Byzantium; he tries to reunite the Eastern and Western branches of the Christian church. Dionysius Exiguus calculates the date of the birth of Jesus, incorrectly; dates start to be calculated Anno Domini instead of Ab Urbe Condita.

the
Medieval and Renaissance World

528 – 1599

528 Justinian appoints a commission to codify all imperial laws, the Corpus Juris Civilis. An earthquake in Antioch kills thousands. Xiao Zhuang Di succeeds Xiao Ming Di as ruler of the Chinese Northern Wei Dynasty. Yasodharman of Malwa defeats the Hun invaders in India. King Seong of Baekje adopts Buddhism as the state religion.

529 St. Benedict founds a monastery at Monte Cassino, south of Rome. The Academy at Athens, founded by Plato in 387, is closed by Justinian. The Church of the Nativity in Bethlehem is burnt down during a revolt by the Samaritans. The Canons of the Council of Orange are established, approving Augustinian doctrine.

530 Byzantine generals Belisarius and Hermogenes defeat the Persians in the Battle of Daras, halting their incursion into Roman Mesopotamia. Hilderic, king of Vandals and Alans is deposed by his cousin Gelimer. Wei Chang Guang Wang succeeds Xiao Zhuang Di as ruler of the Chinese Northern Wei Dynasty

531 Theudis succeeds Amalaric as king of the Visigoths. Khosrau I succeeds Kavadh I as king of Persia.

532 Franks invade the kingdom of Burgundy. The Nika riots in Constantinople; the cathedral is destroyed and 30,000 die; Justinian I orders the building of a new cathedral, the Hagia Sophia. Xiao Wu Di succeeds An Ding Wang in Northern China. Silla conquers Geumgwan Gaya on the Korean peninsula. This is the first year in which the Anno Domini calendar is used for numbering the years, a system invented by the Scythian monk, Dionysius Exiguus.

533 The Byzantine general, Belisarius, lands in North Africa and attacks the Vandals. Theodebert I becomes king of Austrasia, comprising parts of the territory of present-day eastern France, western Germany, Belgium, Luxembourg and the Netherlands.

534 The Frankish kings, Cothar I and Childebert I, overthrow Godomar, king of the Burgundians, and end the kingdom of Burgundy. Belisarius brings the Vandal kingdom of North Africa to an end and the provinces return to the Byzantine Empire. Cynric becomes king of Wessex. Theodahad becomes king of the Ostrogoths.

535 Justinian I orders Belisarius to start the reconquest of Italy. India's Gupta Empire collapses. The beginning of the Western Wei dynasty in China. In this and the following year, the weather is reported to be unusually cold and dark, possibly due to an eruption of Krakatoa.

536 Belisarius takes Naples and enters Rome. The Franks invade Provence. At the Synod of Constantinople, bishops acknowledge the supremacy of the Byzantine Emperor in Church matters.

537
Hagia Sophia in Constantinople is completed.

538 Gabrán mac Domangairt becomes king of Dál Riata. Witiges, king of the Ostrogoths, ends his siege of Rome and retreats to Ravenna, leaving the city in the hands of Belisarius. The Pope becomes the leading ruler in the West for the next 1,260 years. The Kofun era in Japan ends and the Asuka period, the second part of the Yamato period, begins. Around this date, Buddhism arrives in Japan, spreading throughout the country.

539 Emperor Kimmei ascends the throne of Japan.

540 High King Custennin ap Cado of Britain is deposed and returns to Dumnonia. General Belisarius conquers Milan and the Ostrogoth capital Ravenna. Ostrogoth King Witiges is succeeded by Ildibad. The Persian Sassanids attack Daraa in south-western Syria and capture Antioch in modern-day Turkey.

541 Plague appears in Egypt, spreading the following year to Constantinople. More than 100,000 die in Constantinople and several million in the rest of the Empire. Totila becomes king of the Ostrogoths; he reconquers Naples, Benevento and other parts of Italy.

542 Childebert I captures Pamplona and besieges Zaragoza in Spain.

543 The death of St Benedict of Nursia, founder of the Benedictine Order of monks. The Nubian kingdoms in North Africa adopt Christianity.

544 Belisarius returns to Italy to fight the Ostrogoths.

545 The Ostrogoths under Totila besiege Rome.

546 The Ostrogoths retake Rome.

547 Ida founds the kingdom of Bernicia at Bamburgh, in north-east England. Theodebald becomes king of Austrasia.

548 Belisarius is relieved of command of the Byzantine forces in Italy and is replaced by Narses. Theudigisel succeeds Theudis as king of the Visigoths.

549 Totila recaptures Rome. Agila succeeds Theudigisel as king of the Visigoths. Emperor Jinwen succeeds Emperor Wu as ruler of the Liang Dynasty in China.

550 The Franks conquer the Thuringii. The Eastern Wei Dynasty is succeeded by the Northern Qi Dynasty in northern China; Qi Wen Xuan Di is the first ruler of the Northern Qi Dynasty. Around this date: The construction of the Mayan acropolis of Quiriguá; the Nubians in Sudan, north-eastern Africa, become Christian; the Byzantine silk industry is started by monks who smuggle silkworms to Constantinople from China. Hindu mathematicians give zero a numeral representation in a positional notation system.

551 The Byzantine Empire captures part of southern Spain from the Visigoths. Beirut is destroyed by an earthquake and a tsunami. Liang Yu Zhang Wang succeeds Liang Jian Wen Di as ruler of the Chinese Liang dynasty.

552 Cynric, king of Wessex, captures the fort at Old Sarum. In the Battle of Taginae, General Narses defeats and kills Totila, king of the Ostrogoths; Teia succeeds him but Narses recaptures Rome by the end of the year. Göktürks establish the first known Turkic state under the leadership of Bumin Khan. Year One in the Armenian calendar. Liang Yuan Di succeeds Liang Yu Zhang Wang as ruler of the Chinese Liang dynasty.

553 The Fifth Ecumenical Council is held. The Ostrogoth kingdom is conquered by the Byzantines after the Battle of Mons Lactarius.

554 General Narses reconquers Italy. Byzantine forces seize Granada and Andalusia from the Visigoths. Athanagild succeeds Agila as king of the Visigoths. Wei Gong Di succeeds Western Wei Fei Di as ruler of the Chinese Western Wei Dynasty. Baekje and Gaya ally and wage war upon Silla in the Korean peninsula, but are defeated.

555 The beginning of the Nan Liang Dynasty; the first ruler is Nan Liang Xuan Di. In the Chinese Liang Dynasty, Liang Yuan Di is succeeded by Liang Zheng Yang Hou and then Liang Jing Di.

556 Cynric and Ceawlin of Wessex fight against the Britons at Beranburh. The Western Wei Dynasty ends in China.

557 The beginning of the Northern Zhou Dynasty in northern China; the first ruler is Xiao Min Di. In southern China, the end of the Liang Dynasty and the beginning of the Chen Dynasty; the first ruler is Chen Wu Di.

558 Conall mac Comgaill becomes king of Dál Riata. In Constantinople, the dome of the Hagia Sophia collapses. Clotaire I reunites the Frankish kingdom. The Guanghua Temple is built.

559 Glappa succeeds his father Ida as king of Bernicia. The Bulgars raid Byzantine territory, but are driven back near Constantinople by Belisarius. Ara Gaya, a member of the Gaya confederacy, surrenders to Silla in the Korean peninsula.

560 Ceawlin becomes king of Wessex. Æthelbert succeeds his father Eormenric as king of Kent. Adda succeeds his brother Glappa as king of Bernicia. Aella becomes king of Deira in northern England. St Columba quarrels with St Finnian over authorship of a psalter, leading to a pitched battle the next year.

561 Civil war breaks out among the Merovingians in France. Wu Cheng Di succeeds Xiao Zhao Di as ruler of the Chinese Northern Qi Dynasty

562 Belisarius stands trial in Constantinople for corruption. A peace treaty is signed between the Byzantine and the Persian empires. Tikal, a Mayan city state, is defeated by Kalakmul. Nan Xiao Ming Di succeeds Nan Liang Xuan Di as ruler of the Chinese Nan dynasty.

563 St Columba arrives in Scotland from Ireland to spread Christianity and reports seeing a monster in Loch Ness.

565 Justin II succeeds Justinian I as ruler of the Byzantine Empire. Hou Zhu succeeds Wu Cheng Di as ruler of the Chinese Northern Qi Dynasty. In China, the Uyghurs are conquered by the Göktürks.

567 Liuva I succeeds Athanagild as king of the Visigoths. The East Germanic Gothic tribe, the Gepids, are conquered by the Avars.

568 Ceawlin of Wessex defeats Æthelbert of Kent at the Battle of Wibbandun. Æthelric succeeds his brother Adda as king of Bernicia. King Alboin leads the Lombards into Italy; refugees fleeing them go on to found Venice. Leovigild succeeds his brother Liuva I as king of the Visigoths. The Turks and Sassanids destroy the Hepthalite Empire.

570 Ctesiphon, capital of the Sassanid Empire, becomes the largest city in the world. Byzantium and Persia start a 50-year truce. The birth of Muhammad, founder of Islam.

572 The Byzantine Empire begins a war with Persia and is also attacked by the Visigoths in Spain. Emperor Bidatsu takes the throne of Japan.

574 Áedán mac Gabráin becomes king of Dál Riata. Byzantine Emperor Justin II retires, naming Tiberius II Constantine as his heir. Visigothic king, Liuvigild conquers Cantabria in northern Spain.

575 The Kingdom of East Anglia is founded by the Angle groups 'North Folk' and 'South Folk', naming Norfolk and Suffolk, respectively.

577 The Anglo-Saxons under Ceawlin of Wessex defeat the British Celts at the Battle of Deorham.

578 Kongo Gumi, the world's oldest continuously operating company, is founded in Osaka, Japan; it closed in 2006.

579 The Slavs begin to migrate into the Balkans and Greece. The Northern Qi Dynasty comes to an end in China.

580 Ethelbert becomes king of Kent. The Roman Senate sends an embassy to Constantinople, its last recorded act.

581 The Sui Dynasty replaces the Northern Zhou Dynasty, the last of the Northern Dynasties in China; its first ruler is Sui Wen Di.

582 Maurice succeeds Tiberius II Constantine as Emperor of Byzantium. Fire and earthquake ravage Constantinople.

584 The Lombards sack Monte Cassino. The Visigoths take Cordoba from Byzantium.

585 Creoda becomes king of Mercia. There is famine in Gaul. Emperor Yōmei ascends to the throne of Japan. In China, Emperor Xiaojing succeeds Emperor Xiaoming as ruler of the Nan Liang Dynasty. The Suebi kingdom on the Iberian Peninsula is conquered by the Visigoths under King Liuvigild.

586 The Byzantines defeat the Persians at the Battle of Solachon, near Daraa. Reccared succeeds his father Liuvigild as king of the Visigoths.

587 The death of St David, patron saint of Wales. Sledda becomes king of Essex. The Nan Liang Dynasty in China comes to an end. Emperor Sushun ascends to the throne of Japan.

588 Æthelric becomes the first king of Northumbria, after the kingdom is formed from the union of the two Anglian tribes of Bernicia and Deira. Ten people are killed in rural China by a large meteorite impact.

589 Plague in Rome. The Visigoth kingdom renounces Arianism and embraces Catholicism.

591 A locust swarm destroys the harvest in Italy. Jnanagupta translates the Vimalakirti Sutra into Chinese.

592 Ceawlin is deposed as both king of Wessex and as Bretwalda.

593 Æthelfrith succeeds Hussa as king of Bernicia. Pybba becomes king of Mercia. Empress Suiko ascends to the throne of Japan.

594 Empress Suiko issues the Flourishing Three Treasures Edict, officially recognizing the practice of Buddhism in Japan

595 Augustine of Canterbury is sent on a mission to Kent by Pope Gregory I. Muhammad marries Khadija. The decimal system is being used by Indian mathematicians. Construction begins on the Zhaozhou Bridge in Hebei Province, China, the world's oldest open-spandrel stone segmental arch bridge.

597 St Augustine becomes Archbishop of Canterbury. Kōtoku becomes Emperor of Japan.

599 Yemen is conquered by the Sassanid Empire. The Maya–city of Palenque is defeated by another Maya–city, Kalakmul.

600

The population of the world rises to about 208 million. Smallpox hits Europe for the first time. Pope Gregory I codifies what comes to be known as Gregorian chant. The Persians begin to use windmills for irrigation. Around this date: The earliest references to chess in Indian and Persian literature; the beginning of an important period of art and literature in Ireland; the Hopewell culture of North America ceases to be dominant; Tiahuanaco civilization begins in Bolivia; Mayan civilization is at its high point; the rise of Huari in Peru.

601 The earliest dated English words – 'Town' and 'Priest' – are both recorded in the Laws of Æthelbert.

602 Phocas kills Maurice and declares himself Byzantine Emperor. A series of wars begins between the Byzantine Empire and the Sassanid Empire. Slavic tribes start to settle the Balkans. The Vikings invade Ireland.

603 Japan's Prince Shotoku establishes the Twelve Level Cap and Rank system and is said to have authored a 17-article constitution.

604 Saebert succeeds Sledda as king of Essex. Æthelfrith of Northumbria unites Deira and Bernicia. The Visigoths drive the last Byzantines from Spain.

605 Around this time, the Grand Canal is built in China.

606 Shashanka is the first recorded independent king of Bengal.

607 Ceolwulf of Wessex fights the South Saxons. King Songstan unifies Tibet.

609
The Pantheon in Rome is consecrated to the Virgin Mary and all saints.

610 Heraclius overthrows the East Roman Emperor Phocas and becomes Emperor; he changes the official language of the East Roman Empire from Latin to Greek. According to Islamic belief, the archangel Gabriel first appears to Muhammad, reciting to him the first verses of the Surat al-Alaq and beginning the revelation of the Qur'an.

613 Shahrbaraz, a general of the Persian Empire, captures Damascus.

614 Shahrbaraz captures and sacks Jerusalem; the Church of the Holy Sepulchre is damaged by fire and the True Cross is captured.

615 The Turks invade China.

616 Eadbald succeeds Ethelbert as king of Kent. Æthelfrith of Northumbria defeats the army of Powys; he is slain by Rædwald of East Anglia in the Battle of the River Idle, which establishes Rædwald's claim as Bretwalda. Edwin becomes king of Northumbria. Alexandria is captured by Khosrau II of Persia. A shrine is founded on the site of the future Westminster Abbey.

617 Sui Gong Di succeeds Sui Yang Di as Emperor of China.

618 The beginning of the Tang dynasty in China.

619 The Avars attack Constantinople. The calculation of the Chinese calendar begins to use the true motions of the sun and moon modelled using two offset, opposing parabolas.

621 The Byzantine Emperor, Heraclius, invades Persia. Year One of the Islamic calendar, the year that Islam began.

622 Muhammad and his followers emigrate from Mecca to Medina.

622 The first Chinese Encyclopedia, Yiwen Leiju (Collection of Literature Arranged by Categories), is completed.

624 Edinburgh is founded by King Edwin of Northumbria. The Byzantines recapture Andalusia after 70 years of Visigoth rule; they also defeat the Avars and Slavs besieging Constantinople. The Tang court adopts

Buddhism. Emperor Gaozu of Tang China abdicates in favour of his son, Li Shimin.

627 Emperor Heraclius defeats the Persians in the Battle of Nineveh, ending the Roman–Persian Wars.

628 Brahmagupta writes the *Brahmasphutasiddhanta*, an early book on mathematics.

629 Jerusalem is retaken by the Byzantine Empire from the Persian Empire.

630 The start of the Byzantine–Arab Wars. Khan Kubrat establishes Great Bulgaria. Muhammad conquers Mecca bloodlessly.

632 The death of Muhammad; he is succeeded by Abu Bakr.

633 In England, the Mercians defeat the Northumbrians. Li Chung Feng builds a celestial globe.

634 The Arabs invade Palestine.

635 St Aidan founds Lindisfarne in Northumbria, England.

636 In the Battle of Yarmuk, the Byzantine Empire loses Syria to the Arabs. The Arabs invade Persia. The city of Basra in Iraq is founded by Caliph Omar.

637 The Arabs defeat the Persian army, taking the Persian capital of Ctesiphon, Jerusalem and Aleppo. Chang'an, the capital of China, becomes the largest city in the world.

638 The Muslims capture Jerusalem, Antioch, Caesarea Maritima and Akko. The Islamic calendar is introduced.

640 Arabs begin to spread the Muslim faith across northern Africa.

640 The Islamic leader, Caliph Omar, begins the conquest of Egypt

641 The Byzantine Emperor Heraclonas is deposed and his brother Constans II becomes sole emperor.

642 A monastic settlement is established which later becomes Winchester Cathedral. The Arabs conquer Persia at the Battle of Nehawand. Empress Kogyoku ascends to the throne of Japan. The date of the earliest surviving dated Arabic papyrus.

643 Arab armies win their first North African victory at Tripoli. The last Sassanid king of Persia flees to China.

644 The Tang dynasty of China begins invasion of the kingdom of Goguryo in Korea.

645 The Japanese court begins to copy the Chinese style of government. The Byzantines recapture Alexandria from the Arabs. Emperor Kotoku ascends the Japanese throne.

646 Alexandria is recaptured by the Arabs after a Byzantine attempt to retake Egypt fails, ending nearly 10 centuries of Graeco-Roman civilization in Egypt. Emperor Kotoku introduces the Taika reforms, a series of political and social doctrines, in Japan.

649 The Arabs conquer Cyprus.

650 Croats and Serbs occupy the area that is now Bosnia. The Arabs complete the conquest of Persia. Islam becomes the state religion in Iran. The first surgical developments take place in India. Around this time: The revelations of Muhammad are written down, becoming the Qur'an; the Native American Hopewell people establish themselves along the upper Mississippi River; the city of Teotihuacan in Mexico becomes an important trade centre.

651 The bakt between Egypt and Makuria, the longest-lasting treaty in history, at 700 years, is signed. Yazdegard III is killed, ending both Persian resistance to Arab conquest, as well as the Sassanid dynasty; the Muslims conquer Persia. Ali, Muhammad's son-in-law is assassinated; Muuawiyah becomes caliph and establishes the Umayyad dynasty.

652 Christian Nubians and Arabs in Egypt agree on Aswan on the River Nile being the southernmost limit of Arab expansion.

654 The Arabs invade Rhodes; the remains of the Colossus of Rhodes are sold off.

655 The Northumbrians defeat the Mercians in the Battle of Winwaed.

656 Northumbria annexes Mercia.

657 The last Welsh offensive, led by Cadwaladr, is mounted against the Saxons. The Tang Dynasty defeats the Turks. St Hilda founds an abbey on the Yorkshire coast at Whitby.

659 Mercians rebel against Northumbria and proclaim Wulfhere king.

663 A brief outbreak of plague hits Britain. Byzantine Emperor Constans II invades southern Italy. An anonymous monk reaches the summit of Mount Fuji.

664 At the Synod of Whitby, Roman Christianity is chosen in preference to Celtic.

665 The Anglo-Saxons convert to Christianity after the Second Battle of Badon. The Eastern Roman Emperor Constans II is assassinated in his bath.

668 Goguryeo in southern Manchuria and northern Korea, is overthrown by the alliance of Tang China and Silla, leading to the unification of Korea.

670 The city of Kairouan in what is now Tunisia is founded. Around this date, the Syrian chemist, Callinicus, invents Greek Fire, a highly inflammable liquid used by the Byzantine army in battle.

671 King Ecgfrith of Northumbria defeats the Picts at the Battle of Two Rivers. The Jinshin War, a succession dispute following the death of Emperor Tenji, is fought in Japan.

674 The first Arab siege of Constantinople begins. The first glass windows appear in English churches.

675 The Bulgars, a nomadic people from the Russian steppes are, settling the lands south of the Danube.

677 In the Battle of Syllaeum the Arab fleet is destroyed by Byzantines.

680 The Battle of Karbala in Iraq is fought between supporters and relatives of Muhammad's grandson Husayn ibn Ali and forces of Yazid I, the Umayyad caliph.

681 The Bulgars defeat the Byzantine Empire; this is considered to be the birth date of Bulgaria.

683 The end of the reign of Pacal the Great, ruler of the Mayan state of Palenque.

685 Plague kills all the monks in a Northumbrian monastery apart from the abbot and one small boy – the future scholar, Bede. The Arabs reach present-day Morocco.

686 The kingdom of Kent is conquered by the West Saxons under Caedwalla. The Isle of Wight becomes the last place in the United Kingdom to convert to Christianity.

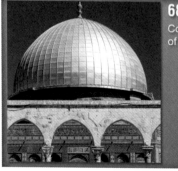

687
Construction work begins on the Dome of the Rock in Jerusalem.

688	Emperor Justinian II of the Byzantine Empire defeats the Bulgarians.
690	Wu Ze Tian comes to power in China, the only woman in history to rule China; she founds the Zhou dynasty.
691	The Dome of the Rock is completed.
692	The Arabs conquer Armenia.
693	The Portuguese city of Viseu is taken from the Byzantine Empire by the Moors.
694	Empress Wu conquers the kingdom of Khotan in Western China. The 13th Mayan ruler of Copán, 18-Rabbit begins a 44-year reign.
695	The Byzantines revolt against Justinian II; Leontius is made emperor and Justinian II is banished.
697	Paolo Lucio Anafesto is elected the first Doge of Venice. Arabs destroy the Byzantine city of Carthage in North Africa.
700	Around this date: Vikings start to invade the British Isles; the copper deposits of south Katanga are mined and traded by the Bantu; the mound-building Mississippi culture emerges in the Mississippi river basin; in eastern Arizona, the Pueblo people start to live in houses above ground and begin farming; the Moche and Nazca civilizations collapse.
702	The Byzantine Emperor Justinian II regains his throne. The Umayyad Mosque, also known as the Grand Mosque, is completed in Damascus.
705	Muslim armies begin a period of expansion, conquering Turkmenistan and Sind and pushing as far as the borders of China. Chinese Chancellor, Zhang Jianzhi, murders the Zhang brothers and restores Emperor Zhongzong, marking the end of the short-lived Zhou Dynasty.
707	The Byzantines lose the Balearic Islands to the Moors.
708	In France, after a reported appearance of the archangel Michael, the island of Mont Tombe is dedicated to him and renamed Mont Saint-Michel. Copper coins are minted in Japan for the first time.
709	A violent storm separates the Channel Islands of Jethou and Herm.
710	The Muslim Kingdom of Nekor is founded in Morocco. Nara, in the Kansai region, south of modern-day Kyoto, becomes the capital of Japan. The first Al-Aqsa Mosque in Jerusalem is finished.
711	Philippicus incites a revolt against Justinian II, and upon the latter's death declares himself Byzantine Emperor. Umayyad Moors conquer the Iberian Peninsula after the Battle of Guadalete. Umayyads found the first Muslim state in India.
712	The *Kojiki*, a history of Japan from its birth, is completed; it is the oldest surviving book in Japan.
713	Emperor Philippicus is deposed; Anastasius II is proclaimed emperor.
716	Theodosius III leads a revolt against Anastasius II and is proclaimed Byzantine Emperor.
717	The Pictish king, Nechtan, son of Derile, expels the monks from the Scottish island of Iona. Leo III usurps the throne of Byzantium. Arabs besiege Constantinople for almost a year.
718	Pelayo defeats the Arabs at Covadonga and establishes the Kingdom of Asturias in the Iberian Peninsula. Emperor Leo III and Khan Tervel defeat the Arab forces besieging Constantinople, stopping an Arab invasion of Europe. The world's oldest hotel, Houshi Onsen, opens in Ishikawa-ken, Japan.
719	The church of Nubia changes its allegiance from the Eastern Orthodox Church to the Coptic Church.
720	The *Nihon Shoki* (The Chronicles of Japan), one of the oldest Japanese history books, is completed.

721	In the Battle of Toulouse, Al-Samh ibn Malik al-Khawlani, the governor of Muslim Spain is defeated by Duke Odo of Aquitaine; an Arab invasion of Gaul is prevented.
722	War breaks out between Wessex and Sussex.
723	The world's first mechanical clock is allegedly built in China.
725	Bede publishes *De Ratione Temporum*, calculating dates from the birth of Christ.
726	The first annual Sumo tournament is staged in Japan by Emperor Seibu.
730	Emperor Leo III of the Byzantine Empire orders the destruction of all icons; the beginning of the First Iconoclastic Period.
731	Pope Gregory II condemns iconoclasm, causing Byzantine Italy to break with the Empire. Bede completes his *Historia Ecclesiastica Gentis Anglorum*.
732	Charles Martel, King of the Franks, defeats the Muslims at Poitiers, bringing to a halt the Muslim advance northwards and establishing a balance of power between Western Europe, Islam and the Byzantine Empire. Egbert becomes Bishop of York; he founds a library and makes the city a renowned centre of learning.
735	Death of the Venerable Bede.
736	The first documented instance of hop cultivation in the Hallertau region of present-day Germany. The Kegon school of Buddhism arrives in Japan from Korea.
739	Charles Martel drives the Moors out of France.
741	Japanese authorities decree that Buddhist temples should be established throughout the country.
742	Emperor Xuanzong of Tang begins to favour Taoism over Buddhism.
745	Bubonic plague begins to sweep through Europe.
748	An earthquake strikes the Middle East, destroying many remnants of Byzantine culture.
750	The last Umayyad caliph is overthrown by the first Abbasid caliph; the caliphate is moved to Baghdad, which develops into a centre of world trade and culture. Teotihuacan is sacked by the Toltec. The Zapotec city of Monte Alban is abandoned.
751	Pepin the Short is elected king of the Franks, marking the end of the Merovingian and beginning of the Carolingian dynasty. Arabian armies defeat Chinese Tang troops at the Battle of Talas near Samarkand. The oldest surviving printed document, a Buddhist scripture, is printed in Korea.
753	Samarkand in Uzbekistan is conquered by the Arabs.
755	The An Lushan rebellion begins in China, resulting in the abdication of Emperor Xuanzong.
756	Pepin the Short defeats the Lombards of northern Italy who have threatened Pope Stephen III. Abd-ar-rahman I conquers Iberia and re-establishes the Umayyad dynasty at Cordoba in modern Spain.
757	Offa, noted for Offa's Dyke, becomes king of Mercia. A major earthquake strikes Palestine and Syria.
758	The Chinese city of Guangzhou is sacked by Arab and Persian raiders.
759	The Franks capture Narbonne; the Saracens are driven out of France. Japanese poet Otomo no Yakamochi compiles the first Japanese poetry anthology, Man'yoshu.
760	The Mayan city of Dos Pilas is abandoned.
762	The Abbasid dynasty, rulers of Iraq, names Baghdad as its capital.
763	Tibetan forces occupy the Chinese capital Chang'an.
764	Offa of Mercia conquers Kent, and installs Egbert II on the throne. According to the historian Theophanes in this year, the Black Sea melts and icebergs float past Constantinople.

768 Charlemagne is crowned king of the Franks on the death of his father, Pepin the Short. The important settlement of Hedeby is founded in Viking Denmark.

772 Offa of Mercia conquers Sussex. Charlemagne starts fighting the Saxons and the Frisians; Saxony is subdued and converts to Christianity.

773
The concept of the number zero is introduced to the city of Baghdad.

774 Charlemagne conquers the kingdom of the Lombards.

775 The Srivijaya kingdom extends from Sumatra and Java to Malaysia.

777 Charlemagne defeats the Saxons.

778 Charlemagne's army suffers a terrible defeat at the hands of the Basques; the 11th-century *Song of Roland* is loosely based on the events of this battle.

781 Charlemagne defines the papal territory.

784 Construction starts on Offa's Dyke, a massive, defensive earthwork between England and Wales, built by Offa, king of Mercia.

786 Harun-al-Rashid's reign coincides with the 'Golden Age' of the Abbasids, rulers of Iraq.

787 The first three Viking ships land in Wessex and the Norsemen start to plunder towns and coastal monasteries.

788 Charlemagne conquers Bavaria. Morocco becomes an independent state under Idris, an Arab chief.

790 A revolt against Empress Irene leads to her son, Constantine VI, being declared sole ruler of the Byzantine Empire.

793 Vikings sack the monastery of Lindisfarne in the first major Viking raid in England.

794 Heian-kyo (Kyoto) becomes the Japanese capital.

796 Charlemagne defeats the Avars.

797 Empress Irene orders Constantine VI captured and deposed.

800 The coronation of Charles the Great (Charlemagne) as Emperor in St Peter's Church, Rome, by Pope Leo III, marks the beginning of the Holy Roman Empire. Celtic monks begin work on the *Book of Kells* on the island of Iona. Around this date: The first castles are built in Western Europe; the Aghlabid dynasty of emirs rules in Tunis in North Africa; Arabs and Persians set up trading posts at Malindi, Mombasa, Kilwa, and Mogadishu on the East African coast; the Hohokam people expand their settlements in southern Arizona; the Maori start migrating to New Zealand from Polynesia; the beginning of the Mississippian Period in the Central North American continent.

801 Empress Irene is deposed and replaced by Nicephorus I.

802 Egbert becomes king of Wessex. Krum becomes Khan of Bulgaria. The Angkorian dynasty is founded in Cambodia by King Jayavarman II.

803 Venice gains independence from the Byzantine Empire.

805 The Mayan city of Copán is abandoned.

806 Vikings slaughter all the inhabitants of the religious community on the island of Iona.

807 Christianized Vikings land on the Cornish coast and form an alliance with the Cornish to fight against the West Saxons.

809 The Byzantine Empire and the Bulgars are at war until 817.

810 The *Book of Kells* is completed by the Celts. Bulgars, under Khan Krum, destroy the Avars. China demands the return of territory captured by Tibet.

811 Khan Krum of Bulgaria defeats the Byzantines and kills the emperor.

813 Louis the Pious is crowned co-emperor of the Franks with his father Charlemagne. At the Third Council of Tours priests are ordered to preach in the vernacular (either Vulgar Latin or German). Al-Mamun rules as Abbasid caliph; the House of Wisdom – a library and translation institute – he founds in Baghdad becomes the most important school in the Arab world.

814 The death of Charlemagne; Louis the Pious succeeds him. The Bulgarians lay siege to Constantinople. Serbia is founded.

820 Musa al-Chwarazmi, a Persian mathematician, develops a system of algebra.

823 Crete is conquered from the Byzantines by the Saracens.

824 The Constitutio Romana establishes the authority of the Holy Roman Emperors over the pope. Iñigo Arista revolts against the Franks and establishes the kingdom of Navarre.

825 Kent, Surrey, Sussex, East Anglia and Essex submit to Wessex.

827 Pope Valentine becomes the 100th pope. Arabs invade Sicily. Chalid Ben Abdulmelik and Ali Ben Isa measure the circumference of the Earth, getting a result of 40,248 km.

828
Egbert of Wessex becomes the first king of England.

829 Egbert of Wessex conquers Mercia and is recognized as Bretwalda.

830 Egbert of Wessex defeats the Welsh. The *Historia Brittonum*, attributed to Nennius, and known for its list of the twelve battles of King Arthur, is written. The Buddhist monument of Borobodur, in Indonesia, is completed after 50 years of work.

831 The legendary date of the genesis of the Flag of Scotland; it is said to have appeared to King Óengus II the night before a battle against the Angles. Byzantine Emperor, Theophilus, forbids the usage of icons. Louis the Pious is reinstated as Emperor of the Franks following the end of the first civil war of his reign. The Saracens capture Palermo. St Ansgar founds the first church in Sweden, at Birka. The second St Mark's Basilica is built in Venice.

836 Egbert of Wessex is defeated by the Danes.

837 Halley's Comet passes within approximately 5 million kilometres of the Earth – its closest ever approach.

838 At Hingston Down, Egbert of Wessex beats the Danish and the West Welsh. The Stone of Destiny is placed at Scone Palace, Scotland. Feidlimid becomes High-King of Ireland.

840 Lothar succeeds Louis the Pious as Emperor.

841 The Norse town of Dyflinn or Dublin is founded in Ireland.

842 Louis the German and Charles the Bald swear the Oaths of Strasbourg, an alliance against Holy Roman Emperor, Lothar.

843 Kenneth MacAlpin unites the kingdom of Scotia, becoming the first king of Scotland (Alba) as well as king of the Picts. The Treaty of Verdun divides the Carolingian Empire between the three sons of Louis the Pious; the kingdom of France becomes a distinct state for the first time.

844 Rhodri Mawr rules as the first prince of all Wales. Louis II is crowned Holy Roman Emperor.

845 Buddhism is banned in China.

846 Arab pirates sack the Vatican.

850 The Arabs perfect the astrolabe, the navigation instrument used until the invention of the sextant in the 18th century. Around this time, Mayan civilization in the southern lowlands of Mexico goes into decline and its cities are abandoned. Irish philosopher John Eriugena posits that Mercury, Venus, Mars and Jupiter circle the Sun.

855 Louis II succeeds Lothar as Western Emperor.

856 An earthquake in Corinth in Greece, kills an estimated 45,000; in Iran an earthquake kills 200,000.

858 The beginning of the control of Japanese emperors by the Fujiwara clan, a powerful family of regents.

859 The University of Al Karaouine, the oldest university in the world, is founded in Fes in Morocco.

860 The Vikings control Novgorod in Russia and attack Constantinople.

862 The East Slavic and Finnish tribes of northern Russia invite the Vikings, led by Varangian chieftain Rurik, to rule them.

865 A Russian expedition threatens Constantinople. Bulgaria, under Boris I, converts to Orthodox Christianity.

866 A Viking army captures York. Louis II beats the Saracen invaders in Italy. Pope Nicholas I forbids the use of torture in prosecutions for witchcraft.

867 Basil I becomes sole ruler of the Byzantine Empire.

868 The First County of Portugal is established by Vímara Peres, after the reconquest of the region north of the Douro river from the Moors. Ahmad ibn-Tulun breaks away from the Abbasid caliphate, establishing the Tulunid dynasty in Egypt. The *Diamond Sutra*, the oldest printed book still in existence, is printed in China.

869 The Western Emperor Louis II allies with Eastern Emperor Basil I against the Saracens.

870 The Viking Great Summer Army invades England and conquers East Anglia. Prague Castle is founded. Malta is conquered by Arabs from Sicily.

871 Alfred the Great becomes king of England.

874 Ingólfur Arnarson arrives in Iceland as the first permanent Viking settler.

875	Harald Fairhair, Viking king, subdues Orkney and Shetland and adds them to his kingdom. Charles the Bald, king of West Francia, is crowned Emperor.
877	Louis the Stammerer becomes king of the West Franks. Indravarman I of the Khmer in Cambodia unites his kingdom.
878	Alfred defeats the Vikings under Guthrum at Ethandune; the Treaty of Wedmore divides England between the Anglo-Saxons and the Danes.
879	Nepal gains independence from Tibet.
881	Charles the Fat is crowned Western Emperor.
882	Oleg of Russia makes Kiev his capital.
884	The Huang Chao rebellion is suppressed by the Tang Dynasty of China with the help of the Shatuo Turks.
885	The Vikings besiege Paris in France, at the time capital of the kingdom of the West Franks.
886	Alfred the Great captures London and renames it Lundenburgh. The Tamil Chola dynasty rules south India from its capital at Tanjore, until 1267. Alfred the Great mints the first halfpenny; previous halfpennies had been pennies cut in half.
887	Fujiwara Mototsune is installed as chief adviser to the Japanese emperor.
889	In Korea, the unified Silla kingdom collects taxes by force, setting off peasant rebellions. The Khmers start to build the first of a series of capital cities at Angkor in Cambodia.
890	Around this time, the Huari Empire goes into decline in Peru.
891	The collection of annals known as the *Anglo-Saxon Chronicle*, the history of the Anglo-Saxons, is written by monks.
894	Northumbrians and East Angles swear allegiance to Alfred the Great, but promptly break their truce by attacking the south-west of England. Japan ceases commercial relations with China.
895	The approximate date of the composition of the *Musica Enchiriadis*, marking the beginnings of Western polyphonic music.
896	The Eastern Franks invade and conquer Italy under the leadership of Arnulf of Carinthia. The Bulgarians, under Simeon I, defeat the Byzantine Empire at Bulgarophygon.

899
The death of Alfred the Great; he is succeeded by Edward the Elder.

900	The world population is approximately 240 million. The Persian scientist Rhazes distinguishes smallpox from measles in the course of his writings. Around this date: Magyars, nomadic people from central Asia, invade Europe, settling Hungary; the Toltec conquer the Central Valley in Mexico and build their capital at Tula.
901	Muslims conquer Sicily. Military governor, Zhu Wen, seizes the imperial Tang dynasty capital.
902	The Wu State is founded in present-day Yangzhou in southern China by Yang Xingmi.

904 Pope Sergius III succeeds Pope Leo V as the 119th pope, beginning the 30-year era of the Pornocracy. Thessalonica is captured by the Saracens. Abbasids invade and take control of the Tulunid emirate of Egypt. Chang'an, the capital of the Tang dynasty and the largest city in the ancient world, is destroyed by Zhu Wen. The Royal Mint is founded in England.

906 A Synod at Scone unites Scottish Christian pastors for gospel reformation without the interference or authority of Pope Sergius III in Rome.

907 The Tang dynasty falls after 300 years, and Zhu Wen establishes the Later Liang dynasty, the first of northern China's Five Dynasties; for the next 50 years, China is divided into many warring states. Paintings on hanging scrolls and handscrolls are established in China.

908 Khitan Mongols under Ye-lu a-pao-chi begin the conquest of Inner Mongolia and several districts of northern China.

909 The Benedictine Cluny Abbey is founded in Burgundy by William I, Count of Auvergne.

911 Rollo, the Viking chief, settles in Normandy, France.

912 Abd-al-Rahman III becomes Umayyad caliph of Cordoba, Spain; during his peaceful reign he develops arts and industry, such as paper-making.

914 Vikings conquer much of Ireland.

916 The Mercian warrior queen Æthelflaed conquers Wales.

920 The Saxons retake East Anglia from the Danes. The golden age of the Ghana empire begins in Africa.

921 In the Later Liang dynasty in China all 'barbarian' tribes are reported to have been pacified by the Khitan.

923 The Later Liang dynasty falls to the Later Tang dynasty, founded by Li Cunxu.

924 Qi State in north-west China falls to the Later Tang dynasty.

925 Former Shu, one of the Ten Kingdoms, surrenders when invaded by the Later Tang.

927 The various small kingdoms within what is now England are unified by King Æthelstan, creating the kingdom of England. The ancient city of Taranto, in southern Italy, is destroyed by the Saracens. Chu State, one of the Ten Kingdoms, is founded by Ma Yin.

930 With the establishment of the Alþing, now the world's oldest parliament, the Icelandic Commonwealth is founded.

931 Eric Bloodaxe becomes second king of Norway.

934 The German king, Henry I, the Fowler, and his Christian forces under king Gnupa defeat the Heathen army and conquer Hedeby. The Eldgjá volcanic eruption in Iceland is the largest basalt flood (an eruption covering an area in basalt lava) ever recorded.

935 Haakon the Good, son of Harald Fairhair, reunites Norway. Córdoba, capital of Al-Andalus, becomes the largest city in the world. Later Shu, one of the Ten Kingdoms, is founded by Meng Zhixiang. Koryo state is founded in west-central Korea.

936 Otto the Great becomes king of Germany; he is crowned Holy Roman Emperor in 962. In China, the Later Tang Dynasty falls to the Later Jin Dynasty founded by Shi Jingtang, posthumously known as Gaozu of Later Jin. Sixteen Prefectures, which includes the area around modern-day Beijing, is absorbed by the Khitan Empire.

937 Æthelstan of England defeats a large army of Scots, Irish and Danes at the Battle of Brunanburh, northern England. The Wu State, one of the Ten Kingdoms, is taken by Li Bian, who then founds the Southern Tang.

938 Vietnam gains independence from China.

939 The Arabs lose Madrid to the kingdom of Leon.

941 The Rus'–Byzantine War is fought. Fujiwara Tadahira becomes civil dictator in Japan.

942 Hywel Dda, king of Deheubarth, annexes Gwynedd to become ruler of most of Wales. The Southern Han Dynasty ends in China.

945 Edmund I of England conquers Strathclyde but Cumberland and Westmorland are annexed by the Scots. Lothair II of Italy takes control of Italy and rules until 950. The kingdom of Min is taken by the Southern Tang.

947 The Khitan empire adopts the dynastic name 'Great Liao'. In China, the Later Jin dynasty falls to the Later Han dynasty founded by Gaozu of Later Han.

949

The orbits of all the planets of the solar system are thought to have been within the same 90% arc of the solar system on this date; it will not occur again until 6 May 2492.

950 Igbo-Ukwu culture begins to flourish in eastern Nigeria. The fall of the Later Han dynasty.

951 In China, the Chu State is absorbed by the Southern Tang, and the Later Zhou dynasty is founded by Guo Wei. The Northern Han dynasty is founded by Liu Min in northern China.

954 On the death of Eric Bloodaxe, Edred becomes king of England.

955 Edwy becomes king of England. Otto the Great, king of the Germans, defeats the Magyars at the Battle of Lechfeld, near Augsburg, and defeats the Slavs at Reichnitz.

957 The Chandra Hindu dynasty ends, thus beginning a time of chaos in the area of modern-day Mongolia.

958 King Harald of Denmark accepts Christianity.

959 Edwy, king of England dies and is succeeded by his brother Edgar the Peaceable who consolidates the English kingdom.

960 Dunstan becomes Archbishop of Canterbury and Edgar's chief adviser; he reforms monasteries and enforces the rule of St Benedict. Mieczyslaw I is the first ruler of Poland. The Song dynasty reunifies China.

961 The Byzantine Empire recaptures Crete from Muslim control.

962 Otto the Great is crowned Holy Roman Emperor; he signs the Diploma Ottonarium with Pope John XII, among other things, granting control of the Papal States to the Pope. Alptigin, a Turkish warrior slave, captures the Afghan fortress of Ghazni and founds the Ghaznavid dynasty.

963 Luxemburg is founded. Mieszko I founds the kingdom of Poland; he is succeeded by Boleslav I, who greatly expands its territory.

964 Al-Sufi's illustrated astronomical text the *Book of Fixed Stars* is published.

965 Northern Song armies invade Later Shu and force them to surrender.

968 Byzantine historian Leo Diaconus makes the first recorded reference to the Sun's corona.

969 John I becomes Emperor of the Eastern Roman Empire. The Fatimid dynasty expands from Tunis and conquers Egypt from the Tulunid dynasty; they build Cairo and make it the Egyptian capital.

970 A decade-long famine begins in France. The Byzantine Emperor John I successfully defends the Eastern Roman Empire from a barbarian invasion. The Fatimids build the al-Azhar University in Cairo, one of the world's first universities. Paper money is introduced by the Chinese government.

971 The Southern Han falls to the Song Dynasty in China.

974 The Byzantine Empire retakes Syria from the Abbasids.

975 King Edward the Martyr is crowned in England. Emperor Taizu of the Song Dynasty conquers the Southern Tang and Hunan Province.

976 Brian Boru becomes king of Munster. Leopold of Babenberg is appointed Margrave of Austria; the Babenberg family rules Austria until 1246. The Yuelu Academy, in Hunan Province, China, is founded.

978 Æthelred II becomes king of England at the age of ten, following the assassination of his half-brother, Edward the Martyr. Vladimir becomes Grand Prince of Kiev. The Toltec merge with the Maya on the Yucután Peninsula. The Wu-Yue State surrenders to the Song Dynasty.

979 The Tynwald, the parliament of the Isle of Man, is founded. The Song Dynasty destroys the Northern Han State.

980 In East Africa, The Zanj Empire is founded by Ali ibn Hasan, succeeding the Kilwa Empire.

981
Viking explorer Eric the Red discovers Greenland. Hundreds of land-starved Vikings flood to it. The Arabs produce the first commercially sold special soap for shaving.

983 A 1,000-chapter encyclopaedia, the *Taiping Yulan*, is produced in China.

985 Chola King Rajaraja I conquers Kerala in south India.

987 Hugh Capet becomes the first Capetian king of France.

988 Al-Azhar University is founded in Cairo, Egypt, the second oldest university in the world.

989 Vladimir of Kiev chooses Orthodox Christianity as the official religion for his people. Sankore University is founded in Timbuktu.

990 Construction work begins on the Al-Hakim Mosque in Cairo. The Toltec people take over the Mayan city of Chichen Itza.

997 Mohammed of Ghazni comes to power in the Afghan empire; he invades India 17 times during his reign.

998 Otto III retakes the city of Rome and reinstates his cousin Pope Gregory V after mutilating and blinding his rival, the Antipope John XVI.

1000 The population of the world is 310 million. The Battle of Svolder or Svold, a naval battle, is fought in the western Baltic between King Olaf Tryggvason of Norway and an alliance of his enemies. The Hungarian state is founded by Stephen I. Around this date: Leif Ericson lands in North America, calling it Vinland; the Hutu arrive in present-day Rwanda and Burundi, soon outnumbering the native Twa; Bantu-speaking peoples set up kingdoms in southern Africa; the kingdoms of Takrur and Gao flourish in West Africa due to the gold trade; gunpowder is invented in China; Maori people settle in New Zealand; Polynesians begin to build stone temples; the Japanese court lady, Murasaki Shikibu, writes the novel *Tale of Genji*; farmers in Peru grow sweet potatoes and corn.

1002   The English king, Æthelred, orders all Danes in England to be killed, leading to the St Brice's Day Massacre. Brian Boru becomes High King of Ireland. All-out war breaks out between Byzantine Emperor Basil II and Bulgarian Tsar Samuil.

1006   The brightest supernova ever recorded, SN 1006, is observed in the constellation of Lupus.

1009   The Church of the Holy Sepulchre is destroyed by Caliph al-Hakim bi-Amr Allah. The Ly dynasty, Vietnam's first independent dynasty, is proclaimed.

1010   Viking explorer Thorfinn Karlsefni attempts to found a settlement in North America. Persian poet Ferdowsi finishes writing his poetic opus, *The Shahnameh*. The Native Ly dynasty is founded in northern Vietnam. Eilmer of Malmesbury attempts flight in a glider of his own construction.

1013   The Danes invade England under King Sweyn I; Æthelred II flees to Normandy, and Sweyn becomes king of England. Kaifeng, capital of China, becomes the largest city in the world.

1014   Æthelred returns to England and retakes the English crown. Brian Boru, High King of all Ireland, defeats the Vikings at the Battle of Clontarf, but loses his life. In the Battle of Kleidion, Basil II defeats the Bulgarian army and massacres 15,000 prisoners. Henry II of Germany is crowned Henry II, Holy Roman Emperor. Rajendra I becomes ruler of the Cholas, who dominate much of India.

1015   Canute the Great, a Viking king, invades England.

1016   Canute becomes king of England, Denmark, Norway and part of Sweden, until 1035. George Tsul, ruler of Khazaria, is captured by a combined Byzantine–Rus' force, effectively ending Khazaria's existence.
Earthquakes partly destroy the Dome of the Rock.

1017   England is divided into the earldoms of Wessex, Mercia, East Anglia and Northumbria. Hamza ibn-'Ali ibn-Ahmad declares that the Fatimid Caliph Al-Hakim bi-Amr Allah is God, founding the Druze religion.

1018   Bulgaria becomes part of the Byzantine Empire. Buckfast Abbey is founded in England.

1019   Sweden and Norway sign a treaty at Kungälv. Ghazni armies from the area of Afghanistan occupy most of northern India. Yaroslav the Wise, ruler of Kiev in Russia, begins the unification of many Russian principalities.

1020   Canute the Great codifies the laws of England. Around this time, Boleslav I of Poland creates a powerful state. Italian towns, including Rome, Florence and Venice, become city states. A hospice is built in Jerusalem by the Knights Hospitaller.

1021   Al-Zahir becomes Fatimid Caliph; Fatimid power declines.

1023   The Judge-Governor of Sevilla seizes power as Abbad I, thus founding the Abbadid dynasty.

1024   The Salian Dynasty of the Holy Roman Empire is founded by Conrad II.

1030   Henry I of France revolts against his father Robert. In Afghanistan, Masud seizes the Ghaznavid throne; his empire stretches from Persia to the Ganges. An Italian monk, Guido of Arezzo, develops the solfège system, for learning music by ear.

1031 Henry I becomes king of France. The Moorish caliphate of Córdoba collapses.

1034 Empress Zoe of Byzantium marries her chamberlain and elevates him to the throne of the Eastern Roman Empire as Michael IV.

1035 Harold I becomes regent in place of his half brother. Normandy in the north of France grows powerful.

1037 Harold I takes the crown of England from his half-brother Harthcanut. The Spanish kingdoms of Castile and Leon unite.

1038 Western Xia in north-western China declares independence.

1040 Harthcanut lands at Sandwich and reclaims the English throne. King Duncan I is killed in battle against his first cousin and rival Macbeth, who succeeds him. The Seljuk Turks defeat the Ghaznavids in Persia and advance on Baghdad. The oldest brewery still active is founded at Weihenstephan in Germany.

1041 Edward the Confessor returns from exile to become the heir to Harthcanut's throne.

1042 Edward the Confessor becomes king of England. Michael V of Byzantium is deposed by popular revolt; Zoe, Empress of the Byzantine Empire becomes Empress with her sister Theodora; she marries for the third time and elevates her husband to the throne as Constantine IX.

1043 The Ziyarids dynasty ends in Persia.

1044 Anawrahta takes power in Burma; he builds a large empire, strengthens his army, and founds a dynasty. Schools are established throughout China to train students for the civil service exams. King Anawrahta seizes the throne of Pagan, Myanmar.

1045 Edward the Confessor begins the construction of Westminster Abbey. El Cid is proclaimed a national hero in Spain. Movable-type printing is invented by Bi Sheng in China.

1047 William the Conqueror secures control of Normandy.

1050 Swedish forces attack Finland. The culture of the Yoruba people of Ife flourishes in Nigeria in West Africa. Anasazi settlers inhabit the Chaco canyon in modern-day New Mexico. The Japanese sculptor, Jocho, founds his school.

1051 Ilarion of Russia becomes the first native Metropolitan of the Eastern Orthodox Church in the East Slavic state of Kievan Rus.

1053 In the Battle of Civitate, 3,000 horsemen of Norman Count Humphrey rout the troops of Pope Leo IX.

1054 A permanent split occurs between the Catholic Church of Rome and the Orthodox Christian Church of Byzantium.

1057 King Macbeth of Scotland is killed in battle against Malcolm III of Scotland. King Anawrahta of Myanmar captures Thanton in northern Thailand, strengthening Theravada Buddhism in the country.

1059 The Almoravids conquer the Moroccan Berbers, the Berghouata.

1061 The Normans conquer Messina in Sicily. Most of West Frisia (Holland) is conquered by imperial German armies and given to the Bishop of Utrecht.

1062 The Almoravids overrun Morocco and establish a kingdom with its capital at Marrakech, stretching from Spain to Senegal.

1064 The Sunset Crater Volcano in Arizona erupts for the first time.

1065 Westminster Abbey is consecrated. The kingdoms of Galicia and Portugal become independent under the rule of Garcia. Muslim Seljuk Turks invade Asia Minor.

1066

At the Battle of Stamford Bridge, King Harold Godwinson of England defeats Harald of Norway marking the end of the Viking era in England. William, Duke of Normandy, defeats Harold at the Battle of Hastings and is crowned king of England. Halley's Comet appears and is recorded in the Bayeux Tapestry.

1067 Work begins on the building of the Tower of London. The Trencavel family takes over in Carcassonne in France.

1069 William the Conqueror rides through the north of England, burning houses, crops, cattle and land, resulting in the deaths of over 100,000 people from starvation and winter cold.

1070 Hereward the Wake begins a Saxon revolt in the Fens of eastern England.

1071 The last Byzantine-controlled city in southern Italy, Bari, is captured by Robert Guiscard. Turkish Seljuks take Jerusalem; they defeat the Byzantine army at the Battle of Manzikert and take control of much of Asia Minor. Constantine the African brings Greek medicine to the West.

1072 William I of England invades Scotland; he defeats Hereward the Wake in the Fens. Norman armies begin the conquest of Sicily.

1073 Rabbi Yitchaki Alfassi finishes writing the *Rif*, an important work of Jewish law.

1075 The rebellion of three earls against William the Conqueror is the last serious act of resistance in the Norman Conquest. Henry IV, Holy Roman Emperor, subjugates Saxony. The Liao Dynasty version of the Buddhist Tripitaka is completed.

1076 Count Dirk V reconquers most of West Frisia (Holland) from the Bishop of Utrecht. The Almoravids capture the Ghanaian capital of Kumbi.

1077 Robert Curthose instigates his first insurrection against his father, William the Conqueror. The first recorded trial by combat is staged in England. Pope Gregory expels the Holy Roman Emperor Henry IV from the Catholic Church; Henry pleads forgiveness, but conflict between the Empire and the Papacy continues into the 12th century. The kingdom of Duklja is founded in Serbia. The Almoravids invade Ghana in Africa. The Bayeux Tapestry is completed.

1078 The cathedral of Santiago de Compostela is begun in Galicia, Spain.

1079 William I of England establishes the New Forest. Abbess Hildegarde of St Ruprechtsberg makes the first surviving reference to the use of hops in brewing. The Persian astronomer Omar Khayyám computes the length of the year as 365.24219858156 days; he is accurate to within one second.

1080 William I of England writes to the pope to remind him that the king of England owes him no allegiance.

1081 Byzantine Emperor Nicephorus III is overthrown by Alexius I Comnenus, ending the Middle Byzantine period and beginning the Comnenan dynasty. Corfu is taken from the Byzantine Empire by Robert Guiscard, Norman king of southern Italy.

1082 Henry IV, Holy Roman Emperor, besieges Rome and gains entry; a synod is agreed upon by the Romans to rule on the dispute between Henry and Pope Gregory VII. The Korean printing of the entire Buddhist Tripitaka is completed.

1083 Pope Gregory VII is besieged in Castel Sant'Angelo by Henry IV, the Holy Roman Emperor. Bosnia is conquered by Duklja.

1085 Around this date, Thule Eskimo culture spreads to Greenland and Siberia.

1086 The Domesday survey is commissioned by William I of England to ensure proper taxation and levies. The power of the Fujiwara family declines in Japan with the introduction of the cloistered emperor system.

1090 Around this date, a mechanical clock, driven by water, is built in Kaifeng in China.

1091 The construction of around 15,000 temples and palaces is under way in Pagan, Myanmar.

1092 The Islamic sect, the Assassins, kill the Seljuk vizier.

1096 The First Crusade is launched to retake Palestine from the Seljuks.

1098 The monastery of Citeaux is founded in France marking the start of the Cistercian Order of monks.

1099 The Crusaders capture Jerusalem.

1100 Jayadeva writes the Indian love poem, *Gitagovinda*. Around this date: Middle English replaces Old English; the Hohokam people of Arizona, North America, are building platform mounds; the first statues are erected on Easter Island; the beginnings of organized societies in the Hawaiian Islands; the earliest settlements by Polynesians in Pitcairn Island; the rise of the Incas in Peru; the Ghana empire in West Africa declines; Katanga in Zaire, Central Africa, is founded; the height of the Chimu civilization at Chan Chan, on the north-west coast of Peru; the Anasazi people in North America build cliff dwellings at Mesa Verde, Chaco Canyon and the Canyon de Chelly; the game of checkers is invented.

1101 Robert Curthose gives up his claim to the Anglo-Norman throne, thus establishing Henry I as king of England. A second wave of Crusaders arrives in the newly established kingdom of Jerusalem.

1102 Raymond IV of Toulouse besieges Tripoli but is imprisoned by Tancred, regent of the principality of Antioch.

1104 The Venetian Arsenal is founded. Alfonso I of Aragon becomes king of Aragon and Navarre. Baldwin I of Jerusalem captures Acre. Baldwin II, Count of Edessa, is taken prisoner by the Seljuk Turks at the Battle of Harran; Tancred becomes regent. The volcano Hekla erupts in Iceland, destroying settlements.

1105 Henry IV, the Holy Roman Emperor, is deposed by his son, Henry V.

1106 Henry I of England defeats his older brother Robert Curthose, Duke of Normandy, at the Battle of Tinchebrai. The Great Comet of 1106 is seen in Wales, Japan, Korea, China and Europe.

1107 Chinese money is printed in three colours to prevent counterfeiting.

1108 St Magnus becomes the first Earl of Orkney.

1109 The Crusaders capture Tripoli.

1110 Henry V invades Italy. The Crusaders conquer Sidon and Beirut.

1112 The German state of Baden is founded. Alfonso I becomes Count of Portugal.

1113 The start of the reign of Suryavarman II of Cambodia; he begins construction of the temple complex of Angkor Wat.

1114 Ramon Berenguer III of Barcelona conquers Ibiza and Mallorca.

1115 The Jurchen establish the Jin Dynasty of China. Paris becomes a centre of religious learning. The beginning of the career of Bernard of Clairvaux, whose abbey becomes the most important monastery in Europe. Pierre Abélard becomes canon of Notre Dame de Paris.

1116 Baldwin I of Jerusalem invades Egypt. The modern book format of separate pages stitched together is invented in China.

1117
The earliest recorded use of a compass for navigational purposes.

1118 A rebellion against Henry I of England breaks out in Normandy. Ramon Berenguer III captures Tarragona from the Moors. Alfonso the Battler expels the Moors from Zaragoza. The Knights Templar are founded, to protect the road to Jerusalem.

1119 Bologna University is founded in Italy.

1120 Welcher of Malvern creates a system of measurement for the Earth using the degrees, minutes and seconds of latitude and longitude. The Chinese play with painted playing cards.

1121 The Concordat of Worms condemns Pierre Abélard's writings on the Holy Trinity; later in the year, Fulbert of Chartres, uncle of Heloïse, with whom Abélard has had an affair, has Abélard castrated. The king of Georgia with an army of 55,000 defeats the 200,000-strong Muslim coalition troops at Didgori, Eastern Georgia.

1123 St Bartholomew's Hospital is founded in London. The Republic of Venice and the Kingdom of Jerusalem sign the Pactum Warmundi treaty.

1124 David I kills Alexander I and becomes king of Scotland. Tyre falls to the Crusaders.

1125 Lothair of Saxony becomes Holy Roman Emperor on the death of Henry V. Troubadour and trouvère music becomes popular in France.

1126 Alfonso VII is crowned king of Castile and León in Spain. The Jin Dynasty is established in the north of China with the Sung Dynasty's loss in battle at the Huang He river valley.

1127 Constantinople, capital of the Byzantine Empire, becomes the largest city in the world. Jurchen forces sack the Song Chinese capital, Kaifeng, and more than a century of political division begins between north and south in China.

1128 Holyrood Abbey is founded in Edinburgh by David I, King of Scotland. Prince Alfonso of Portugal defeats his mother, Teresa of León, in battle and gains control of the country.

1130 Magnus the Blind and Harald Gille become joint kings of Norway and the country's civil war era begins.

1131 Fulk of Anjou and Melisende become king and queen of Jerusalem.

1132 St Denis Abbey, the first Gothic church, is built by Abbot Suger in Paris.

1133 Durham Cathedral is completed.

1134 Narbonne is seized by Alphonse I of Toulouse. The Zeeland archipelago is created by a massive storm in the North Sea. Magnus IV of Norway defeats Harald IV of Norway at the battle at Färlev.

1135 The domination of Baghdad by the Seljuk Turks ends.

1136 Owain Gwynedd of Wales defeats the Normans at Crug Mawr. Pierre Abélard writes the *Historia Calamitatum*, detailing his relationship with Héloïse.

1138 The English defeat David I of Scotland in the Battle of the Standard. A deadly earthquake in Aleppo, Syria kills around 230,000 people.

1139 Following the Battle of Ourique, Prince Alfnso becomes King Alfonso I of an independent Portugal.

1141 The Jin dynasty and the Southern Song dynasty sign the Treaty of Shaoxing and enjoy peace for the next 20 years. The Italian winemaking company Ricasoli is founded.

1143 Robert of Ketton makes the first European translation of the Qur'an, into Latin.

1144 Normandy comes under Angevin control under Geoffrey of Anjou. Giordano Pierleoni founds the revolutionary Commune of Rome.

1145 Pope Eugene III issues *Quantum Praedecessores*, calling for the Second Crusade. Merv in the Seljuk Empire becomes the largest city in the world.

1146 St Bernard of Clairvaux preaches the Second Crusade in Burgundy.

1147 King Alfonso I of Portugal and the Crusaders capture Lisbon from the Moors. The Almohads, Berber Muslims opposed to the Almoravids, seize Marrakech and go on to conquer Almoravid Spain, Algeria and Tripoli.

1148 King Alfonso I of Portugal takes Abrantes from the Moors.

1149 Nur ad-Din defeats the principality of Antioch at the Battle of Inab. The Christian armies of the Second Crusade lose to the Turks in Asia Minor; they abandon the siege of Damascus.

1150 The ferry across the Mersey begins running between Liverpool and Birkenhead. The University of Paris, now known as the Sorbonne, is founded. The Zagwe dynasty rules in the Ethiopian highlands. Around this time: The end of Hopewell culture in North America; the Chimu civilization flourishes on the coast of Peru; Maoris begin to settle in the river mouth areas in the north of the South Island in New Zealand.

1151 Ghazni in Afghanistan is burned by the princes of Ghur. The Toltec Empire in Mexico comes to an end. Explosives are used in battle for the first time, by the Chinese.

1152 The Church of Ireland acknowledges the pope's authority. Frederick I Barbarossa is elected king of the Germans. The Almohad dynasty conquers Algeria.

1153 Malcolm IV becomes king of Scotland. The Treaty of Winchester allows Empress Matilda's son, Henry of Anjou, to become king of England. The Angevin dynasty takes control of Gascony and Guyenne. Constantinople, capital of the Byzantine Empire, again becomes the largest city in the world. Baldwin III of Jerusalem takes control of the Kingdom of Jerusalem from his mother Melisende, and also captures Ascalon. Islam is introduced to the Maldives.

1154 Henry Plantagenet becomes King Henry II of England. Sweden's King Eric introduces Christianity to Finland. Nur ad-Din gains control of Damascus, uniting Syria under one ruler. Muhammad al-Idrisi completes his atlas of the world, which will remain one of the most accurate maps until the 15th century. Birmingham in England and the Birmingham Bull Ring are founded.

1155 Frederick I Barbarossa becomes Holy Roman Emperor.

1156 Prince Yuriy Dolgorukiy fortifies Moscow, regarded as the date of the founding of the city. The Carmelite Order is established. Mosan artists create the Stavelot Triptych, a reliquary to house what were purported to be pieces of the True Cross. The Hogen disturbance, a civil war about succession, takes place in Japan.

1158 The British Pound Sterling is introduced.

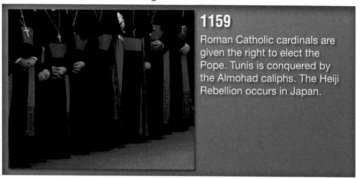

1159
Roman Catholic cardinals are given the right to elect the Pope. Tunis is conquered by the Almohad caliphs. The Heiji Rebellion occurs in Japan.

1160 Yasovarman II succeeds his uncle Dharanindravarman as ruler of the Khmer Empire.

1162 Thomas Becket is consecrated as Archbishop of Canterbury.

1163 Owain Gwynedd is recognized as ruler of Wales. The Council of Tours names and condemns the Albigensians. The first stone of Paris's Notre Dame Cathedral is laid by Pope Alexander III. The birth of Genghis Khan, creator of the Mongol Empire.

1164 Thomas Becket argues with Henry II and leaves England to solicit support from the pope and the king of France.

1165 The Muslims take Caesarea Philippi from the Crusaders.

1167 William Marshal, said to be the greatest knight that ever lived, is knighted. Alfonso I of Portugal is defeated by the kingdom of Léon. The Lombard League defeats Frederick I in the Battle of Legnano. Taira no Kiyomori becomes the first samurai to be appointed Daijo Daijin, chief minister of the government of Japan.

1168 Prince Richard of England becomes Duke of Aquitaine and later becomes King Richard I of England. To prevent Old Cairo being captured by the Crusaders, its caliph orders the city to be set on fire; it burns for 54 days.

1169 The start of the conquest of Ireland. Richard Fitz Gilbert de Clare ('Strongbow') makes an alliance with the exiled Irish chief, Dermot MacMurrough, to help him recover the kingdom of Leinster. Eleanor of Aquitaine leaves England to establish her great court in Poitiers. Nur ad-Din invades Egypt, and his nephew Saladin becomes sultan of the conquered territory.

1170 Thomas Beckett, Archbishop of Canterbury, is assassinated in Canterbury cathedral. Henry II of England sponsors the Norman invasion of Ireland, sparking eight centuries of conflict and war between Ireland and England; Dublin is captured by the Normans. Fes in the Almohad Empire becomes the largest city in the world.

1171 Rhys ap Gruffydd of Wales agrees to negotiate with Henry II of England. Saladin, Muslim warrior and commander in the Egyptian army, overthrows the Fatimid dynasty, restoring Sunni rule.

1172 Henry II conquers Ireland. The Council of Avranches absolves Henry of the assassination of Thomas Becket. The Synod of Cashel ends the Celtic Christian system and brings it under the authority of Rome.

1173 Construction starts on the Tower of Pisa. Eleanor of Aquitaine and her sons rebel unsuccessfully against her husband Henry II of England in the revolt of 1173–4. Saladin declares himself sultan of Egypt. The first recorded use of algebraic chess notation.

1174 William I of Scotland is captured by Henry II of England; Henry occupies Scotland. Saladin captures Damascus. Vietnam is given the official name of Annam by China. The first known racetrack of the post-classical era opens at Newmarket in England. Fire destroys most of Padua in Italy.

1175 Ruaidri Ua Conchobair (Rory O'Conner), the last High King of Ireland, submits to Henry II with the Treaty of Windsor.

1176 Construction begins on the first London Bridge. The first recorded Welsh Eisteddfod is held by Rhys ap Gruffydd at Cardigan. The Cathedral of Sens installs the first 'horologe'.

1177 Baldwin IV of Jerusalem and Raynald of Chatillon defeat Saladin at the Battle of Montgisard. A fire devastates Kyoto. The Cham sack the Khmer capital of Angkor Wat.

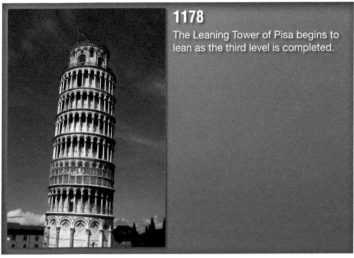

1178
The Leaning Tower of Pisa begins to lean as the third level is completed.

1179 The Norwegian Battle of Kalvskinnet changes the tide of the civil wars. The Third Council of the Lateran condemns Waldensians and Cathars as heretics, and creates the first ghettos for Jews. Westminster School is founded by the monks of Westminster Abbey. The Drigung Kagyu school of Kagyu Buddhism is founded.

1180 Philip II Augustus becomes ruler of France, conquering Angevin lands in the west. Alfonso I of Portugal is taken prisoner by Ferdinand II of Léon. The Chola kingdom in southern India goes into decline. The last major volcanic eruption of Sunset Crater, in Arizona. In Japan, Prince Mochihito instigates the Genpei War between the Taira and Minamoto clans. Hangzhou, capital of Southern Song China, becomes the largest city in the world.

1181 Chinese and Japanese astronomers observe a supernova, one of only eight observed in recorded history. Jayavarman VII defeats the Cham and assumes control of the Khmer kingdom.

1182 The Jews are expelled from Paris by Philip II of France.

1183 The Siege of Kerak is waged between the Ayyubids and the Crusaders. Taira no Munemori and the Taira clan flee with the three-year-old Emperor Antoku and the three sacred treasures to western Japan to escape pursuit by the Minamoto clan.

1184 The streets of Paris are paved by order of Philip Augustus. The papal bull, *Ad Aboldendam*, is issued against several European heretical groups: the Cathars, the Waldensians, the Patarines and the Humiliati.

1185 Knights Templar settle in London and begin the building of New Temple Church. Peter and Asen establish the Second Bulgarian Kingdom. In the Byzantine Empire, Isaac II Angelus deposes Andronicus I Comnenus and takes the throne of the Byzantine Empire. In the Genpei War in Japan, the naval battle of Dan-no-ura leads to a Minamoto victory.

1186 Guy of Lusignan becomes king of Jerusalem. The last Ghaznavid ruler is deposed by Mohammed of Ghur, the Muslim founder of an empire in North India.

1187 Pope Gregory VIII proposes the Third Crusade. Saladin defeats the Crusaders and takes Jerusalem. Ghorin Muhammed conquers the Punjab. The Toltecs are deposed at Chichen Itza. Zen Buddhism arrives in Japan. King of Angkor Wat, Jayavarman VII, defeats the Cham conquerors.

1188 Newgate Prison is built in London. Richard the Lionheart allies with Philip II of France against his father, Henry II of England. Recruitment is undertaken in Wales for the Third Crusade and the 'Saladin Tithe', a tax, is levied in England and France.

1189 Troops assemble for the Third Crusade. Richard the Lionheart is crowned as king of England. The Siege of Acre begins. The Crusader castles of Montreal and Kerak are captured by Saladin. The year 1189 is fixed in 1276 as the end of 'time immemorial' in English law.

1190 The Third Crusade begins. There is a massacre and mass-suicide of the Jews of York. The Teutonic Order of knights, a military society, is set up in Germany to defend Christian lands in Palestine and Syria. Richard I of England threatens war against Tancred of Sicily, and captures Messina. Frederick I Barbarossa drowns in the Saleph River while leading an army to Jerusalem. The Japanese Feudal Era begins.

1191 Saladin's garrison surrenders, ending the two-year siege of Acre; Richard I of England defeats Saladin at Arsuf. Tea comes to Japan from China.

1192 A truce between Richard I of England and Saladin ends the Third Crusade. Richard is taken hostage by Leopold V of Austria. Conrad I, king of Jerusalem, is assassinated. In Japan, Minamoto no Yoritomo is granted the title of shogun, establishing the first shogunate in Japan's history.

1193 Saladin dies, and the lands of the Kurdish Ayyubid dynasty of Egypt and Syria are split among his descendants. Qutb-ud-Din, a Ghurid slave commander and founder of the Slave dynasty, captures Delhi.

1194 Richard I of England is ransomed from Henry VI, Emperor of the Holy Roman Empire. In China, the Yellow River experiences a major change in course and takes over the Huai River drainage system for the next 700 years. The *Elder Edda*, a collection of Scandinavian mythology, is written.

1196 In London, there is a popular uprising of the poor against the rich. Water boards are established in the region of present-day Netherlands, creating one of the oldest democratic entities still in existence in the world today.

1199 King Richard I of England is killed at the siege of Châlus and John 'Lackland' becomes king of England.

1200 The Mongols defeat Northern China. Around this date: The Early Gothic period begins in England; King Lalibela of Ethiopia builds churches cut from rock; the Kanem-Bornu Empire is established in northern Africa; in North America, Cahokia, a city of temple mounds, is at its height; complexes of apartment blocks and circular kivas are built at Cliff Canyon and Fewkes Canyon, Colorado; the Incas in Peru gravitate to the growing settlement of Cuzco; the Tui Tonga monarchy builds a coral platform for ceremonial worship on the island of Tonga in the South Pacific.

1201 The Fourth Crusade is launched.

1202 The military order, the Livonian Brothers of the Sword, is founded. Leonardo Fibonacci publishes *Liber Abaci*, introducing the Arabian zero to Europe. The first jesters appear in European courts.

1203 Philip II of France enters Rouen, leading to the eventual unification of Normandy and France. The Fleet of the Fourth Crusade enters the Bosphorus and Constantinople is captured; Alexius IV is named Byzantine Emperor. Boniface of Montferrat, a leader of the Fourth Crusade, founds the kingdom of Thessalonica.

1204 Jersey enjoys self-government thanks to the division of the Duchy of Normandy. Baldwin, Count of Flanders is crowned Emperor of the Latin Empire. Valdemar II, king of Denmark, is recognized as king in Norway. Byzantine Emperor Alexius IV is overthrown in a revolution; Alexius V is proclaimed Emperor.

1205 Henry of Flanders is crowned Emperor of the Latin Empire.

1206 The former Turkestan slave Aibak founds the new sultanate of Delhi in north India. Qutb ud-Din proclaims the Mameluk dynasty in India, the first dynasty of the Delhi Sultanate. The Mongol Empire is founded by Genghis Khan.

1207 King John issues letters patent, creating the new Borough of Liverpool.

1208 An inferior Swedish force defeats the invading Danes in the Battle of Lena.

1209 London Bridge is completed. Cambridge University is founded. The Albigensian Crusade against the Cathars begins; Simon de Montfort, leader of the Albigensian Crusade, takes Carcassonne. St Francis of Assisi founds the Franciscan religious order. Genghis Khan conquers Turkestan.

1211 Genghis Khan invades Jin China. Construction begins on Notre Dame de Reims. The oldest recorded example of double-entry bookkeeping dates from this time.

1212 Most of London is burned to the ground. Crusaders push the Muslims out of northern Spain. Kamo no Chomei writes the Hojoki, one of the great works of classical Japanese prose.

1213 In the Battle of Damme, the English fleet destroys a French fleet in the first major victory for the fledgling Royal Navy. Pope Innocent III calls for the Fifth Crusade to recapture Jerusalem.

1214 In France, Philip II defeats John of England.

1215 English King John seals the Magna Carta, giving more power to the barons. The Fourth Lateran Council meets, adopting the doctrine of transubstantiation. The Dominican Order is founded.

1216 Henry III becomes king of England. Prince Louis of France invades England in the First Barons' War.

1217 The Treaty of Lambeth ends the First Barons' War. The kingdom of Serbia is founded. The Fifth Crusade begins with a failed Christian attack on Egypt.

1218 The Livonian Brothers of the Sword begin the conquest of Estonia. Genghis Khan destroys the Kara-Khitai Empire. The Ayyubid Empire breaks up but Ayyubids rule Egypt until 1250.

1220 Trial by ordeal is abolished in England. Building work begins on Salisbury Cathedral. Genghis Khan takes Bukhara and Samarkand.

1221 Merv is sacked and its people massacred by Genghis Khan's forces. The Maya of the Yucatán revolt against the rulers of Chichen Itza.

1222 The University of Padua is founded. The Manden Charter establishing human rights and abolishing slavery is proclaimed in Mali.

1224 The University of Naples is founded.

1227 The Estonians' fight for independence ends; there is foreign rule in the country for the next seven centuries. The monk, Dogen, brings Zen Buddhism to Japan from China.

1228 The Sixth Crusade is launched. Conrad IV of Germany becomes titular king of Jerusalem, with Frederick II as regent. Sukaphaa, the first Ahom king, establishes his rule in Assam; Ahom kings reign for 600 years.

1229 The Christians regain Jerusalem. The island of Majorca is captured by the Catalans from the Muslims. There are student riots and a two-year strike at the University of Paris.

1230 The kingdom of Léon unites with the kingdom of Castile. The returning Crusaders introduce leprosy to Europe. The *Carmina Burana* poetry and song collection is compiled. Around this time, the Hafsid monarchy takes over from the Almohads in Tunisia.

1232 The first edition of Tripitaka Koreana, Buddhist scriptures, is destroyed by Mongol invaders.

1233 The Inquisition is established. Mustansiriya University is founded in Baghdad.

1234 The Mongols bring the Jin dynasty to an end.

1235 The Berber kingdom of Abd al-Wadids is founded in the Maghreb in Africa. Around this time, the great warrior leader Sun Diata, founds the Mali Empire in West Africa.

1236 Córdoba is retaken for Christianity. Lithuanians and Semigallians defeat the Livonian Brothers of the Sword in the Battle of Saule. Volga Bulgaria is conquered by the Mongol khan, Batu.

1237 The Mongols invade Russia.

1238 Valencia is captured from the Moors. The Khmers are expelled from Luang Phrabang in Laos. The Sukhothai Kingdom is founded in Thailand.

1240 The Russian Alexander Nevsky defeats the Swedes at the Neva River, preventing a full-scale invasion from the north. The civil war era in Norway comes to an end.

1241 Lübeck and Hamburg form a Hansa (association) for trade and mutual protection, marking the beginning of the Hanseatic League.

1242 The Mongols invade the Seljuk sultanate. Arab physician Ibn Nafis suggests that the right and left ventricles of the heart are separate and describes the circulation of blood.

1244 The Cathars of Montségur surrender after a nine-month siege; they are massacred.

1245 The rebuilding of Westminster Abbey begins. In Portugal, there is a rebellion against King Sancho II of Portugal in favour of his brother Alphonso. Pope Innocent IV sends an envoy to the Mongol court, suggesting that the Mongols convert to Christianity.

1246 Güyük Khan is enthroned as the 3rd Great Khan of the Mongol Empire.

1247 The Thuringian War of Succession begins. Egypt takes control of Jerusalem from the Kharezmians. Ch'in Chiu-Shao publishes the original form of the Chinese remainder theorem.

1248 The Seventh Crusade begins. Seville is taken from the Moors. The Moors begin construction of the Alhambra palace in Granada. The Gothic chapel of Sainte-Chapelle is consecrated in Paris, France. The foundation stone of Cologne Cathedral is laid. Roger Bacon publishes a major scientific work, including writings about convex lens spectacles for treating long-sightedness and the first publication in the Western world of the formula for gunpowder.

1249 University College, the first college of Oxford University, England, is founded. Faro in the Algarve is recaptured from the Moors, ending the Portuguese Reconquista.

1250 The Great Interregnum in the Holy Roman Empire lasts 23 years; the Empire passes from the Hohenstaufen dynasty to the Habsburgs. The Lombard League is dissolved. The Bahri dynasty of Mamelukes seize power in Egypt. The Kanem kingdom in Lake Chad region begins to break up into rival factions. The Welayta state is founded in present-day Ethiopia. Chimu people are expanding their empire along the northern coast of Peru. The Aztecs arrive in central Mexico. There is a Maya revival; a new capital is built at Mayapan. The Rialto Bridge in Venice is converted from a pontoon bridge to a permanent, raised wooden structure. Albertus Magnus isolates the element arsenic. Notre Dame Cathedral in Paris is completed.

1251 The First Shepherds' Crusade is launched, a French peasants' crusade to rescue Louis IX from captivity in Egypt. Alexander Nevsky signs the first peace treaty between Kievan Rus' and Norway. Möngke Khan is elected as Khan of the Mongol Empire. The Tripitaka Koreana, a collection of Buddhist scriptures, is carved on 81,000 wooden blocks.

1252 Pope Innocent IV authorizes the torture of heretics in the medieval Inquisition. The Swedish city of Stockholm is founded. In astronomy, work begins on the recording of the Alfonsine tables dividing the year into 365 days, 5 hours, 49 minutes, 16 seconds. The first European gold coins are minted in the Italian city of Florence, and are known as florins.

1253 A series of naval wars begins between Genoa and Venice, continuing sporadically until 1371. The Mongol Empire attacks Baghdad and Cairo; it also destroys the kingdom of Dali (Yunnan) in Laos, incorporating the region into the empire. Nichiren Buddhism is founded.

1254 In England, lesser barons are replaced on the King's Council by elected representatives from the shires and cities. The Seventh Crusade is abandoned. King Louis IX of France expels all Jews from France. In Portugal, the first session of the Cortes (Portugal's general assembly) is held. The Horses of St Mark, once supposed to have adorned the Arch of Trajan in ancient Rome, are installed at St Mark's Basilica in Venice. Copenhagen receives its city charter. Malmö is founded.

1255 The Hundred Rolls, an English census, is conducted. The final Cathar stronghold in southern France falls. Lisbon becomes capital of Portugal. Hulagu Khan, grandson of Genghis Khan, is dispatched by his brother Möngke Khan to destroy the remaining Muslim states in south-western Asia. The Gothic cathedral at Bourges, France, is completed.

1256 Hulagu Khan founds the Mongol kingdom of Persia; it will become one of the four main divisions of the Mongol Empire.

1257 The first high-denomination gold coin is minted in England.

1258 King Henry III of England is forced to accept the Provisions of Oxford, requiring the calling of a parliament and ending absolute monarchy in England. Llywelyn the Last is the final ruler of an independent Wales. Hulagu Khan's Mongol forces burn Baghdad to the ground, killing 1,000,000 citizens.

1259 The Treaty of Paris is signed between kings Henry III of England and Louis IX of France. The Mongol Golden Horde attacks Lithuania and Poland.

1260 The Mongols take Palestine. Kublai, grandson of Genghis, becomes Great Khan. Mameluke commander Baybars takes over as sultan of Egypt. The Sena Dynasty of Bengal falls. The Hindu Silharya Dynasty, which ruled an area around Mumbai, comes to an end. The German musical theorist, Franco of Cologne, publishes a new theory of musical notation, a system still in use today. Nicola Pisano sculpts the pulpit of the Pisa Baptistery.

1261   Constantinople is recaptured by Nicaean forces, re-establishing the Byzantine Empire.

1262   King Henry III of England obtains a papal bull releasing him from the Provisions of Oxford, leading to the Second Barons' War. Iceland and Greenland come under Norwegian rule. King Mengrai of the Lannathai kingdom in present-day Thailand, founds the city of Chiang Rai as the kingdom's first capital. Adam de la Halle writes the first operetta, *Le Jeu de la feullée*.

1263   Alexander III of Scotland defeats the Vikings in the Battle of Largs. The Venetians defeat the Genoese at the Battle of Settepozzi.

1264   The Second Barons' War, a civil war in England, begins. The first definitively known meeting of the Irish legislature takes place at Castledermot in County Kildare. The Thuringian War of Succession ends. Kublai Khan moves the empire's capital from Karakorum in Mongolia to the Chinese city of Khanbaliq (now Beijing). The title, Baron de Ros, the oldest continuously held peerage title in England, is created. Thomas Aquinas completes his theological work, *Summa contra Gentiles*.

1265

In Westminster, the first elected English parliament (De Montfort's Parliament) takes place. The Battle of Evesham is fought in the Second Barons' War, with Edward's army defeating Simon de Montfort and killing him. The *Book of Aneirin*, a Welsh manuscript of poetry, is written. The brewing of Budweiser Budvar beer begins in Bohemia.

1266   The war between Scotland and Norway ends with Norway ceding the Western Isles and the Isle of Man to Scotland in exchange for a large monetary payment. Niccolo and Maffeo Polo, brother and uncle of Marco Polo, reach Kublai Khan's capital Khanbaliq (now Beijing) in China.

1267   Henry III of England acknowledges Llywelyn ap Gruffydd's title of Prince of Wales in the Treaty of Montgomery. A Spanish invasion of Morocco is repelled. Vienna forces Jews to wear the *Pileum cornutum*, a cone-shaped headdress, in addition to the yellow badges they were already forced to wear. Malik ul Salih establishes Samudra Pasai, the first Muslim state in Indonesia. Roger Bacon completes his work *Opus Majus* which contains wide-ranging discussion of mathematics, optics, alchemy, astronomy, astrology, and other topics, including the first description of a magnifying glass.

1268   Conradin, the last legitimate male heir of the Hohenstaufen dynasty of the kings of Germany and Holy Roman Emperors, is replaced by Charles I of Sicily, a political rival and ally to the hostile Roman Catholic Church. King Stephen V of Hungary launches a war against Bulgaria. The House of Bourbon first rises to prominence. The principality of Antioch falls to the Mameluke Sultan Baibars. The Battle of Xiangyang is fought, a six-year battle between the Chinese Song Dynasty and the Mongol forces of Kublai Khan. The carnival in Venice is first recorded. An earthquake in Cilicia (modern Turkey) kills an estimated 60,000 people.

1269   King Otakar II of Bohemia inherits Carinthia and part of Carniola, making him the most powerful prince in the Holy Roman Empire. The Berber

Marinid completes the conquest of Morocco, replacing the Almohad dynasty. Pélerin de Maricourt first describes magnetic poles.

1270 The Eighth Crusade is launched; Louis IX of France dies while besieging Tunis. The *Summa Theologiae*, by Thomas Aquinas, considered within the Roman Catholic Church to be the paramount expression of its theology, is completed around this time. Ashkelon is captured from the Crusader states and destroyed by the Mameluke sultan Baibars. Yekuno Amlak overthrows the Ethiopian Zagwe dynasty, claims the throne and establishes the Solomonic dynasty. Witelo translates Alhazen's 200-year-old treatise on optics, *Kitab al-Manazir*, from Arabic into Latin. The Sanskrit fables known as the *Panchatantra*, dating from as early as 200 BC, are translated into Latin. Hangzhou, in China, is the most populous city in the world.

1271 Edward I of England and Charles of Anjou arrive in Acre, starting the unsuccessful Ninth Crusade. Mameluke sultan Baibars captures the Krak des Chevaliers castle from the Knights Hospitaller in present-day Syria. Caerphilly Castle, the largest in Wales, is completed. Venetian explorer Marco Polo sets out for China.

1272 Charles I of Anjou occupies Durres in Albania and establishes an Albanian kingdom. The first recorded reference is made to cricket. In London, the Worshipful Company of Cordwainers acquires the right to regulate the leather trade.

1273 Rudolph I becomes first Habsburg ruler of Austria. Followers of the recently deceased Jalal al-Din Muhammad Rumi establish the Sufi order of the Whirling Dervishes in the city of Konya. Firearms are used in warfare for the first time in the six-year battle of Xiangyang in which the Song Dynasty's forces surrender to Kublai Khan.

1274 King Edward I of England returns from the Ninth Crusade to be crowned king. He orders all English Jews to wear yellow badges.

1275 The first of the Statutes of Westminster are passed by the English Parliament; they include equal treatment of rich and poor, and free and fair elections. The verge escapement, a simple type of escapement used in clocks, is invented around this time. Marco Polo reportedly visits Xanadu, Kublai Khan's summer capital of the Mongol Empire. Jean de Meun writes the French allegorical work of fiction, *Roman de la Rose*.

1276 A 23-year drought begins in the Grand Canyon area; the agriculture-dependent people of the Anasazi culture are forced to migrate. The court of the Southern Song dynasty of China flees in the face of an invasion by the Mongol Empire.

1277 Baibars invades Anatolia and captures the emirates which once composed the Sultanate of Rüm. Burma's Pagan Empire begins to disintegrate after being defeated by Kublai Khan. The leaders and citizens of the Southern Song dynasty of China become the first recorded inhabitants of Macau, as they flee the invading Mongols. The St George's cross is first used as the flag of England.

1278 Rudolph I of Germany and Ladislaus IV of Hungary defeat Otakar II of Bohemia in the Battle of Marchfield, the largest battle of knights of the Middle Ages; the Habsburgs will continue to rule Austria and other captured territories until the end of the First World War in 1918. The earliest known written copy of the *Avesta*, a collection of ancient sacred Persian Zoroastrian texts, is completed.

1279 The Chola dynasty of South India falls under attacks by the Hoysala Empire and Pandyan kingdom. Kublai Khan completes the Mongol conquest of China and exterminates the Song dynasty. The Dai-Gohonzon, the supreme object of veneration of Nichiren Shoshu Buddhism, is inscribed by Nichiren. In England, the second of the Hundred Rolls surveys is undertaken; it lasts until 1280.

1280 King Edward I of England forms the Court of the King's Bench. The Asen dynasty of tsars of Bulgaria ends. Construction is begun on the northern section of the Grand Canal of China.

1281 A French and Venetian crusade against Constantinople is forced to turn back. Osman I, founder of the Ottoman Empire, becomes bey of the Söğüt tribe in central Anatolia. The Mongols abandon an invasion of Japan because of a storm, said to be the kamikaze or divine wind. Kublai Khan orders the burning of sacred Taoist texts.

1282 The Sicilian rebellion known as the Sicilian Vespers begins against the rule of Angevin King Charles I of Sicily. The technology of watermarks is introduced by paper-manufacturers in Bologna.

1283 The Archbishop of Canterbury orders the closure of all London synagogues. Death by drawing and quartering is first used as a form of execution by King Edward I of England in his execution of Dafydd ap Gruffydd, the last ruler of an independent Wales. Kublai Khan invades the Khmer empire; Jayavarman VIII pays tribute rather than fight the invasion. The construction of Caernarfon Castle, Conwy Castle and Harlech Castle is begun in Wales by King Edward I of England.

1284 The creation of the Statute of Rhuddlan, formally incorporating Wales into England in the entity England and Wales. The Italian city state of Genoa defeats its rival Pisa in the naval Battle of Meloria, hastening Pisa's decline in power. The Mongol Golden Horde attacks Hungary. Peterhouse, the first college of Cambridge University, is founded. Venice begins coining the ducat, a gold coin that is to become the standard of European coinage for the following 600 years. Sequins are first made in Venice.

1285 Mameluke sultan Qalawun captures the Crusader fortress of Margat in present-day Syria, a major stronghold of the Knights Hospitaller thought to be impregnable. Vietnamese forces defeat an invading Yuan dynasty Mongol army.

1286 Alexander III of Scotland dies, initiating the first war of Scottish Independence. Rudolph I of Germany withdraws all political freedoms from the Jews.

1287 King Alfonso III of Aragon conquers the island of Minorca from the Moors. A barrier between the North Sea and a shallow lake in Holland collapses; it causes the fifth largest flood in recorded history and creats the Zuider Zee inlet; 50,000 people die and Amsterdam gains sea access, allowing its development as a port.

1288 Pope Nicholas IV proclaims a crusade against King Ladislaus IV of Hungary. The Scottish Parliament creates a law allowing women to propose marriage to men during leap years.

1289 Sultan Qalawun captures the County of Tripoli, thus extinguishing the Crusader state. The 17,887 feet-high volcano Popocatépetl is first ascended by members of the Tecuanipas tribe in present-day Mexico. Franciscan friars begin missionary work in China.

1290 Edward I of England banishes all Jews from England. The Mongol Empire invades the Bessarabia region of Moldavia. The Mameluke dynasty of the Sultanate of Delhi is overthrown by Jalal-ud-din Feroz Khalji of the Khalji dynasty. An earthquake in China kills an estimated 100,000. Around this time, spectacles are invented in Italy.

1291 Scottish nobles recognize the authority of King Edward I of England in mediating a resolution of the succession crisis created by the death of King Alexander III. Three Swiss cantons join together to begin a struggle for independence from the Habsburgs. The independence of San Marino is confirmed by a papal bull. Mameluke Sultan of Egypt Khalil captures Acre, exterminating the Crusader Kingdom of Jerusalem, the final Christian landholding, and ending the Ninth and final Crusade. All glassmakers in Venice are forced to move to the island of Murano in order to contain the risk of fire, thus establishing the glass industry there. Engineer and astronomer Guo Shoujing creates the artificial Kunming Lake as a reservoir for Beijing.

1292 John Balliol is selected as king of Scotland. The Lanna kingdom of northern Thailand conquers the Mon kingdom of Haripunchai. The Vaghela dynasty in Gujarat is subjugated by the Deccan Yadava dynasty of Daulatabad.

1293 The Hindu Majapahit Empire of the Malay Archipelago is founded by Kertarajasa. The Javanese defeat a Mongol expeditionary force. Dante Alighieri completes his book of verse, *La Vita Nuova*.

1294 John Balliol, king of Scotland negotiates the Auld Alliance with France and Norway. The death of Kublai Khan allows the four khanates of the Mongol Empire to become independent.

1295 Edward I summons the Model Parliament. Marco Polo returns to Italy from his travels to China.

1296 Edward I storms Berwick-upon-Tweed, slaughtering the inhabitants; he defeats the Scots at the Battle of Dunbar.

1297
William Wallace begins his revolt against the English, defeating them at the Battle of Stirling Bridge. Monaco gains independence from Genoa; it has been ruled by the Grimaldi family ever since.

1298 King Edward I of England defeats William Wallace in the Battle of Falkirk, reconquering Scotland. While in prison in Genoa, Marco Polo dictates his travels to a local writer.

1299 Osman I declares independence from the Seljuk Turks, marking the birth of the Ottoman Empire. The Mexicans settle Chapultepec, a former Toltec stronghold.

1300 Around this date: Trade fairs take place in Bruges, Antwerp, Lyons and Geneva. The spinning wheel is invented; Imperial China has roughly 60 million inhabitants; Ife culture in West Africa produces famous brasses; the Tuareg establish a state centred on Agadez; Hawaiian peoples start to develop a class structure as a result of economic growth through agriculture; the Incas begin to expand their empire throughout the central Andes; stone temple complexes are erected on Rarotonga on the Cook Islands, and on Moorea Island in the Society Islands; huge stone statues are erected on Easter Island.

1301 Edward of Caernarvon (later King Edward II of England) becomes the first Prince of Wales. Robert I of Scotland makes peace with Edward I of England. Osman defeats the Byzantines at Baphaion. Dante is sent into exile from Florence.

1302 In the Battle of the Golden Spurs, Flanders defeats the French. The War of the Sicilian Vespers over the rule of the Angevin king Charles I ends.

1303 The University of Rome is founded.

1304 Edward I of England takes Stirling Castle, the last rebel stronghold in the Wars of Scottish Independence.

1305 The measurements, the yard and the acre, are standardized by Edward I of England. The great Gothic artist Giotto paints frescoes in Sta Maria dell' Arena in Padua.

1306 Robert the Bruce becomes king of Scotland. The Earl of Pembroke defeats Bruce's Scottish rebels at the Battle of Methven. Philip IV of France exiles all Jews from France and confiscates their property.

1307 Edward II becomes king of England. Dante Alighieri begins to write *The Divine Comedy*.

1308 The papal court moves to Avignon; the Great Schism follows. The beginning of the reign of the Capet-Anjou family in Hungary.

1309 Pope Clement V settles the papal seat in Avignon.

1310 The first purpose-built accommodation for students, Mob Quad, is completed at Merton College, Oxford, England.

1311 A committee of 21 English barons draws up a series of ordinances, which replace the king with ordainers as the effective government of the country.

1312 The Knights Templar are forcibly disbanded. Mansa Mansa becomes king of Mali.

1313 The Order of the Rose Cross, the Rosicrucian Order, is founded.

1314 Robert the Bruce defeats the English at the Battle of Bannockburn and Scotland regains its independence. The Mappa Mundi (Map of the World) is made.

1315 The Swiss defeat Leopold of Austria at the Battle of Morgarten, ensuring independence for the Swiss Confederation. A Muslim prince of Nubian royal blood ascends the throne of Dongola in present-day Sudan. The Great Famine in Europe kills millions (until 1317). Cairo, capital of Mameluke Egypt becomes the largest city in the world.

1316 The Second Battle of Athenry ends with over 5,000 dead and ends the power of the Ua Conchobair (O'Connors) as kings of Connacht.

1318 The Scots capture Berwick-upon-Tweed from the English. The kingdom of Maharashtra is conquered by the Sultanate of Delhi.

1319 Magnus VII unites Norway and Sweden.

1320 The Scots reaffirm their independence by signing the Declaration of Arbroath. Ghiyas al-Din Tughlaq founds the Tughlaq dynasty of the Delhi Sultanate. Around this time, Mansa Mansa commissions the building of the great Friday Mosque in Timbuktu.

1322 The Battle of Ampfing, often called the last battle of knights, takes place; Louis IV, Holy Roman Emperor, defeats Frederick I of Austria.

1323 The Treaty of Nöteborg regulates the Swedish–Russian border. The Pharos Lighthouse of Alexandria, one of the Seven Wonders of the World, is destroyed by a series of earthquakes.

1324 The publication of *Defensor Pacis*, laying the foundations of modern doctrines of sovereignty, by Marsilius of Padua. Malian Emperor Mansa Musa makes a legendary pilgrimage to Mecca, taking an entourage numbering in the thousands as well as hundreds of pounds of gold.

1325 The Aztecs found the city of Tenochtitlan (now Mexico City) on an island in Lake Texcoco. The Hohokam people begin building Casa Grande, the largest structure south of the Gila River in modern-day south-western United States. Ashikaga Takauji, a Japanese general, rebels against the emperor and becomes the first of the Ashikaga shoguns.

1326 Isabella, Edward II's wife, invades England with her lover Roger Mortimer, capturing the king. The Treaty of Novgorod delineates the border between Russia and Norway in Finnmark. The Ottoman Orhan takes Brusa in north-western Turkey from the Byzantines and makes it his capital.

1327 Edward III becomes king of England.

1328 England recognizes Scotland as an independent nation. The sawmill is invented.

1330 The Bulgars under Michael III are beaten by the Serbs at Velbuzhd; large parts of Bulgaria fall to Serbia.

1332 The first record of the division of the English Parliament into two Houses. Lucerne forms the Swiss Confederation with Uri, Schwyz, and Unterwalden. The great African philosopher and historian, Ibn Khaldun is born.

1333 In Japan, Emperor Godaigo overthrows the Hojo clan and captures Kamakura.

1334 Giotto begins the building of the campanile in Florence. The Alhambra palace in Granada is completed. The first recorded outbreak of the Black Death occurs in Hubei, in China.

1335 Abu Said dies and the Ilkhanate division of the Mongol Empire disintegrates.

1336 The Hindu Empire of Vijayanagar in India, founded by Harihara I, becomes a centre of resistance to Islam. The Ashikaga shogunate is established in Japan.

1337 Edward III of England claims the French throne and the Hundred Years' War (1337–1453) begins. Edward, the Black Prince, becomes the first English Duke. William Merlee of Oxford makes the first weather forecasts.

1338 The Ottomans reach the Bosphorus.

1339 Construction starts on the Kremlin in Moscow. Kashmir is conquered by the Muslims.

1340 Edward III of England is declared king of France.

1341 Petrarch is crowned poet laureate in Rome, the first man since antiquity to be given this honour.

1344 Edward III introduces three new gold coins, the florin, the leopard and the helm. The Bardi and the Peruzzi, two great Florentine banking houses, are declared bankrupt.

1345 York Minster is completed. The Serbian Empire is proclaimed.

1346 The English defeat the French at the Battle of Crécy. An earthquake in Constantinople damages the eastern arch of Hagia Sophia.

1347 The English defeat the French at the Battle of Croytoye. Bahman Shah establishes an independent sultanate in the Deccan, in southern India. Bubonic plague or Black Death reaches Europe.

1348 A truce is signed between England and France; it lasts until 1352. Giovanni Boccaccio writes The *Decameron*. Egypt is devastated by the Black Death; one third of the population dies. Hangzhou in Mongolian China becomes the largest city in the world. The Order of the Garter is created.

1349 The Jewish population of Basel in Switzerland is rounded up and incinerated because it is claimed that they are the cause of the plague.

1350 An English fleet personally commanded by King Edward III defeats a Spanish fleet in the Battle of Les Espagnols sur Mer. The last Hindu Javanese kingdom of Majapahit begins to spread in south-east Asia. Hohokam villages in what is now Arizona begin to be abandoned. Edward III begins the rebuilding of Windsor Castle. Li Xingdao writes *The Chalk Circle*, a play about justice and retribution. The beginning of Noh Theatre in Japan. Maoris begin to flourish in North Island, New Zealand. Around this time: Nahuatl becomes the predominant language of the Valley of Mexico; the four-liwan architectural style is introduced into the building of mosques and schools in the Middle East.

1351 Zürich joins the Swiss Confederation. The Turks cross the Dardanelles into Europe for the first time. An uprising weakens the Mongolian Yuan dynasty of China. In the past four years, 75 million Europeans have died of Black Death. In England, tennis begins to be played in the open air.

1352 Ibn Battuta, a Berber scholar, travels across Africa and writes an account of his journey.

1353 Giovanni Boccaccio finishes the *Decameron*.

1354 The Ottomans occupy Gallipoli. The Lao kingdom of Lan Xang is established.

1355 Civil war breaks out in Portugal.

1356 Edward Balliol surrenders his title of king of Scotland to Edward III of England. In the Battle of Poitiers the English, commanded by the Black Prince, defeat the French, capturing King John II of France in the process. The Hanseatic League, a trading alliance between many cities in northern Europe, is officially founded. The king of Raška in Serbia, Stefan Dušan, is proclaimed Tsar of all Serbs, Arbanasses and Greeks. The majority of the Great Pyramid of Giza's limestone casing stones are removed by Bahri Sultan An-Nasir Nasir-ad-Din al-Hasan to build fortresses and mosques in Cairo.

1358 The Jacquerie Revolt takes place; a peasant uprising north of Paris. Muhammad II becomes ruler of the Merinid dynasty in present-day Morocco. Nanjing in Mongolian China becomes the largest city in the world.

1360 The Treaty of Brétigny marks the end of the first phase of the Hundred Years' War. The first francs are minted in France.

1361 Black Death reappears in England. Buda becomes capital of Hungary. Anarchy reigns in the Mongol Blue Horde; there are 20 khans in 17 years.

1362 Louis I of Hungary conquers northern Bulgaria. The Byzantine Empire is reduced to the city of Constantinople. The Grote Mandrenke, a massive south-westerly Atlantic gale, kills 25,000 in England, the Netherlands, northern Germany and Schleswig. English replaces French as England's national language, for the first time since the Norman Conquest of 1066.

1363 Guy de Chauliac writes a book on surgery, *Chirugia Magna*.

1364 Charles V becomes king of France. The Ava dynasty is established in present-day northern Burma.

1365 Bahmani Sultan Mohammed Shah I invades the Vijayanagara Empire in southern India. The Sukhothai kingdom in northern Thailand becomes a tributary state of the Ayutthaya kingdom.

1366 The Stella Artois brewery in present-day Belgium is founded.

1367 The French and English help to restore Pedro as king of Castile. In France, Charles V creates the first royal library.

1368 Moscow attacks Tver. Tver makes a counter-attack with the aid of Lithuania and the Blue Horde. The Mongol leader Tamerlane sacks Delhi. The Mongols are driven out of China; Zhu Yuanzhang founds the Ming dynasty. Work begins on the current Great Wall of China.

1369 War breaks out between France and England; the French recapture most of Aquitaine. Hugues Aubriot founds the Bastille, in Paris. The Thai kingdom of Ayutthaya conquers Cambodia for a second time.

1370 Tamerlane completes his conquest of Central Asia and parts of Persia, establishing the Tamerlaneid Empire. Geoffrey Chaucer writes his first book, *The Book of the Duchess*. The steel crossbow is first used as a weapon of war.

1371 Robert II becomes the first Stuart king of Scotland. The Byzantine co-emperor John V Palaiologos pledges loyalty to the Ottoman Empire to prevent the Turks invading Constantinople. The Ottomans gain control of all of Macedonia, apart from Salonika.

1372 The French gain control of the English Channel for the first time since 1340.

1373 The treaty of Anglo-Portuguese friendship is signed, the oldest active treaty in the world. Merton College Library is built in Oxford, England.

1374 Edward III of England grants the English writer Geoffrey Chaucer a gallon of wine a day for the rest of his life. The dancing mania illness begins in Aix-la-Chapelle, possibly caused by ergot poisoning.

1375 The English sign the Treaty of Bruges, leaving them with only the coastal towns of Calais, Bordeaux and Bayonne. The Mamelukes from Egypt conquer the Armenian kingdom of Cilicia. Robin Hood first appears in English literature.

1376 The Good Parliament is held in England; it attempts to reform the corrupt Royal Council. The Black Prince dies. Acamapitchili becomes the first Tlatoani of the Aztec-Mexican dynasty.

1377 In England, Edward III of England dies; he has reigned for 50 years. Richard II becomes king; the Bad Parliament undoes the work done by the Good Parliament. The Papacy moves back to Rome from Avignon. Ibn Khaldun begins work on the Muqaddimah, an early Muslim view of history. Movable metal type is used for the first time, to print a Korean Buddhist text.

1378 John Wyclif makes his theses public. The Great Schism occurs following the death of Pope Gregory XI – a split in the Catholic Church with one pope in Rome, one in Avignon. In Florence, the Revolt of the Ciompi briefly provides the first European government representing all social classes. Halley's Comet appears.

1379 The independent principality of the Turkomans of the Black Sheep Empire is established in present-day Armenia.

1380 Russian forces resist a large invasion by the Blue Horde, Lithuania and Ryazan. Norway enters the Kalmar Union with Denmark. Tamerlane defeats Persia, Russia, Georgia and Egypt. Khan Tokhtamysh of the White Horde dethrones Khan Mamai of the Blue Horde. The two hordes unite to form the Golden Horde. Around this time, the Kongo kingdom is founded in the Congo river-mouth region of Zaire, central Africa. John Wyclif and Nicholas of Hereford complete the first English translation of the Bible.

1381 The Peasants' Revolt in England is led by Wat Tyler. Venice wins the three-year War of Chioggia against Genoa. Tamerlane conquers east Persia, ending the rule of the Sarbadar Dynasty.

1382 The Ottomans take Sofia from the Bulgarians. Khan Tokhtamysh of the Golden Horde overruns Moscow. John Wyclif's teachings are condemned by the Synod of London. Winchester College is founded in England.

1383 A period of civil war and anarchy, known as the 1383–5 Crisis, begins in Portugal. Löwenbräu beer is first brewed. The construction of the Bastille is completed in Paris.

1385 Albania is conquered by the Ottomans, beginning 80 years of resistance to Turkish rule. The Golden Horde conquers parts of the Jalayirid Empire in western Persia.

1386 The English defeat an invading French and Castilian naval force in the Battle of Margate. Winning the Battle of Sempach, the Swiss safeguard their independence from Habsburg rule. The Venetians take control of the island of Corfu. The Ruprecht-Karls University of Heidelberg, the oldest university in Germany, is founded.

1387 Tamerlane conquers the Muzaffarid Empire in central Persia. Geoffrey Chaucer begins writing *The Canterbury Tales*.

1388 The Wyclif Bible is completed. The construction of Milan Cathedral is begun.

1389 England and France sign a truce in the Hundred Years' War. Queen Margaret of Norway and Denmark also becomes ruler of Sweden.

Christian Serbs are defeated by Ottoman Turks at Kosovo in Serbia. Yilderim Bayezid becomes sultan and conquers the Christian army of Sigismund of Hungary at Nicopolis. The Kanem-Bornu Empire (now eastern Chad and Nigeria) loses its land in present-day Chad to the Bilala.

1390 Robert III becomes king of Scotland. Templo Mayor, the main temple of the Aztec capital of Tenochtitlan, is built. Around this time: Samarkand in Central Asia is reconstructed and becomes Tamerlane's capital; Ottoman Turks complete the conquest of Asia Minor; the kingdom of Kaffa is established in present-day Ethiopia; Viracocha becomes the eighth Inca ruler.

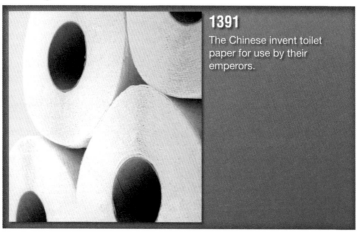

1391
The Chinese invent toilet paper for use by their emperors.

1392 The Earl of Orkney takes control of the Shetland Islands and the Faeroe Islands. The end of the division of Japan into northern and southern courts; the Ashikagas become shoguns of Muromachi. In England, foreigners are banned from selling goods.

1393 Tamerlane ends the Muzaffarid dynasty in Persia. Bosnia resists an invasion by the Ottoman Empire and signs a peace treaty with Hungary. Ottoman Turks capture the capital city of East Bulgaria.

1394 Charles VI of France orders the expulsion of all Jews from France. The Ottomans begin an eight-year siege of Constantinople. Tamerlane sacks Astrakhan. Hanseong (now Seoul) becomes capital of the Joseon dynasty in present-day Korea.

1396 The Ottomans conquer Bulgaria.

1397 The Kalmar Agreement unites Denmark, Norway and Sweden.

1398 Tamerlane sacks Delhi – 100,000 are massacred. Jan Hus, the Bohemian religious reformer, lectures on theology at Prague University.

1399 The death of John of Gaunt; his son Henry Bolingbroke deposes Richard II and takes the throne as Henry IV of England.

1400 Richard II is murdered. Owen Glendower declares himself Prince of Wales and starts a rebellion. Wenceslas, the Holy Roman Emperor, is deposed because of his drunkenness. The first reference to the dulcimer. Around this date: Europe's population falls to 60 million; gold from mines in Zimbabwe is exported to Asia via Sofala on the east coast; the Iroquois Confederacy is formed, featuring five Native American tribes – the Mohawk, the Oneida, the Onondaga, the Cayuga and the Seneca; the Aztec Empire expands in Mexico; the Inca Empire also enters a period of expansion; Islam reaches Malacca; the Tonga people build a major ceremonial centre at Mu'ac; the Pueblo people abandon northern sites and gather in large towns; the Inca are using the quipu as a numeric device for counting; Aztec priests sacrifice tens of thousands of people each year to ensure the rebirth of the Sun every day.

1401 Tamerlane takes Damascus and Baghdad.

1402 Henry IV fights Owen Glendower in Wales. David Stewart, Duke of Rothesay, the heir to the throne of Scotland, dies while being kept prisoner by his uncle, Robert Stewart, the 1st Duke of Albany. Genoa recaptures Monaco. Tamerlane defeats the Ottomans at the Battle of Ankyra in Turkey and overruns their empire. Zhu Di seizes the throne as the Yongle Emperor in China; he becomes one of China's greatest emperors. Seville Cathedral is begun.

1403 Henry IV defeats Harry 'Hotspur' Percy at the Battle of Shrewsbury. Between this date and 1409, an encyclopaedia of over 20,000 chapters, *Yongle Dadian*, is compiled in China. Lorenzo Ghiberti sculpts human bodies in realistic style for bronze doors of Florence Baptistery, heralding the Renaissance.

1405 The French arrive in Wales to support Owen Glendower against Henry. Tamerlane dies. The first Chinese maritime expedition is undertaken to the Indian Ocean. Japan begins to trade with China.

1406 James I becomes king of Scotland. Henry, Prince of Wales defeats the Welsh. The building of the Forbidden City is begun in Beijing.

1407 Bethlehem hospital in London becomes an institution for the insane.

1408 The Italian sculptor Donatello creates *David* and *St John*.

1409 The Council of Pisa tries to resolve the 30-year Great Schism, deposing both popes and electing Alexander V.

1410 John XXII is elected antipope; he is backed by the Medici family. In the Battle of Tannenberg, Ladislaus II of Poland beats the Teutonic Knights.

1411 Sigismund of Hungary is elected Holy Roman Emperor. Ahmad Shah of Gujarat comes to power and builds the capital city of Ahmadabad. St Andrews University is founded in Scotland.

1412 The birth of Joan of Arc.

1413 Henry V becomes king of England.

1414 The English king, Henry V, adopts the French claims of Edward II. In Florence, the Medicis become official bankers to the papacy.

1415 Henry V defeats the French at Agincourt, mainly thanks to the longbow. King John of Portugal seizes Ceuta in Morocco. The religious reformer, Jan Hus is burnt at the stake. Around this time, Brunelleschi develops a system of linear perspective in painting.

1416 Owen Glendower dies. Drift nets are used for the first time by Dutch fishermen. Around this time, the Limbourg brothers create *Les Très Riches Heures*, a masterpiece of manuscript illumination.

1417 The Great Schism in the Catholic Church finally comes to an end; a single pope, Martin V, is elected in Rome.

1418 Nezahualcoyotl, poet-king of the Texcocan, takes the throne.

1419 Korea prospers under King Sejong; he introduces an official Korean script. Brunelleschi designs the Foundling Hospital in Florence and constructs the dome of Florence Cathedral.

1420 The Treaty of Troyes acknowledges Henry V as heir to the French throne. Portuguese sailors begin to explore the west coast of Africa and settle Madeira. Cosimo (the Elder) becomes manager of the Medici bank in Florence. The Songhai people in the Gao region of West Africa, begin raids on the Mali empire. The Chinese Ming capital moves from Nanjing to Beijing.

1422 Henry VI becomes king of England and Charles VII, king of France.

1426 The Aztecs at Tenochtitlan form a Triple Alliance with the neighbouring cities of Texcoco and Tlacopan; Emperor Itzcoatl reorganizes the state to concentrate all power in his hands.

1428
Joan of Arc leads the French against England; the English begin the siege of Orléans.

1429 Joan of Arc raises the Siege of Orléans; she beats the English at the Battle of Patay, forcing them to leave the Loire Valley.

1430 Joan of Arc is taken prisoner. The Ottomans become master cannon-makers. The Khmer Empire in south-east Asia begins to collapse; Angkor Wat is abandoned after being sacked by the Thai army. The sultans of Kilwa on the East African coast begin a grand building programme. The Pawnee people begin to settle along the major rivers in Nebraska. Gutenberg, a German metalworker, experiments with printing, using movable type. Around this time, Middle English is replaced by Modern English. Josquin Desprez, often called the 'Prince of Music', is a leading composer of the Renaissance.

1431 Joan of Arc is burnt at the stake by the English; she is 19. Henry VI of England is crowned king of France in Paris. Chinese mariner Zheng He makes his seventh and final voyage; he sails as far as the east coast of Africa. Margery Kempe writes the first English autobiography, *The Book of Margery Kempe*.

1433 The double eagle becomes the symbol of the Holy Roman Empire. Tuareg nomads occupy Timbuktu.

1434 Cosimo de Medici becomes ruler of Florence. The reign of Christian emperor, Zera Yacub, begins in Ethiopia; he expands the Church and promotes great monasteries. The Khmer capital moves from Angkor Wat to Phnom Penh. Holland is the centre for European music. Dutch painter Jan van Eyck paints scenes of bourgeois life such as the *Arnolfini Marriage Group*.

1437 James I of Scotland is assassinated by Sir Robert Graham and others.

1438 The Inca Emperor Viracocha dies; his successor Pachacuti expands the Inca Empire northwards into Ecuador.

1440 Incas begin the construction of the great fortress at Cuzco. The Aztec Emperor Moctezuma I gains power; he conquers large areas of eastern Mexico. The Platonic Academy is founded in Florence.

1443 The Korean syllabary, the Hangul, is created on the orders of King Sejong.

1444 The Ottomans conquer Hungary at the Black Sea, opening their route to Constantinople. Copenhagen becomes the capital of Denmark.

1447 Casimir IV of Poland unites the Polish kingdom with the Grand Duchy of Lithuania. Skanderberg defeats Murad II, gaining independence for Persia, India and Afghanistan.

1448 Thailand expands for the next 40 years under King Trailok; he brings about major administrative and legal reforms.

1449   The Ashikaga Yoshimasa rule in Japan until 1474.

1450   Under the leadership of the Medicis, Florence becomes the centre of the Renaissance and humanism. The Vatican Library is founded. Building at Great Zimbabwe, southern Africa, is at its height. In Peru, the Inca city of Machu Picchu is constructed on a high ridge above the Urubamba River; around this time, the Incas build 20,000 miles of road in the Andes.

1452   The first association of professional midwives is founded in Germany. Leonardo da Vinci is born.

1453   Henry VI of England becomes insane; Richard, Duke of York becomes regent. The Hundred Years' War ends; the English are expelled from France, retaining only Calais. The Ottomans besiege and capture Constantinople, ending the Byzantine Empire and the Middle Ages.

1455   The Wars of the Roses between the houses of York and Lancaster begin in England. The first Bible is printed in Europe by Gutenberg. The Palazzo Venezia is built in Rome. Cadamasto, a Venetian sailor, explores the Senegal and Gambia rivers and discovers the Cape Verde Islands. A huge temple is built in Tenochtitlan to the Aztec war god Huitzilopochtli.

1456   The Ottoman Turks capture Athens. The Hungarians, under nobleman John Hunyadi, storm Belgrade and drive out the Turks.

1459   The Ottoman Turks capture Serbia.

1460   The Earl of Warwick and Edward, Earl of March, eldest son of the Duke of York, seize London; at the Battle of Northampton they defeat a Lancastrian army and capture King Henry; York becomes Henry's heir, but dies in the Battle of Wakefield. James II is killed at the Battle of Roxburgh. The imperial porcelain works at Jingdezhen in China successfully export Ming pottery.

1461   Edward of York becomes king of England. The Turks conquer Trebizond, the only surviving Byzantine state.

1462   Castille takes Gibraltar from the Arabs. Ivan III (the Great) becomes Grand Prince of Muscovy, until 1505. Sonni Ali becomes ruler of the Songhai and goes on to build an empire.

1463   War (until 1479) between the Ottoman Turks and the Venetians; the Turks are eventually triumphant. Sultan Mehmet II builds a mosque in Istanbul, surrounded by eight colleges, the peak of the Ottoman educational system.

1465   Henry VI is imprisoned by Edward IV. The first printed music appears.

1466   Desiderius, the Dutch scholar, is born; he leads a revival of learning in northern Europe.

1467   A period of civil war begins in Japan and lasts for more than 100 years. The name of the Swiss hero William Tell appears for the first time, in a ballad.

1468   Lorenzo and Giulliano Medici become rulers of Florence. Songhai King Sonni Ali drives the Tuareg nomads out of Timbuktu.

1470   Henry VI is restored to the English throne. Chimu culture in northern Peru collapses. Around this time, Sir Thomas Mallory writes *Morte d'Arthur*.

1471   Henry VI dies, probably murdered, in the Tower of London. The Ottomans rule from the Taurus Mountains to the Adriatic. Topa Inca expands the Inca Empire into Bolivia, Chile and Argentina. German artist Albrecht Dürer is born.

1473   The Sistine Chapel is built. Tenochtitlan absorbs the neighbouring Aztec city, Tlatelolco.

1474   Louis XI of France declares war on Charles the Bold, Duke of Burgundy. Topa Inca becomes emperor, succeeding Pachacutec. William Caxton prints the first book in English. The German astronomer

Regiomontanus describes the method of finding longitude by using lunar distance.

1475 Edward IV invades France. The peace of Piquigny is agreed between England and France. The Turks conquer the Crimea. Michelangelo is born.

1476 William Caxton sets up a printing press at Westminster.

1477 Charles the Bold is defeated and killed by the Swiss. The marriage of Maximillian of Austria to Mary of Burgundy makes the Habsburgs heirs to one of the most powerful European states. Caxton prints *The Canterbury Tales*. Venetian painter Titian is born.

1478 Hungary gains Moravia and Silesia. The Turks conquer Albania.

1479 Spain is united under Ferdinand and Isabella. In the Treaty of Constantinople, Venice agrees to pay tribute to the Ottoman Empire for trading rights in the Black Sea. Brussels becomes the centre of European tapestry-making.

1480 The Spanish Inquisition is introduced to uncover heresy. Tsar Ivan III of Russia stops paying tribute to the Mongols. Leonardo da Vinci invents the parachute.

1481 The death of Muhammed II, founder of the Ottoman Empire.

1482 The Portuguese explore the Congo River estuary and establish settlements on the Gold Coast.

1483 The death of Edward IV of England; he is succeeded by Edward V. Richard III deposes Edward and becomes king of England. The Russians start exploring Siberia. The Portuguese land in Angola; missionaries arrive the following year. Ashikaga Yoshimasa completes the building of the Silver Pavilion Temple, or Ginkakuji, at Kyoto in Japan. The Italian artist Raphael is born.

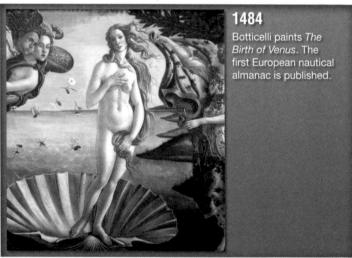

1484
Botticelli paints *The Birth of Venus*. The first European nautical almanac is published.

1485 Henry VII becomes the first Tudor king of England and Wales after the defeat of the last Plantagenet king, Richard III, at the Battle of Bosworth Field; the Wars of the Roses end. Hungary captures Vienna and Lower Austria, becoming the most powerful state in central Europe.

1486 The Aztec Emperor Ahuitzotl rules, until 1502; the Aztec Empire is at the height of its power in Mexico.

1488 James IV becomes king of Scotland. The first major Ikko-ikki, or Uprising of Ikko Buddhists, occurs in Japan. Ming emperors order the rebuilding of the Great Wall to defend China from northern invaders. Choe Pu presents his diary of travels in China to the Korean king. The Portuguese explorer Bartholomew Diaz rounds the Cape of Good Hope.

1489   The plus (+) and minus (-) symbols come into use; they are first used in the book *Mercantile Arithmetic* by Johannes Widmann.

1491   After six years of war, the Mamelukes and the Ottoman Turks make peace. The Portuguese baptize the ruler of the Congo kingdom as a Christian.

1492

The Christian Spanish capture Granada in Spain from the Muslims, ending Muslim influence in Spain. Sikander Lodi, sultan of Delhi, annexes Bihar and moves his capital to Agra so that he can conquer Rajasthan. Martin Behaim of Nuremberg constructs a terrestrial globe. Christopher Columbus lands on the Bahama Islands, Cuba and Hispaniola; he is the first European to reach the Americas since the Vikings.

1493   The pope divides the newly discovered lands of the New World between Spain and Portugal. The Songhai Empire reaches its peak under Askia Mohammed, who takes over much of the Mandingo Empire.

1494   Charles VIII invades Italy. Returning to the Americas, Columbus lands in Jamaica. Luca di Pacioli writes *Summa de arithmetica, geometrica, proportioni et proportionalita*, a collection of the mathematical knowledge of his time.

1495   Charles VIII is defeated by the Holy League. Friar John Cor makes the first known written reference to a batch of Scotch whisky.

1497   The Italian navigator John Cabot discovers Newfoundland. Vasco da Gama rounds the Cape of Good Hope, sailing on to India.

1498   The Italian religious reformer Savonarola is burnt at the stake. Columbus discovers Trinidad and South America.

1499   Louis XII invades Italy and conquers Milan. The Italian navigator, Amerigo Vespucci explores the north-east coastline of South America. Christopher Columbus quashes a revolt in Hispaniola by Spanish settlers. John Cabot dies exploring the North American coast.

1500   Pedro Cabral claims Brazil for Portugal. Hieronymus Bosch paints the *Ship of Fools*. The first successful caesarean birth is recorded in Switzerland. A regular postal service starts between Brussels and Venice, later extending to other cities. Around this date: Black-lead pencils are being used in England; card games gain popularity in Europe; the Songhai Empire in West Africa enters its period of greatest expansion and power under Askia Mohammed Turré; trade encourages the growth of the Hausa states in West Africa; Tutsi herders move into Hutu lands; French exploration in Canada begins.

1501   France and Spain occupy Naples. Russia and Poland are at war. The reign of Ismail, first Safavid shah of Persia, begins. Book burning is authorized by papal bull. Around this time, Italian painter Andrea Mantegna creates a scandal when he depicts Christ realistically in *The Dead Christ*.

1502   War breaks out between France and Spain. Moctezuma II becomes ruler of the Aztec dominions. In Germany, Peter Heinlein makes the first working watch movement. Columbus sets out on his fourth and final voyage; he reaches Honduras, Nicaragua, Costa Rica, Panama and Colombia.

1503

Scotland and England sign the Treaty of Everlasting Peace; it lasts ten years. France is defeated in the battles of Cerignola and Garigliano. Leonardo da Vinci begins painting *La Gioconda* (the *Mona Lisa*). Canterbury Cathedral is finished; it took 433 years to build.

1505 In the Treaty of Blois, France keeps Milan but gives Naples to Spain. The Portuguese found Mozambique and begin to trade with the Africans. Zhengde becomes Emperor of China. Scipione del Ferro, an Italian mathematician, is solving cubic equations.

1506 King Alfonso of Kongo, in south-western central Africa, introduces European customs. Christopher Columbus dies. Work begins on the construction of the basilica of St Peter's in Rome. The Swiss Guard becomes the protective force of the Vatican and the pope. Niccolò Machiavelli creates a militia in Florence.

1507 Nzinga Mbemba, Christian and Portuguese ally, becomes king of the Kongo kingdom in central Africa. Martin Waldseemuller creates a map of the world, using the name 'America' for the first time. Leonardo da Vinci completes the *Mona Lisa*.

1508 Maximillian I becomes Holy Roman Emperor. The pope grants Spain the right to control missionary activities in the New World. Michelangelo begins painting the ceiling of the Sistine Chapel in the Vatican (completed in 1512).

1509 Henry VIII becomes king of England; he will reign for 38 years. The Battle of Diu establishes Potuguese control over the Indian seas. A catastrophic earthquake devastates Constantinople.The first slaves are brought from Africa to the New World by the Spanish.

1511 Around this time, Portuguese navigators begin to explore the Pacific; the Portuguese capture Malacca in Malaysia.

1512 The French are driven out of Milan. Copernicus suggests that the Sun is the centre of the universe.

1513 James IV of Scotland is killed by the English at the Battle of Flodden Field. The Ottoman geographer Piri Reis includes the Americas in his map of the world. Pope Leo X uses concave lenses to improve his sight while hunting. Vasco Núñez de Balboa, Spanish explorer, first sights the Pacific Ocean. The Portuguese reach China.

1514 Turkey and Persia are at war; the Persians lose the Battle of Chaldiran.

1515 Thomas Wolsey, Archbishop of York, becomes Lord Chancellor of England and a cardinal. Francis I becomes king of France. Sunni Islam becomes the state religion of the Ottomans. The French regain Milan from the Swiss. France opens the first national factories for the manufacture of weapons and textiles. German artist Matthias Grünewald paints the Isenheim altarpiece.

1516 In the Treaty of Noyon, between France and Spain, France relinquishes its claim to Naples. The Songhai Empire, at its height, has its capital at Timbuktu. Sir Thomas More writes *Utopia*.

1517 Martin Luther, German scholar, publishes his 95 Theses questioning Catholic practices, launching the Reformation. Ottomans defeat the Mamelukes and conquer Egypt and Syria. The first coffee from the Americas arrives in Europe.

1518 Eyeglasses are made using ground lenses. Philippus Paracelsus, a Swiss physician, uses laudanum as a painkiller. Italian architect Andreo Palladio is born.

1519 Ulrich Zwingli preaches reformation in Switzerland. Charles, Archduke of Austria (and king of Spain) is elected Holy Roman Emperor; he retires in 1556. Hernan Cortés lands on the coast of Yucutan, marches on the Aztec capital, Tenochtitlán, and kills Moctezuma; horses appear in the New World for the first time. The navigator Vasco Nunez de Balboa is beheaded in Spain for desertion and treason. Ferdinand Magellan attempts a voyage around the world: he dies en route and his crew complete the voyage in 1522.

1520 Francois I of France and Henry VIII of England meet on the Field of Cloth of Gold; they fail to form an alliance. Christian II becomes king of Denmark, Norway and Sweden. The reign of Suleyman the Magnificent begins; the Ottoman Empire is at its peak. The first chocolate from the New World arrives in Europe.

1521 The Diet of Worms excommunicates Martin Luther; Luther begins to translate the Bible into German, completing it in 1534. France and Spain go to war over Italy. Suleyman captures Belgrade and Rhodes. Cortés claims Mexico for Spain. A Spanish colony is established in Venezuela.

1522 Charles V drives the French out of Milan. Albrecht Dürer designs a flying machine. Paracelsus writes the first modern surgery manual. Only one ship from Magellan's expedition makes it back to Europe.

1523 Gustavus Vasa of Sweden leads a revolt against Danish rule and is elected King Gustavus I. The Portuguese are expelled from China.

1524 France recaptures Milan. The Italian Giovanni da Verrazano discovers New York Bay. The first turkeys from the Americas arrive in Europe.

1525 Diego Ribeiro, official mapmaker for Spain, makes the first scientific charts covering the Pacific.

1526 Babur, a descendant of Mongol ruler Genghis Khan and of Tamerlane, the first Mughal emperor, invades India. The Portuguese land on Papua New Guinea.

1527 Charles V's troops sack Rome and capture Pope Clement VII. The Incas begin a bloody civil war.

1529 Wolsey is dismissed for failing to obtain a divorce for Henry VIII; Sir Thomas More becomes Lord Chancellor; Henry begins to cut ties with the Church of Rome. France renounces its claims to Italy in the Peace of Cambrai. The Muslims defeat Christian Ethiopian forces at the Battle of Shimbra Kure and overrun the kingdom until 1543, when Portuguese troops help to defeat them.

1530 The Knights of St John are established on Malta by Charles V. Charles V is crowned king of Italy. Civil war breaks out in Switzerland; the Catholics defeat the Protestants. The Portuguese begin to organize the transatlantic slave trade. The Spaniards conquer Ecuador, Paraguay, and a part of Chile.

1532 Sir Thomas More resigns over Henry's divorce. John Calvin starts a Protestant movement in France. Spanish Conquistador Francisco Pizarro invades Peru and destroys the Inca Empire, killing its ruler Atahualpa, even though he gave him a vast amount of gold. Sugar cane is first cultivated in Brazil. François Rabelais writes the bawdy satire *Pantagruel*.

1533

Henry VIII's marriage to Catherine of Aragon is annulled; he marries Anne Boleyn and is excommunicated by Pope Clement VII; Thomas Cranmer becomes Archbishop of Canterbury. Barbarossa becomes Chief Admiral of the Ottoman fleet. North Vietnam splits into the kingdoms of Tonking and Annam.

1534 Henry VIII of England breaks with Rome; he declares himself head of the English Church. The Turks take Tunis, Baghdad and Mesopotamia. The Frenchman Jacques Cartier explores Labrador and the St Lawrence River. Loyola founds the Jesuits. Martin Luther publishes his translation of the New Testament.

1535 Sir Thomas More is executed. France and Spain are at war. Manco Inca founds the state of Vilcambamba in the Peruvian highlands, lasting until 1572.

1536 Anne Boleyn is executed; Henry VIII marries Jane Seymour. France allies with Turkey and invades Savoy and Piedmont. Akbar becomes Emperor of India. Spain annexes Cuba.

1537 Jane Seymour dies after giving birth to the future Edward VI.

1538 The Truce of Nice is signed between France and Spain.

1540 Henry VIII marries Anne of Cleves, divorces her and marries Catherine Howard. The Spanish arrive in California. Spanish physician Michael Servetus describes pulmonary circulation.

1541 John Knox brings the Reformation to Scotland. The Turks conquer Hungary. Hernando de Soto discovers the Mississippi. The Greek painter El Greco is born.

1542 Catherine Howard is executed. James V of Scotland dies at the Battle of Solway. Mary Stuart becomes queen of Scotland.

1543 Henry VIII marries Catherine Parr. The Holy Roman Empire and England form an alliance against France and Scotland and invade France. The Portuguese introduce firearms to Japan. Nicolas Copernicus publishes *De revolutionibus orbium coelestium*, in which he states that the Sun, not the Earth, is the centre of the solar system.

1544 The Act of Succession restores Elizabeth to the Line of Succession to the throne of England. Charles V invades France again. Swedish succession is tied to the male line.

1545 The Council of Trent attempts to reform the Catholic Church. English warship the *Mary Rose* is sunk at the Battle of the Solent.

1546 Songhai forces conquer Mali. Tabinshwehti assumes the title of king of all Burma. The Flemish geographer Gerardus Mercator describes the Earth's magnetic poles.

1547 Henry VIII dies; Edward VI becomes king of England. Henry II becomes king of France. Ivan the Terrible becomes Tsar of Russia.

1548 The Holy Roman Empire annexes the Netherlands.

1549 Ivan IV creates Russia's first national assembly. The Jesuit St Francis Xavier takes Christianity to Japan. *The Book of Common Prayer* is published in England.

1550 The Wolof Empire in West Africa disappears. The Tutsi establish the kingdom of Rwanda around this time. The Mongols besiege Beijing. The Spanish discover gold in Chile and Colombia. Tang Xi Anzu, Ming playwright and author of *The Peony Pavilion*, is born. A German mathematician, Georg Rheticus, publishes trigonometric tables.

1551 Turkey and Hungary go to war until 1562. Bayinnaung inherits the Burmese throne and overruns Thailand.

1552 War breaks out between Charles V and Henry II of France. Mary Queen of Scots plays golf.

1553 Lady Jane Grey is declared queen of England after the death of Edward; her reign lasts nine days and the Catholic Mary I becomes queen. Roman Catholic bishops are restored in England.

1554 Lady Jane Grey is executed. Mary I marries Philip, heir to the Spanish throne. The Turks conquer the coast of North Africa.

1555 England returns to Roman Catholicism; Protestants are persecuted. In the Religious Peace of Augsburg, Protestant princes are granted freedom of worship. Great Zimbabwe is completed. A total of 835,000 people die in an earthquake in north-west China. Tobacco is brought to Spain from the New World.

1556 Philip II becomes king of Spain. Akbar the Great becomes Mughal ruler of India; he defeats the Hindus and begins the conquest of the entire subcontinent, completed in 1605.

1557 France is defeated by England and Spain at the Battle of St Quentin. The Portuguese establish a colony at Macao. The Livonian War begins, involving Poland, Russia, Sweden and Denmark; it lasts until 1582. The architect Sinan completes Suleyman I's mosque complex.

1558

Elizabeth I becomes queen of England and reigns for 45 years; Catholic legislation is repealed. England loses Calais. Mary, queen of Scots marries François, heir to the French throne. Gioseffo Zarlino creates definitions of the modern major and minor musical scales. The Flemish painter Pieter Breughel begins a prolific ten-year period.

1559 François II becomes king of France. Spain now controls almost all of Italy. Work starts on the palace of Escorial outside Madrid.

1560 The Treaty of Berwick is signed between England and the Scottish reformers. Catherine de Medici becomes regent of France until 1574. The French Wars of Religion begin (until the 1590s): the Protestant minority is in conflict with the Catholic majority, as nobles fight for power under the weak Valois kings. Charles IX becomes king of France. Around this time, mercury is discovered at Huancavelica in Peru.

1561 Mary, queen of Scots returns, widowed, to Scotland. The Cathedral of St Basil the Blessed in Moscow is completed.

1562 Sir John Hawkins starts the English slave trade, transporting slaves from West Africa to the Americas.

1563 The Thirty-nine Articles establishing the Anglican Church are published. Ivan the Terrible conquers part of Livonia.

1564 The Peace of Troyes is signed between England and France. A reign of terror begins in Russia. The pope gives his approval to the publication of an Index of Prohibited Books. The birth of William Shakespeare, Christopher Marlowe and Galileo Galilei.

1565 The Portuguese found Rio de Janeiro. Flemish painter Pieter Breughel the Elder paints *The Return of the Hunters*.

1567 Following the murder of Lord Darnley, husband of Mary, queen of Scots, Mary marries the Earl of Bothwell, is imprisoned and forced to abdicate; James VI becomes king of Scotland. Typhoid kills two million in the Americas. Alvaro de Menda, a Spanish sailor, sets sail from Callao in Peru westwards to cross the Pacific; he reaches the Solomon Islands.

1568 Mary, queen of Scots is imprisoned by Elizabeth I in England. A Dutch campaign for independence from Spanish rule begins; it is finally achieved in 1648. Bottled beer is produced for the first time in London.

1569 Poland and Lithuania merge.

1570 French Huguenots, reformed Protestants, are given conditional freedom of worship. Around this time, the Kanem-Bornu kingdom in central Africa is at its most powerful under Idris III.

1571 Don John of Austria routs the Ottoman fleet under Ali Pasha at the Battle of Lepanto.

1572 In the Massacre of St Bartholomew, in Paris, 8,000 Protestants are killed. The Spanish behead the last Inca leader, Tupac Amaru.

1573 Venice abandons Cyprus and makes peace with Turkey. Don John of Austria recaptures Tunis. Emperor Wan Li comes to power in China, ushering in a period of great paintings and porcelain-making.

1574 Turkey retakes Tunis and controls most of North Africa. *Taiping Guangzhi* is published, the first Chinese book printed with movable type. Richard Burbage gains a licence to open a theatre in London.

1575 The Portuguese begin to colonize Angola; more than a century of warfare follows. Stephen Batory, prince of Transylvania in Romania, is elected king of Poland.

1576 Protestantism is banned in France. Rudolf II becomes Holy Roman Emperor until 1612.

1577 Akbar the Great completes the annexation of northern India. English seaman Francis Drake sets out on a voyage round the world, completed in 1580. Ralph Holinshed writes the two-volume *Chronicles of England, Scotland and Ireland*. El Greco is painting his greatest works. Flemish artist Peter Paul Rubens is born.

1578 The Muslims defeat the Portuguese at the Battle of Al Kasr Al-Kabil. Sir Francis Drake claims Vancouver for England.

1579 The English and the Dutch form an alliance against Spain. The Dutch northern provinces form the Union of Utrecht.

1580 Spain conquers Portugal in Europe and Argentina in the Americas.

1581 The Union of Utrecht declares independence from Spain, calls itself the Dutch Republic and elects William of Orange as its ruler. Poland invades Russia. The Russians complete the conquest of Siberia. Akbar of India conquers Afghanistan. Galileo investigates the pendulum.

1582 Peace is declared between Poland, Russia and Sweden. Edinburgh University is founded. The Gregorian Calendar is introduced in Roman Catholic countries; it is accurate to within one day every 3,300 years.

1583 The first life insurance policies are issued in London.

1584 William of Orange of the Dutch Republic is assassinated by a supporter of the Spanish. Sir Walter Ralegh sends an expedition to Virginia in North America, followed a year later by a colonizing expedition, which fails. The Chinese tempered musical scale is defined.

1585 England sends troops to the Dutch Republic.

1586 Mary, queen of Scots is involved in a conspiracy against Elizabeth I. A period of national unification in Japan begins when feudal lord

Oda Nobunaga captures the capital, Kyoto. Francis Drake makes an expedition to the West Indies.

1587 Mary, queen of Scots is executed. England is at war with Spain (until 1603); Drake destroys the Spanish fleet at Cadiz.

1588 The English fleet defeats the Spanish Armada off the south coast of England; Spanish power declines. Henri of Guise is murdered. Shah Abbas becomes ruler of the Safavid Empire, creating reforms and rebuilding Isfahan. In Japan's reorganized society, only Samurai are permitted to carry weapons.

1589 The first English knitting machinery is invented by William Lee. Henry III of France is murdered and the Protestant Henri of Navarre becomes king. Forks are being used as eating implements at the French court.

1590 Burma begins to break up into small states. Shakespeare begins his career as a playwright; he writes around 38 plays before his death in 1616. Galileo studies falling bodies. Around this time, the Royal Mosque is built in Isfahan.

1591 The Songhai Empire is overthrown by the Moroccan army. Hideyoshi unifies Japan.

1592 Akbar the Great takes Sind. Portuguese traders settle in Mombassa. Korea succeeds in beating off the first of a number of Japanese invasions. The Nguyen and Trinh lords take power in Vietnam; they rule unti 1788. The ruins of Pompei are discovered in Italy.

1593 Henry IV, the first Bourbon king of France, converts to Catholicism, ending the French religious wars. War breaks out between Austria and Turkey, until 1606.

1595 Sweden gains Estonia in the Treaty of Teusina with Russia. Mercator dies, having published his atlas in parts since 1578.

1597 A rebellion in Ireland against the English is led by Hugh O'Neill, Earl of Tyrone.

1598 Henry IV grants equal rights to Protestant Huguenots. The first Dutch trading posts are established on the coast of Guinea, West Africa, around this time. The Koreans invent an iron-clad ship.

1599 Irish rebels defeat the Earl of Essex; a truce is arranged. China invades Burma. The Globe Theatre is built in London. Spanish painter Velázquez is born.

the Enlightened World

1600 – 1799

1600 Elizabeth I grants a charter to the English East India Company. Astronomers Tycho Brahe and Johannes Keppler work together near Prague. In North America, five Algonquin tribes form a confederacy under Wa-hun-sen-acawh. In the Battle of Sekigahara in Japan, Tokugawa Ieyasu defeats his rivals and takes power and the Tokugawa or Edo period begins. Around this time: Religious wars erupt across Europe; the Kalonga kingdom, north of the Zambezi River, becomes rich through trading ivory; Great Zimbabwe is replaced by several regional capitals in the Transvaal, Botswana and Zimbabwe; the Tutsis gain control of Urundi (Burundi); the Masai move south from the Rift Valley; statue-building dies out on Easter Island; in Tonga, political leadership passes from the Tu'i Tonga dynasty to the Tu'i Konokupolu dynasty.

1601 The Earl of Essex attempts rebellion against Elizabeth I and is executed. Elizabethan Poor Law charges the parishes with providing for the poor.

1602 Savoy attacks Geneva. The Dutch East India Company is founded. Holy war breaks out between Persia and Turkey, lasting until 1618. Matteo Ricci, an Italian Jesuit missionary working in China, publishes a Chinese atlas of the world.

1603 The Union of the Crowns in Britain; James VI of Scotland becomes James I of England. James orders the arrest of Sir Walter Ralegh for treason. The Russians settle Siberia. Ieyasu is appointed shogun, undisputed ruler, in Japan; Edo (Tokyo) becomes the capital. German astronomer Johann Bayer catalogues the sky, employing a system still used today.

1604 England and Spain make peace. The French East India Company is founded. A Cossack settlement is founded at Tomsk in Siberia.

1605 The Gunpowder Plot fails in England. Boris Godunov's reign as Tsar ends in Russia. Jahangir becomes Emperor of India; he follows the teachings of both Muslim saints and Hindu yogis. *Don Quixote* by Miguel de Cervantes is published.

1606 Laws are passed against Roman Catholics in England. The Ottomans and Habsburgs acknowledge each other's sovereignty by signing the Treaty of Tsitva. Cossack and peasant uprisings occur in Russia. Luis Vaez de Torres from Spain sails around New Guinea and reaches the straits now named after him. Dutch navigator Willem Jansz sights Australia. Dutch painter Rembrandt van Rijn is born.

1607 Jamestown Colony, the first permanent English settlement in North America, is founded in Virginia. Confucianism becomes the main force in Tokugawa politics and Japanese society.

1608 The Protestant Union is formed in Germany by Frederick IV. Quebec in Canada is founded by French settlers. Galileo Galilei builds a telescope and in 1610, observes Jupiter's satellites.

1609 The Twelve Years' Truce virtually ensures independence for the Netherlands. The Catholic League is formed in opposition to the Protestant Union. Italian Galileo Galilei confirms that the Sun is the centre of the universe. Johannes Keppler publishes his first two laws of planetary motion. The Blue Mosque is built in Constantinople. The *San-ts'ai t'u-hui*, an illustrated encyclopedia, is published in China.

1610 The Hudson Bay is explored by Henry Hudson. Tea is introduced to Europe. Thomas Harriot discovers sunspots.

1611 Scottish and English colonists settle in Ulster. Gustavus Adolphus the Great becomes king of Sweden. James I's authorized version of the Bible is completed.

1612 Heretics are burned at the stake for the last time in England. Christians are persecuted in Japan (until 1639). The Safavids reconquer Azerbaijan. Tobacco is grown as a commercial crop by Virginia colonists.

1613 Michael I becomes Tsar of Russia; the Romanov dynasty begins. Transylvanian prince, Bethlen Gabor, comes to power in Hungary. Smallpox and measles ravage Native Americans from Florida northward. Native American Powhatan chief's daughter, Pocahontas, is captured at Jamestown, Virginia. In London, the Globe theatre is destroyed by fire.

1614 The Scottish mathematician John Napier publishes tables of logarithms.

1615 Northern Chinese tribes begin to form Manchus, military organizations. Ming landscape artist Dong Qichang is working in China.

1616

Sir Walter Ralegh, released from prison, leads an expedition to find El Dorado. Dutch sailor William Schouten rounds Cape Horn. William Baffin discovers Baffin's Bay in Canada. Pocahontas sails to England with her English husband.

1617 Sir Thomas Rowe is granted the right by Emperor Jahangir to maintain warehouses in port cities in India, marking the beginning of the trading advantage enjoyed by the English in India.

1618 The thirty Years' War begins, involving almost all of Europe except Britain. The French explorer Paul Imbert reaches Timbuktu.

1619 The first American parliament meets at Jamestown. The Dutch establish a virtual monopoly of the spice trade in the Moluccas and other Indonesian islands. The first slaves arrive in Virginia. Englishman William Harvey discovers the circulation of the blood.

1620 Queen Nzinga of Ndongo continues the struggle against the Portuguese in Angola. The Caribbean Islands are captured from Spain by the English, the Dutch and the French over a period ending in 1635. The Japanese relax their policy of restricting contact with the outside world. The Pilgrim Fathers sail to America in the *Mayflower*. The Dutchman Cornelius Drebbel invents a human-powered submarine.

1621 The Dutch West Indies Company is founded. Riga comes under Swedish control.

1622 James I dissolves the English Parliament. Spain occupies the Valtelline Pass; war follows with France. The reforming Murad IV becomes Ottoman sultan following the assassination of Osman II. Native Americans begin ten years of attacks on the settlements in Virginia.

1624 Cardinal Richelieu becomes First Minister in France. English settlers arrive in eastern India. Virginia becomes a crown colony. The pope publically burns Martin Luther's translation of the Bible. William Oughtred, an English mathematician, invents the slide rule.

1625 Charles I becomes king of England and dissolves Parliament. Christian IV of Denmark enters the war against the Holy Roman Emperor, Ferdinand II. Dutchman Hugo Grotius publishes *De Jure Belli ac Pacis*, which becomes the basis of international law. There is rampant inflation in the Ottoman Empire. The kingdom of Dahomey is founded. The French begin to settle in the Caribbean.

1626   In the Battle of Dessau, Catholic forces defeat the Protestants. Christian IV loses the Battle of Lutter. The Dutch buy Manhattan Island from the Native American Lenape for 60 guilders worth of trade goods (about $24).

1627   The Huguenots in La Rochelle are besieged by Richelieu. The hereditary rule of the Habsburgs is confirmed in Bohemia. Imperial troops subdue much of Protestant Germany. The Manchus overrun Korea. Heinrich Schütz writes *Dafne*, reckoned to be the first opera.

1628   The Petition of Right is created in England; Parliament curtails the king's powers. The Huguenots surrender to Richelieu, losing political power. An English trading post is established in Bengal. The Dutch occupy Java and the Moluccan Islands.

1629   Charles I dissolves Parliament and, until 1640, rules personally. The Treaty of Lübeck is signed between Ferdinand II, Holy Roman Emperor, and Christian IV of Denmark and Norway. Ferdinand II issues the Edict of Restitution, allowing Catholics to reclaim Protestant lands. Massachusetts is founded. Italian architect Giovanni Branca invents a steam turbine, but does not build it.

1630   Gustavus Adolphus of Sweden enters the war against Ferdinand II. The Turks capture Hamadan. English Puritans set up a colony at Massachusetts Bay; migration begins from England to Massachusetts.

1631

The Dutch painter Rembrandt van Rijn begins his most productive period, painting a masterpiece almost annually for the next 20 years.

1632   Gustavus Adolphus of Sweden is victorious, but dies in the Battle of Lützen; Queen Christina takes the throne. In the Ottoman Empire, Murad IV executes literary and cultural figures with unorthodox views. The English drive the Portuguese from Bengal. Shah Jahan begins work on the Taj Mahal in India; it is completed in 1653.

1633   Galileo is convicted of teaching Copernican doctrine.

1635   Ferdinand revokes the Edict of Restitution and makes peace with Saxony; most Protestant rulers accept the treaty. France declares war on Spain. Dutch settlements are established in Ceylon. A postal service is set up between London and Edinburgh.

1636   Harvard College is founded in Massachusetts.

1637   The English begin to restrict immigration to the American colonies. In Japan, the Shimbara Rebellion leads to the expulsion of the Portuguese and the banning of Christianity. *Ch'ung-chen*, an encyclopedia of Chinese technology, is published. Descartes writes 'I think, therefore I am'.

1638   Scottish Presbyterians sign the Solemn League and Covenant. Ferdinand III becomes Holy Roman Emperor. The Turks capture Baghdad. Christianity is completely stamped out in Japan. The first printing press reaches America. Russian explorers reach the Pacific Ocean, having crossed Siberia.

1639   The First Bishops' War occurs between Charles I and the Scottish Church. Quinine is used for the first time in Europe to combat fever. English settlements are set up in Madras in India. The Cossacks advance to the Pacific coast. Ottoman administrator Evliya Chelebi begins to travel throughout the empire, describing his journeys in *Travels*. The first comic opera, *Chi Soffre Speri* by Virgilio Mazzocchi and Marco Marazzoli, premieres in Rome.

1640   The Second Bishops' War in Britain ends with the Treaty of Ripon. The Long Parliament takes place (until 1660). Portugal gains independence from Spain. A Fante state is founded in Ghana. Coke is first produced from coal. The Ottoman Sultan Mad Ibrahim lines his palace with fur. The *Bay Psalm Book* is the first book published in the English colonies.

1641   In a Catholic revolt in Ireland, 30,000 Protestants are massacred. The Dutch capture Malacca on the Malay Peninsula. The French philospher, René Descartes writes *Meditations on First Philosophy*. England produces cotton cloth.

1642   Civil war erupts in England between Cavaliers (Royalists) and Roundheads (Paliamentarians), lasting until 1647. Cardinal Jules Mazarin succeeds Richelieu as French Chief Minister. Shah Abbas II comes to power in Persia until 1666; he is the last great Safavid builder and patron of the arts. Montreal, in Canada, is founded by the French. London theatres are closed by the Puritans. Molière starts a theatre group in Paris that evolves into the Comédie Française. The French philosopher Blaise Pascal invents an adding machine.

1643   The Solemn League and Covenant is signed by the English Parliament. Louis XIV becomes king of France. France defeats Spain in the Battle of Rocroi. Denmark and Sweden fight for Baltic supremacy. Italian physicist Torricelli invents the barometer.

1644   Oliver Cromwell wins the Battle of Marston Moor. The Manchu (Ta Ch'ing) dynasty takes over in China, lasting until 1912. The Dutch settle Mauritius. Dutch navigator Abel Tasman reaches Tasmania and New Zealand.

1645   Cromwell forms his New Model Army; Parliamentarians win the Battle of Naseby. The Candian War between Venice and Ottoman Turks for control of Crete begins. The Brazilians begin to force the Dutch from colonial Brazil, succeeding by 1654. The Manchus massacre the population of the Chinese city of Yangzhou. Following the installation of the Qing government, the Han Chinese are forced to wear the queue, a shaved head with a single braid at the back.

1646   Charles I surrenders to the Scots. The Bahamas are colonized by the English.

1647   Charles I is handed over to the English Parliament; he escapes and makes a secret treaty with the Scots. The first public school system in America is established in Massachusetts.

1648   Scotland invades England and is defeated by Cromwell at the Battle of Prestonpans. The Frondes, five years of revolts, take place against Mazarin's rule in France. The Treaty of Westphalia ends the Thirty Years' War; the Dutch and Swiss republics are recognized. George Fox founds the Society of Friends (Quakers).

1649   Charles I of England and Scotland is executed; the Commonwealth is founded; England is a republic until 1660. Serfdom is completely established in Russia.

1650   Charles II lands in Scotland and is proclaimed king. The Portuguese fight with Muslims in the Zambezi region. Ethiopia expels Portuguese missionaries and diplomats. The first Roman Catholic church is opened in Beijing. The English begin to drink tea, imported from China; the coffee house phenomenon begins in France, England and Germany.

1651 Charles II invades England but loses the Battle of Worcester and flees to France. Philosopher Thomas Hobbes writes *Leviathon*, a defence of monarchy. Italian astronomer Giovanni Riccioli creates a map of the Moon.

1652 England and the Dutch Republic go to war. The Dutch found Cape Town in South Africa.

1653 Cromwell dismisses the Rump Parliament; he becomes Lord Protector of England.

1654 England and the Dutch Republic sign the Treaty of Westminster. The Portuguese take Brazil from the Dutch. Blaise Pascal and Pierre de Fermat create a theory of probability.

1655 The English capture Jamaica from Spain. Sweden declares war on Poland and occupies Warsaw.

1656 Russia, Denmark and the Holy Roman Empire declare war on Sweden. The Venetians rout the Turkish fleet off the Dardanelles. The Dutch take Colombo in Ceylon from the Portuguese. The rings of Saturn are discovered by Dutch scientist Christian Huygens.

1657 Jews in New Amsterdam (later New York) are granted the rights of burghers, but may not worship in public. Tokugawa Mitsukuni begins the compilation of his huge history of Japan, *Dai Nihon shi*.

1658 The death of Cromwell; he is succeeded by his son, Richard. In the Battle of the Dunes, England and France defeat Spain; England gains Dunkirk. Emperor Aurangzeb, the last great Mughal emperor, comes to power.

1659 The English army forces Richard Cromwell to resign and the Rump Parliament is restored. The Treaty of the Pyrenees establishes the border between France and Spain.

1660

Charles II is restored to the English throne. Mawlay-al-Rashid restores the sultanate of Morocco. Poland cedes Livonia to Sweden. In the Indian subcontinent, the Mughal Empire is at its most powerful. Samuel Pepys begins writing his diary. The Royal Society of London is chartered to promote the sciences. The first female players appear on the stage in England and Germany.

1661 The death of Mazarin; Louis XIV becomes absolute monarch in France. Russia and Sweden make peace and restore all conquests to each other. The English acquire Bombay. Emperor Kangxi extends the Chinese Empire, and books and scholarship flourish.

1662 Christopher Wren designs his first building.

1663 Charles II of England grants land for settlement in North Carolina.

1664 The English capture New Amsterdam from the Dutch and rename it New York. The Dutch force the king of Thailand to give them sole rights to deerskin exports and seaborne trade with China.

1665 The Great Plague hits London. The Second Anglo-Dutch War begins. Newton discovers gravity. Caleb Cheeshatemauk is the first Native American to obtain a degree from Harvard. Jan Vermeer paints the *Girl with a Pearl Earring*.

1666
The Great Fire of London destroys large parts of the city. Antonio Stradivari's workshop produces the first signed Stradivarius violins in Cremona in Italy.

1667 The Dutch fleet defeats the English on the Medway. The War of Devolution; France invades the Spanish Netherlands.

1668 The Triple Alliance of England, the Netherlands and Sweden is created against the French. Spain recognizes Portugal's independence. The end of the War of Devolution; France retains its conquests in Flanders. The English East India Company controls Bombay.

1669 Venice surrenders Crete to Turkey. Aurangzeb, Emperor of India, bans the Hindu religion. Rembrandt dies.

1670 William II becomes ruler of the Netherlands. Poland and Turkey go to war for control of the Ukraine. Peasant and Cossack uprisings occur in Russia. The French settle in Senegal. Ashanti clans unify on Africa's Gold Coast; Osei Tutu becomes leader, founding the Ashanti Empire. The Hudson's Bay Company is founded. Christopher Wren enters his most prolific period, designing more than 50 buildings, including St Paul's Cathedral. Around this time, playwright Aphra Behn is the first English woman to make a living as a writer.

1672 The Test Act deprives Catholics and Nonconformists of the right to hold public office in England. The Third Anglo-Dutch War begins. French troops invade southern Netherlands.

1673 In a revolt against the Qing, China's southern provinces break away and the War of the Three Feudatories begins. The Boston Post Road links settlements between Boston and Philadelphia.

1674 The Holy Roman Empire declares war on the French in defence of the Dutch. Jan III becomes king of Poland after defeating the Turks and the Cossacks.

1675 Native Americans attack settlers in New England. Gottfried Leibniz describes differential and integral calculus. Greenwich Observatory is established in London. Matthew Locke composes *Psyche*, the first surviving English opera.

1676 In the Treaty of Zuravno, Turkey gains the Ukraine. Sikh rebellions take place in India.

1677 Russia goes to war with Turkey. Benedicte de Spinoza dies; a religious philosopher with a wide following of European intellectuals.

1678 An imaginary Catholic plot to overthrow Charles II of England is invented by Titus Oates. John Bunyan writes *The Pilgrim's Progress*.

1679 The Act of Habeas Corpus in England ensures no imprisonment without trial. Vietnam and Cambodia go to war; Vietnam takes the Mekong Delta.

Father Louis Hennepin, a French explorer, reaches the Niagara Falls in Canada.

1680 France occupies Strasbourg, Luxemburg and Lorraine. The Ashanti kingdom in West Africa rises to prominence. The Butua kingdom flourishes on the Zimbabwe plains; the Portuguese are driven into the Zambezi Valley, and eastwards. Around this time, the Masai expand southwards in Africa; Basho, the Japanese haiku poet, is at the height of his popularity.

1681 Territory in North America, known as Pennsylvania, is granted to the English Quaker, William Penn.

1682 Peter the Great becomes Tsar of Russia. Turkey and Austria go to war. Ihara Saikaku writes *The Life of an Amorous Man*, an example of the literature of 'the floating world', a term used to describe the culture of Edo period Japan which lasts from 1600 to 1867.

1683 The Turks besiege Vienna; they are beaten off by Polish King John III Sobieski. Formosa (Taiwan) becomes Chinese territory.

1684 Venice, Austria and Poland unite against Turkey with the founding of the Holy League by Pope Innocent XI. Street lighting is established in parts of London.

1685 James II of England and VII of Scotland takes the throne; the Duke of Monmouth's rebellion against the king is quashed. The revocation of the Edict of Nantes in France; all religions except Catholicism are forbidden; more than 50,000 Huguenot families leave the country. Chinese ports are opened to European trade. Composers Johann Sebastian Bach and George Frederick Handel are born.

1686 James II ignores the Test Act and Catholics are appointed to public office. The League of Augsburg is formed – the Holy Roman Empire, Spain, Sweden, Saxony, Bavaria and the Palatinate against France. Louis XIV of France officially annexes Madagascar.

1687 James II extends tolerance to all religions in England. The Habsburg succession to the Hungarian throne is confirmed. The Parthenon in Athens is damaged by a Turkish bombardment.

1688 The Glorious Revolution deposes James II and brings William of Orange to the throne. Algonquin tribes side with the French against the English in King William's war in America. Isaac Newton publishes *Philosophae Naturalis Principia Mathematica*, in which he uses mathematical laws to describe the natural world. Louis XIV's Palace of Versailles is completed.

1689 A Grand Alliance of the Habsburgs, the Dutch and the English is formed against France. Peter the Great becomes Tsar of Russia. The Dutch colonize Natal in southern Africa. China's first treaty with a European power, the Treaty of Nerchinsk, is signed with Russia, defining border and trade rights.

1690 William III invades Ireland to quash a rebellion by supporters of James II; he wins the Battle of the Boyne. France defeats an Anglo-Dutch fleet in the Battle of Beachy Head. The Turks retake Belgrade from the Austrians.

1691 In Paris, a directory of street addresses is published.

1692
The Salem witchcraft trials take place in New England.

1695 The first synagogue in the English colonies is established in New York.

1696 Russia conquers Kamchatka.

1697 The Treaty of Ryswick is signed between France and the Grand Alliance. Peter I (the Great) of Russia begins several years of travel through Western Europe incognito. Isaac Newton becomes director of the English Mint. English artist William Hogarth is born.

1698 The Portuguese are expelled from Mombasa on the eastern coast of Africa.

1699 The Treaty of Karlowitz; the Austrian Habsburgs gain almost all of Hungary. Oman controls the coast of East Africa. An area on the Gulf coast of Mississippi is named Louisiana in honour of the French king.

1700 Philip V becomes king of Spain; much of Europe becomes involved in the War of Spanish Succession until 1713. In the Great Northern War, Russia is victorious and replaces Sweden as the dominant power in north-eastern Europe. Around this time: The Age of Enlightenment introduces revolutionary new ideas to Europe; the Agricultural Revolution begins in Britain and later spreads across Europe; the Ethiopian Empire divides into feudal states; the first contact takes place between Tahitians and Europeans.

1701 The Act of Settlement establishes Protestant Hanoverian succession in Britain; the exiled James II dies. Frederick III takes the Prussian throne. A Grand Alliance is formed against France in the War of Spanish Succession by England, the Netherlands, the Holy Roman Empire and the German states. Osei Tutu creates a free Ashanti nation in West Africa. The city of Detroit is founded in North America by Antoine de Cadillac to control passage between Lakes Erie and Huron. English agricultural pioneer Jethro Tull invents the seed drill, leading to improved crop yields.

1702 Princess Anne, sister of Queen Mary, becomes queen of England and Scotland. Street lighting appears in German cities. Queen Anne's war between the English and the French in America is fought until 1713. The French settle in Alabama.

1703 The Methuen Agreement, a trade treaty, is signed between England and Portugal. Revolt begins in Hungary against Austrian rule. Peter the Great founds St Petersburg. In Japan, the country's national legend is created when 47 ronin, or samurai, commit suicide after avenging the death of their leader. Vivaldi becomes violin master at Venice's La Pieta orphanage; he writes more than 400 concertos for La Pieta.

1704 Britain captures Gibraltar from Spain. In the Battle of Blenheim, allies under the Duke of Marlborough and Prince Eugène of Savoy-Carignan defeat the French. Isaac Newton publishes *Optics*. Johann Sebastian Bach writes his first cantata, beginning a career lasting until the 1740s. The *Boston News-Letter*, the first newspaper in America, is published.

1705 Bey Husain ibn Ali founds a dynasty at Tunis in North Africa. In Africa, Kongo prophetess Dona Beatrice founds a new religious cult and helps to end the civil war.

1706 At the Battle of Ramillies, Marlborough defeats the French; Prince Eugène also defeats the French at the Battle of Turin. Poland and Sweden sign the Treaty of Altranstädt.

1707 The Act of Union unites England and Scotland as Great Britain. In the Battle of Almanza, allied forces lose to Spain. The death of Mughal Emperor Aurangzeb leads to the disintegration of his empire. Mount Fuji in Japan erupts.

1708

The Duke of Marlborough and Prince Eugène defeat the French at the Battle of Oudenarde. Sweden invades Russia. Frenchman Denis Papin invents a steam boiler, a forerunner of the steam engine. St Paul's Cathedral in London is completed.

1709 The French are defeated at the Battle of Malplaquet, but 20,000 allied troops are killed. Russia defeats Sweden at the Battle of Poltava. The Afghan Ghilzai people under Mir Vais defeat the Persian army; Afghanistan ceases to be an obedient province of the Persian Empire. England invades Arcadia in Canada. Shogun Tsunayoshi of Japan dies; he is succeeded by Tokugawa Ienobu. Russians are sent to Siberia as punishment for the first time. Italian instrument-maker Bartolomeo Cristofori invents the pianoforte.

1710 American Mohawk leaders travel to England to ask for support against their enemies. The German engraver Jakob Christophe Le Blon invents a three-colour printing process.

1711 Peace is declared between Austria and Hungary. The Ottomans begin the reconquest of Greece from the Russians, but lose Bosnia. The Tuscarora War starts between settlers and Native Americans in North Carolina.

1712 Religious warfare breaks out in Switzerland. In England, Thomas Newcomen invents a workable steam pump for use in mines.

1713 The Treaty of Utrecht ends the War of Spanish Succession; Philip V becomes king of Spain. Frederick William I becomes king of Prussia; he establishes a standing army of 80,000 men. Smallpox ravages the Cape colony.

1714 George I becomes the first Hanoverian king of Great Britain and Ireland. The Spanish Netherlands are ceded to Austria by France. France captures the island of Mauritius in the Indian Ocean.

1715 The first Jacobite rising takes place in Britain in support of James, the Old Pretender, son of James II. Louis XV becomes king of France. The Yamasee nation attacks the South Carolina colony, killing hundreds of English settlers. A total of 30,000 slaves work in the gold mines of Minas Gerais in Brazil.

1716 Manchu Emperor Kangxi sends troops to expel the Junkar people from Tibet. The reforming shogun Tokugawa Yoshimune comes to power in Japan, until 1745. The first theatre in the English colonies is opened at Williamsburg, Virginia.

1717 Spain seizes Sardinia from Austria and establishes the Viceroyalty of New Granada in South America. Lady Mary Wortley Montague encourages innoculation against smallpox in Britain, having seen it practised in Turkey. The English Grand Lodge of Freemasonry is founded in London.

1718 Spain seizes Sicily from Savoy. The Quadruple Alliance – Austria, Britain, France and the Netherlands – is formed against Spain. Sweden, Prussia, Hanover, Denmark, Savoy and Poland sign the Treaties of Stockholm. The city of New Orleans is founded on the Mississippi River. The death of William Penn, the Quaker founder of the state of Pennsylvania. Texas becomes a Spanish possession. The game of lacrosse, played by the Potawatomie in the American Upper Midwest, is first described.

1719

Daniel Defoe publishes *Robinson Crusoe*; Jonathan Swift, Henry Fielding, Richard Congreve, John Gay and Richard Steele are also active.

Crusoe discovering footprints in the sand.

1720 The South Sea Bubble; the South Sea Company fails in England causing financial panic. The Treaty of the Hague is signed between the Quadruple Alliance and Spain. The Yoruba state of Oyo dominates the territory to the west of the Niger River in West Africa. Tibet becomes a Chinese protectorate. The Spanish occupy parts of Texas. The 'Tulip Period' begins in Ottoman culture; decorations, festivals and flower displays occupy the sultan and his followers.

1721 Robert Walpole becomes the first and longest-serving British Prime Minister, remaining in office until 1742. The Treaty of Nystadt between Russia and the Swedes confirms Russia as a great power. A regular postal service begins between London and New England. Bubonic plague occurs for the last time in Europe.

1722 Russia and China sign the Treaty of Kiakhta; the Siberian–Mongolian border is defined. Manchu Emperor Yongzheng, fourth emperor of the Manchu Qing Dynasty, comes to power in China. The Dutch navigator Jacob Roggeveen discovers Easter Island and reaches Samoa. The ban on foreign books in Japan is lifted. Daniel Defoe publishes *Moll Flanders*.

1723 Afghan tribesmen put an end to the Safavid regime in Iran. The Ashanti conquer the kingdom of Bono-Mansu in West Africa.

1724 Asaf Jah, a minister of the Mughal emperor, retires to the Deccan; he becomes an independent ruler and is declared first Nizam of Hyderabad. King Agaja of Dahomey in West Africa temporarily disrupts the slave trade in his country; it is reintroduced in the 1740s. The teaching of Christianity is banned in China; missionaries are expelled. Peter the Great founds the Russian Academy of Sciences. The first levees are built along the Mississippi.

1725 The Treaty of Vienna is signed by Spain and Austria. An alliance is formed between Britain, France, Prussia, Sweden, Denmark and the Netherlands. Catherine I, widow of Peter the Great, succeeds to the Russian throne. The Spanish found the city of Montevideo in Uruguay to stop further Portuguese colonization southwards from Brazil. Vivaldi writes *The Four Seasons*.

1727 George II becomes king of Great Britain. Spain is at war with Britain and France (until 1729). The death of Mulai Ismail is followed by 30 years of anarchy in Morocco. Dahomey, in Africa, is at the height of its power. In Brazil, coffee is first planted by Europeans and diamonds are discovered in the Minas Gerais area where gold is already mined. The Society of Friends, the Quakers, advocates the abolition of slavery. English painter Thomas Gainsborough is born.

1729 In China, Emperor Yongzhen bans opium smoking. The Ottoman ban on printing books in Turkish or Arabic is lifted. The *Gujin Tushu Jicheng* (Complete Collection of Illustrations and Writings from the Earliest to Current Times) is printed in China using movable copper type; it contains 800,000 pages and over 100 million Chinese characters.

1730 Russia, Persia and the Holy Roman Empire wage war against the Ottoman Empire (until 1743). In India, the Hindu Maratha government becomes dominant. The period of religious fervour known as the Great Awakening begins in America. Vitus Bering, a Danish explorer employed by Russia, reaches the strait between Asia and North America that is named after him.

1732 The colony of Georgia is founded in America. Istanbul's aqueduct system is rebuilt and expanded.

1733 France, Spain, Austria and Russia fight the War of Polish Succession.

1734 France invades Lorraine. Swedish scientist Emanuel Swedenborg builds a following as a philosopher and mystic. Orientalist George Sale translates the Qur'án into English.

1735 The end of the War of Polish Succession. Nadir Shah, ruler of Persia, conquers Afghanistan and invades northern India. North and South Carolina agree their boundaries. The libel trial of John Peter Zeuger in New York helps establish freedom of the press in North America. William Hogarth paints *A Rake's Progress*. Swedish taxonomist Carolus Linnaeus publishes *Systema Naturae*, including a classification system for plants, animals and minerals.

1736 Russia and Austria go to war with Turkey. Natural rubber is discovered in the humid rainforests of Peru. Qianlong becomes Chinese Qing emperor; the empire's boundaries reach their farthest limits, the population increases greatly and frequent rebellions are crushed. Rubber is first imported to Britain from the West Indies. The first successful appendectomy is carried out in France.

1738 The pope publishes an edict against Freemasonry.

1739 The Treaty of Belgrade ends the war that set Austria and Russia against Turkey; the Ottomans regain Bosnia and the Crimea. Nadir Shah invades India and sacks Delhi, taking the Peacock Throne of the Mughal emperors back to Persia. Britain and Spain fight the inconclusive War of Jenkins' Ear for control of North American and Caribbean waters. South Carolina is shaken by slave revolts. John and Charles Wesley found the Methodist movement.

1740 Frederick II, the Great, becomes king of Prussia, greatly expanding its territory and making Prussia a major power in Europe. Prussia attacks Austria and drags much of Europe into the War of Austrian Succession until 1748. The Holy Roman Emperor Charles V is succeeded by his daughter, Marie-Theresa. In Istanbul, urban craftsmen protest against increasing Westernization. The Lunda, in the present day Democratic Republic of Congo, create a prosperous new kingdom. The power of the Hindu Marathas of central India expands into northern India. The population of the 13 colonies in America reaches 1.5 million, 250,000 of whom are slaves; Boston and Philadelphia are the largest cities. The Native American Lakota tribe is decimated by smallpox.

1741 Elizabeth I, daughter of Peter the Great, comes to power in Russia.

1742 Juan Santos takes the name Atahualpa II and leads the Native Americans of Peru in an unsuccessful revolt against the Spanish. Handel's *Messiah* premieres in Dublin to an enthusiastic audience

1743 The French are defeated at the Battle of Dettingen by an army commanded by George II of Britain. Sweden and Russia sign the Treaty of Abo.

1744 King George goes to war with France in North America, until 1748. Benjamin Franklin develops the Franklin stove.

1745 The 'Forty-Five' – a Jacobite rebellion in Britain led by Charles Edward Stuart, the 'Young Pretender'; Government forces are defeated at the Battle of Prestonpans. In the War of Austrian Succession, French forces defeat an Anglo-Dutch-Hanoverian army in the Battle of Fontenoy. A British force captures the French fortress of Louisbourg in Canada. The last execution for witchcraft takes place in France. The famous courtesan, Madame de Pompadour, is presented at court in France.

1746
The Jacobites are defeated at the Battle of Culloden; Charles Stuart flees, Highland clan culture is suppressed – including the banning of the kilt – and many Scots emigrate. The French capture Madras from the British. The Mazrui dynasty in Mombasa, East Africa, becomes independent from Oman. Spanish painter Francisco Goya is born.

1747 Nadir Shah, founder of the Afsharid dynasty, is assassinated. Ahmad Shah becomes ruler of Afghanistan. The Summer Palace at Beijing is designed for the emperor by Jesuits. London's first venereal disease clinic opens. The Jacobite Lord Lovat is the last man to be executed by axe in Britain. Scottish physician James Lind proves that eating citrus fruits cures scurvy. Samuel Johnson begins work on a dictionary of the English language.

1748 Britain swaps the fortress of Louisburg in Canada for Madras in India with the French. The treaty of Aix-la-Chapelle ends the War of Austrian Succession.

1749 Spaniard Giacobbo Rodrigues Periere invents a sign language system. John Cleland writes *Fanny Hill* while in a debtors' prison.

1750 The population of the world is 791 million. Sebastian de Carvalho (later Marquis of Pombal) is appointed Portuguese foreign secretary and acts as chief minister to José I of Portugal. Ahmad Shah Durrani, leader of a united Afghanistan, invades India and takes Lahore. The kingdom of Darfur begins to expand in East Africa. The Chinese capture Lhasa and take over the state of Tibet. Wu Jingzi writes *The Scholars*, a satirical novel about the Chinese examination system, and Cao Xueqin writes *Dream of the Red Chamber* about the decline of a wealthy family. Half of English farmland is enclosed by this date. Bach dies, marking the end of the Baroque period in music.

1751 France begins publication of the *Encyclopédie, ou dictionnaire raisonné des sciences, des arts et des métiers* a leading book of the Enlightenment. Robert Clive seizes Arcot and ends French plans for supremacy in India. Mason and Dixon begin to establish American territorial frontiers.

1752 Darfur dominates the Sahel in Africa. Benjamin Franklin invents the lightning conductor. The British Empire adopts the Gregorian calendar; 11 days have to be skipped and 2 September is followed by 14 September that year.

1753 Alaungaya reunites Burma; founds the last Burmese dynasty, the Kombaung, lasting until 1885. The French occupy the Ohio valley in North America. Thomas Chippendale begins making furniture in England. The Japanese painter Utamaro is born.

1754 A Concordat with the Vatican gives the Spanish Church independence from Rome. The golden age of Tripoli lasts until 1793, with piracy the primary economic activity. The French and Indian War starts in North America, lasting until 1763. The Albany Convention of New England Colonies proposes an American Union. The Royal and Ancient Golf Club of St Andrews is founded.

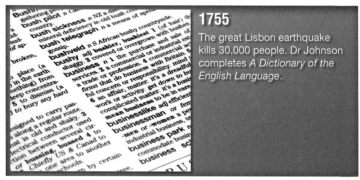

1755
The great Lisbon earthquake kills 30,000 people. Dr Johnson completes *A Dictionary of the English Language*.

1756 The start of the Seven Years War caused by colonial rivalry between Britain and France and rivalry between Austria and Prussia. The 'Black Hole' of Calcutta: 146 British are imprisoned in a small room by Siraj-ud-Daulah, Nawab of Bengal; 123 die. Composer Wolfgang Amadeus Mozart is born.

1757 The Battle of Rossbach: Frederick the Great of Prussia defeats the French and the Austrians. Muhammed III becomes sultan of Morocco. Robert Clive defeats Siraj-ud-Daulah at the Battle of Plassey, establishing British rule in India. English poet, artist and mystic William Blake is born.

1758 Britain takes Senegal from the French. Aoki Konyo, a Japanese scholar, completes a Dutch/Japanese dictionary.

1759 Charles III's reign in Spain begins Bourbon reforms. Britain captures Quebec. The British Museum opens to the public. Voltaire publishes *Candide*.

1760 George III becomes king of Great Britain and Ireland. Canada passes into British hands. Boers begin to settle the interior of southern Africa. Canton becomes the only port in China authorized for foreign trade. Japanese 'floating world' painter Hokusai is born.

1761 The Battle of Panipat between the Marathas and Ahmad Shah Durrani of Afghanistan results in a great Afghan victory.

1762 Britain declares war on Spain. Catherine the Great becomes Empress of all the Russias. The British fleet captures Manila in the Philippines from Spain. A British expedition against Cuba seizes Havana from Spain. Sandwiches, named after the Earl of Sandwich, are invented in England. John Harrison invents a marine chronometer for working out longitude at sea. French philosopher Jean Jacques Rousseau's *Du contrat social* is published.

1763 Britain becomes the dominant power in India and gains control of Canada in the Treaty of Paris that ends the Seven Years War. Rio de Janeiro becomes the capital of Brazil. Ottowa Chief, Pontiac, leads a revolt against the British.

1764 Stanislas Poniatowski becomes the last king of Poland. Osei Kwadwo, becomes ruler of the Ashanti in West Africa. The spinning jenny, a multi-spool spinning wheel, is invented by James Hargreaves in England.

1765   Britain passes the Stamp Act, the first direct taxation on the colonies in the Americas. The Manchu Chinese invade Burma.

1766   The unpopular Stamp Act is repealed. Benjamin Franklin invents bi-focal spectacles.

1767   The Townsend Acts impose taxes on imports into North America from England. Russia and Turkey go to war until 1774; the Ottomans suffer major losses. Catherine the Great commissions a new code of laws in Russia. The Mason-Dixon Line between Maryland and Pennsylvania separates slave states from free states. Burma invades Thailand, forcing the Thais to accept Burmese rule; a Chinese invasion of Burma forces the Burmese to withdraw. British Captain Samuel Wallis is the first European to reach Tahiti.

1768   Ali Bey, a Mameluke army officer, seizes power in Egypt. British Captain James Cook sets out on the first of his three voyages to the Pacific; he discovers Australia. The Scottish explorer James Bruce travels in Ethiopia.

1769   Egypt revolts against rule by the Ottomans. Scottish inventor and engineer James Watt takes out a patent on the modern steam engine. Richard Arkwright invents a water-powered spinning frame. A famine in Bengal kills ten million people; the worst natural disaster in human history.

1770   The Townsend Acts are repealed, apart from the tax on tea. The Tukolor kingdom gains power in former Songhai region of West Africa. William and Caroline Herschel begin their study of comets and nebulae. Composer Ludwig van Beethoven is born.

1771   Russia conquers the Crimea. The Tây So'n Rebellion begins in Vietnam, lasting 30 years. The *Encyclopedia Britannica* is first published. English chemist Joseph Priestley discovers that plants release oxygen. German chemist Carl Scheele discovers oxygen.

1772   Captain Cook sets out on his second voyage to the Pacific. Poland is divided between Russia, Austria and Prussia. The Scottish explorer James Bruce finds the source of the Blue Nile. The Shakers, a Protestant religious denomination, are founded in Manchester by Ann Lee, known as Mother Ann; they move to America in 1774.

1773   The Jesuits are suppressed by Pope Clement XIV. Emelian Pugachev leads an uprising of Cossacks and peasants in Russia. Ali Bey dies a week after being wounded in a battle with rebels led by Abu'l-Dhahab. The Boston Tea Party: colonists in North America rebel against British taxes. The Qianlong emperor launches a project to compile all China's literary heritage in one volume, the *Complete Library of the Treasuries*.

1774   The six-year Russo-Turkish War comes to an end. Louis XVI becomes king of France. Mustafa III, sultan of the Ottoman Empire, is succeeded by Abd-ul-Hamid I. Britain passes repressive Acts against the North American colonies. Warren Hastings becomes governor-general of British India.

1775   War breaks out between the British and the Marathas in India. James Watt and Matthew Boulton form a partnership to produce the first commercial steam engines. The American Revolution begins with fighting at Lexington and Concord in Massachusetts.

1776   Abdelkader leads the Muslims in a holy war along the Senegal River in West Africa. The United States Declaration of Independence is proclaimed on 4 July. The Spanish create the Viceroyalty of La Plata in South America. The British capture the Malvinas from the Spanish and name them the Falkland Isles. Cook makes his third voyage; he dies in Hawaii. Siam (modern-day Thailand) wins independence from Burma. Scottish economist Adam Smith publishes *The Wealth of Nations*.

1777 Maria becomes queen of Portugal. Sidi Mohammed, ruler of Morocco, abolishes Christian slavery. The Treaty of San Idelfonso defines Spanish and Portuguese possessions in Brazil. Christianity is introduced to Korea by Chinese Jesuits.

1778 The War of Bavarian Succession begins between Prussia and Austria. France supports the colonies in the American War of Independence. French philosopher Voltaire dies.

1779 British troops surrender to the Marathas in India; they are forced to return all territories won since 1773. Spain unites with the Americans against Britain. Captain James Cook dies on the Sandwich Islands. The first all cast-iron bridge ever constructed is built across the River Severn in Shropshire.

1780 Riots against Catholics are led by the Protestant Lord George Gordon in London. Joseph II, co-ruler of Austria with his mother Maria Theresa, becomes sole ruler on her death, beginning a ten-year period of important reforms. Benedict Arnold betrays West Point to the British. The British capture Charleston, South Carolina. Tupac Amaru II, descendant of the last indigenous leader of the Incas, leads a revolt in Peru. Sumo wrestling begins to take place in public in Japan. The Derby horse race is first run at Epsom.

1781 The Tijaniyya Islamic order is set up in Algeria. Lord Cornwallis surrenders at Yorktown, ending the American Revolution. Boer settlers massacre the Xhosa. William Herschel discovers Uranus.

1782 The Treaty of Salbai ends the war between Britain and the Marathas. Rama I comes to power in Thailand; he founds the Chakri dynasty and repels Burmese invasions.

1783 Russia annexes the Crimea. US independence is recognized by Britain in the Treaty of Paris. Severe famine cripples Japan. The Montgolfier brothers build the first successful hot-air balloon.

1784 Prime Minister William Pitt the Younger establishes political control over India. Edmund Cartwright invents a steam-powered loom, revolutionizing the manufacture of textiles and hastening the factory system.

1785 The League of German Princes is formed by Frederick the Great against Austria. Omani rulers reassert their influence in Zanzibar. Frenchman Jean-Pierre Blanchard and American John Jeffries cross the English Channel in a hot-air balloon.

1786 Robert Burns publishes *Poems, Chiefly in the Scottish Dialect*. Mozart's *The Marriage of Figaro* premieres in Vienna.

1787 The Assembly of Notables in France is dismissed after failing to draw up financial reforms. Turkey fights Russia until 1792 in an attempt to regain the Crimea, but is defeated. The Tuaregs, Sahara nomads, abolish the Moroccan pashalik of Timbuktu. The first freed British slaves settle at Freetown, Sierra Leone. The US Constitution is drawn up. Lieutenant William Bligh journeys in the *Bounty* to the Pacific to find breadfruit plants; his crew mutiny and put him to sea. Famine in Edo, Japan, causes riots.

1788 The first British convicts are shipped to Botany Bay in Australia. The first edition of *The Times* is published.

1789 In France, the Estates-General meets at Versailles; the French Revolution begins; the Third Estate forms the National Assembly; the Bastille is stormed; the Declaration of the Rights of Man and the Citizen is issued. George Washington becomes the first president of the United States; the United States adopts a constitution that gives greater power to the federal government. The Conspiracy of Tiradentes, to gain independence, takes place in Brazil and a revolt takes place in the Minas Gerais gold mines. Smallpox decimates the Aboriginals of New South Wales in Australia.

1790   Revolt in Haiti against French rule, led by former slave Toussaint Louverture, who for a time runs the country. Ninety per cent of males in Scotland are able to read. Around this time, the great age of European orchestral music begins.

1791

Wolf Tone founds the National Society of United Irishmen, appealing to both Catholics and Protestants to rid themselves of English rule. Amidst the turmoil in France, Louis XVI and his family flee but are captured; Louis accepts the new constitution. Russia gains the Black Sea Steppes from the Ottomans. The Bill of Rights; the first ten amendments are added to the American Constitution. The Canada Act divides Canada into French- and English-speaking territories.

1792   France is declared a republic. Austria and Prussia form a coalition against France; France declares war on them. The death of Sheikh Mohammed Ibn Abdul Wahhab, founder of Saudi Arabia. China invades Nepal. Mary Wollstonecraft publishes *Vindication of the Rights of Woman*, one of the earliest works of feminist literature. The dollar is introduced as the unit of currency in the United States.

1793   Louis XVI and Queen Marie Antoinette of France are executed. Revolutionary France declares war on Britain, the Netherlands and Spain. France introduces the decimal system. Alexander Mackenzie completes the first east to west crossing of Canada. The first free British settlers reach Australia.

1794   The execution of Danton and Robespierre; the Reign of Terror in France draws to a close. Aga Mohammed founds the Kajar dynasty and unites Persia until 1925. American inventor Eli Whitney patents the cotton gin, a mechanical device which removes the seeds from cotton.

1795   The Directoire rules France; France overruns the Netherlands and creates the Batavian Republic. In the Third Partition of Poland, the remainder of the country is divided between Russia, Prussia and Austria. The Hawaiian Islands are united by King Kamehameha I. The British capture Cape colony from the Dutch for the first time. Frenchman Nicholas Jacques Conté invents the modern pencil. Scottish explorer Mungo Park begins his exploration of the Gambia and Niger rivers.

1796   Napoleon Bonaparte, leading the French army, conquers most of Italy. Edward Jenner discovers a smallpox vaccine. The British take Ceylon from the Dutch. Emperor Qianlong of China relinquishes power, but still directs the government, until 1799.

1797   The last invasion of Britain, by a French force led by American Colonel William Tate, at Fishguard; they surrender three days later. Napoleon conquers Venice, ending more than a thousand years of independence. Fath Ali, second Qajar Sha of Iran, establishes a dynasty (until 1834), making Teheran its capital and encouraging the arts. John Adams succeeds George Washington as American president. London haberdasher John Hetherington wears a top hat in public for the first time and attracts a crowd of onlookers; he is fined £50 for causing a public nuisance. The Bank of England issues the first one pound notes. Composer Franz Peter Schubert is born.

1798 A rebellion by United Irishmen wanting separation from Britain, takes place at Vinegar Hill. The French occupy Rome, creating a Roman Republic, and establish the Helvetic Republic in Switzerland; Bonaparte invades Egypt and takes Cairo; in the Battle of the Nile, the British fleet, under Horatio Nelson, defeats the French. In India, Ranjit Singh, the Lion of the Punjab, founds the Sikh kingdom. The strait between mainland Australia and Tasmania is navigated by Bass and Flinders. Thomas Malthus publishes *Essay on the Principle of Population*.

1799 Bonaparte invades Syria. A coalition is formed of Britain, Austria, Russia, Portugal and the Ottoman Empire against the French. Bonaparte returns to France and becomes First Consul. The French are driven out of Italy. Tippoo Sahib, last ruler of Mysore, dies in battle with the British; Britain controls most of southern India. The Combination Laws prohibit trade unions in Britain. The discovery of the Rosetta Stone enables Egyptian hieroglyphics to be understood. Civil war breaks out in Tonga.

the Nineteenth Century

1800 – 1899

1800 The population of the world is 978 million. The Act of Union formally unites Great Britain and Ireland as the United Kingdom. The French defeat the Austrians at the battles of Marengo and Hohenlinden. The Treaty of Lunéville between France and Austria leads to the break-up of the Holy Roman Empire. Washington becomes the home of the United States government. William Young makes shoes designed specifically for the right and left feet. The Italian scientist Volta invents the electric battery. William Herschel discovers infra-red light.

1801 Napoleon signs a Concordat with the Catholic Church, seeking to reconcile the Catholics under his control. Alexander I becomes Tsar of Russia. Thomas Jefferson becomes the third US president. Toussaint Louverture declares Haiti independent. French philosopher, Joseph Lalande catalogues 47,390 stars.

1802 In France, Napoleon Bonaparte is created First Consul for Life. Portuguese explorers cross Africa from west to east. The Tây So'n Rebellion is suppressed by Emperor Gia Long who unifies Vietnam.

1803 War breaks out between Britain and France. The Louisiana Purchase doubles the size of the United States. The Second Maratha War between the British East India Company and the Maratha Empire disrupts central India. Matthew Flinders circumnavigates and names Australia.

1804 Napoleon becomes emperor of France; his civil code is created and adopted by many other countries. Haiti gains independence from France and becomes the first black republic. In England, the Royal Horticultural Society is founded. Beethoven writes his Third Symphony, the 'Eröica', marking the beginning of the Romantic period in music.

1805

The Battles of Trafalgar (Nelson wins a British naval victory) and Austerlitz (French army victory); the French defeat the Austrians at the Battle of Ulm. Mohammed Ali is appointed pasha of Egypt; Egypt breaks away from Ottoman Empire. Seishu Hanaoka, a Japanese doctor, uses general anaesthesia for the first time.

1806 Louis Bonaparte, brother of Napoleon, becomes king of Holland. Napoleon dissolves the Holy Roman Empire, replacing it with the Confederation of the Rhine. Turkey goes to war with Britain, until 1812. Noah Webster publishes the first American dictionary. The Cape colony in southern Africa becomes a British colony.

1807 Britain abolishes the slave trade; slavery continues until 1833. France invades Portugal and takes Lisbon; Portuguese king, John VI, flees to Brazil. The Ashanti invade the Fante confederacy of states. US engineer Robert Fulton builds the first practical steamboat in Virginia. Beethoven completes his Fifth Symphony.

1808 France occupies Spain; Napoleon's brother, Joseph, becomes king of Spain; the Peninsular War begins, lasting until 1814. Russia and Sweden go to war, until 1809. Sierra Leone becomes a British colony. The Fulani invade Bornu near Lake Chad. Rebellions break out against Spain in South America.

1809 The British lose the Battle of Corunna to the French in the Peninsular War. Napoleon defeats the Austrians in the Battle of Wagram. Sweden cedes Finland to Russia. A military coup ousts Gustav IV Adolf of Sweden. Ecuador declares independence from Spain. The Two Thousand Guineas Stakes horse race is first run in England.

1810 George III of the United Kingdom is declared insane; George, Prince of Wales, becomes regent. France annexes Holland, but retreats from Portugal; Jean-Baptiste Bernadotte, Marshal of France, is elected Crown Prince of Sweden. Kamehameha I becomes king of Hawaii. Miguel Hidalgo leads revolts against Spanish rule in Mexico. Beethoven composes 'Für Elise'. Composer Robert Schumann is born.

1811 The French are driven out of Portugal. Paraguay, Bolivia and Venezuela become independent from Spain. The British conquer Java in the East Indies.

1812 Napoleon invades Russia and reaches Moscow but is forced to retreat; 100,000 survive of an army of 600,000. Mohammed Ali massacres the ruling Mamelukes in Cairo. The United States goes to war with Britain until 1814. Britain annexes Mauritius and the Seychelles. The cylindrical printing press is invented and used to print *The Times* of London. The first tin cans are produced in England for preserving food. Luddite riots break out in England against the mechanization of the textile industry. The Brothers Grimm publish their fairy tales.

1813 Napoleon is defeated in the Battle of the Nations at Leipzig. The French are driven out of Spain by Wellington. Allied forces invade France and enter Paris. The waltz, invented in Vienna, becomes popular everywhere. English novelist Jane Austen publishes *Pride and Prejudice*.

1814 Britain, Austria, Russia and Sweden form the Third Coalition against France; Napoleon abdicates and is exiled to Elba; Louis XVIII becomes king of France. Persia and Russia go to war over the annexation of Georgia. Denmark cedes Norway to Sweden; Norway declares independence. The Fulani begin a holy war in northern Nigeria. Lewis and Clark explore beyond the Mississippi. British troops burn down the White House in Washington. The first oil lamp is made in England, designed by a Frenchman, Aimé Argand. English inventor George Stephenson builds the first practical steam locomotive, the *Rocket*.

1815 The Hundred Days: Napoleon escapes from Elba and marches on Paris. At the Battle of Waterloo, Napoleon is defeated by Wellington and exiled to St Helena. The Congress of Vienna follows the defeat of Napoleon; the Austrian and Prussian monarchies are restored; the kingdom of Netherlands formally unites Belgium and Holland. The Serbs revolt against Turkish rule; Milosh Obrenovich becomes Prince of Serbia. Simón Bolivar and José de San Martin begin struggles for independence from Spanish rule in South America. Java is restored to the Dutch by the British. English Corn Laws restrict corn imports.

1816 The United States purchases Florida from Spain. Simón Bolivar defeats the Spanish in Venezuela; independence is confirmed in 1819. Argentina achieves independence from Spain. The *Savannah* is the first steamship to cross the Atlantic. Gioacchino Rossini's *The Barber of Seville* debuts in Rome.

1817 The last Maratha War; the British victory means they rule all of India except the Punjab, Sind and Kashmir. The Elgin Marbles are first displayed in the British Museum.

1818 France joins the four great powers in the Quintuple Alliance. Mohammed Ali overruns the Arabian Peninsula, bringing the first Saudi empire to an end. Chile gains independence from Spain. Shaka founds the Zulu empire.

1819 The Peterloo Massacre in England. Kashmir is conquered by the Sikh leader, Ranjit Sing. Spain gives Florida to the United States. Singapore is founded by Sir Stamford Raffles. Simón Bolivar gains independence for Greater Colombia. The death of Kamehameha I of Hawaii; his heir, Kamehameha II, abolishes the system which restricted contact between men and women.

1820 George IV becomes king of Britain. The Cato Street Conspiracy to assassinate the British prime minister fails. Liberal revolutions occur in Spain, Italy and Portugal. Egypt begins the conquest of Sudan. The US Missouri Compromise ensures a balance between pro- and anti-slavery states. The North Pacific whaling industry begins. The Fulani emirate is founded in Adamawa, West Africa. Around this time, Romanticism dominates European literature, with work by Byron, Shelley, Keats, Chateaubriand, Heine, Turner and Delacroix.

1821 The Greek War of Independence against Turkish rule begins. Shaka founds the Zulu empire in South Africa. Peru, Panama, Guatemala, El Salvador, Honduras, Nicaragua, Costa Rica and Mexico gain independence from Spain. The Republic of Greater Colombia (a federation covering much of present-day Venezuela, Colombia, Panama and Ecuador) is established; Simón Bolívar is named president. Michael Faraday invents the electric motor and generator.

1822 Liberia is established in West Africa as a home for freed slaves. Brazil, Colombia and Ecuador gain independence. Charles Babbage proposes a difference engine, a special-purpose mechanical digital calculator.

1823 The Spanish Revolution fails. In the Monroe Doctrine, US President Monroe warns European states not to interfere in America. Simón Bolívar becomes president of Peru. John Constable paints Salisbury Cathedral.

1824 War breaks out between Britain and the West African Ashanti. The first Anglo-Burmese War; Britain begins the annexation of Burma. Peru defeats the Spanish at the Battle of Ayacucho; Simón Bolívar is declared emperor of Peru. Kamehameha II of Hawaii visits England and dies there. Beethoven premieres his Ninth Symphony in Vienna.

1825 In Russia the Decembrist Rising takes place against the Tsar. The Persian–Russian War breaks out, until 1826. Uruguay declares independence from Brazil. The first photographic image is produced by Frenchman, Joseph-Nicéphore Niepce. The Stockton and Darlington Railway the world's first permanent steam locomotive public railway, opens. The first horse-drawn omnibuses operate in London. London becomes the largest city in the world.

1827 The Treaty of London: Britain, Russia and France guarantee Greek independence and destroy the Egyptian fleet in the Battle of Navarino. Passenger traffic is first carried on a steam locomotive railway, on George Stephenson's Stockton and Darlington Railway.

1828 The Egyptians found the city of Khartoum in Sudan and invade Greece. Indian Hindu, Raja Ram Mohan Roy, founds the reforming Hindu society, Brahmo Samaj. Shaka, the Zulu ruler, is assassinated by his half-brother Dingane who takes over as ruler of the Zulu nation. The Erie Canal opens in North America. Andrew Jackson becomes president of the United States. Bolivia becomes independent. The Dutch annexe Irian Jaya, the western part of New Guinea. The Javanese revolt against the Dutch.

1829 The Catholic Emancipation Act in England allows Roman Catholics to hold public office. Greece gains independence from the Turks. Greater Colombia is divided into Colombia, Venezuela, Ecuador and New Granada. Minh Mang becomes emperor of Vietnam and expels all Christians. Sir Robert Peel founds a police force in London. The Ottomans ban the turban in favour of the fez. The practice of sati (widow burning) is made illegal in India.

1830 William IV becomes king of Britain. The July Revolution in France; Charles X is overthrown and replaced by Louis Philippe. Revolutions occur in Belgium, Poland, Italy and Germany. Greece gains independence from the Ottomans. France invades Algeria. Britain establishes a protectorate over Africa's Gold Coast. The first wagon trains to cross the Rockies arrive in California. Tahitian Protestant missionaries arrive in Fiji.

1831 Leopold I becomes the first king of the Belgians. Mohammed Ali of Egypt seizes Syria; he rules it until 1840. Charles Darwin sets out on HMS *Beagle* on a five-year voyage to the Pacific for scientific research. Guiseppe Mazzini founds the Young Italy movement. Football is played at Eton and other British public schools. The French Foreign Legion is founded.

1832 The Reform Act extends the vote in Britain. Louis Braille, a Frenchman, invents a reading system for the blind. War breaks out between Egypt and Turkey. Abd-al-Kadir leads Arab resistance to France in Algeria. Up to 3,000 die of cholera in London. Edouard Manet, French Impressionist artist, is born. German poet Johann Wolfgang von Goethe dies.

1833 The Factory Act in Britain limits the employment of children. Slavery is abolished in the British Empire. Famine in Japan leads to rioting.

1834 In England, the Tolpuddle Martyrs are transported for forming a trade union. The Pretender Don Carlos tries to take the Spanish throne, leading to the Carlist Wars until 1839. Charles Babbage invents the 'analytical machine', forerunner of the computer. French Catholic missionaries arrive in Mangareva in Tuamotu Islands in South Pacific. The Palace of Westminster is destroyed by fire. French painter Edgar Degas is born.

1835
Hans Christian Andersen publishes his first book of fairy tales. The first revolver is patented by Samuel Colt.

1836 The Chartist movement, demanding votes for all adult males, begins in Britain. The siege of the Alamo; Texas wins independence from Mexico.

1837 Victoria becomes queen of Britain. The Great Trek of the Boers (Dutch farmers) begins away from the British in South Africa; they found the Republic of Natal in 1838 and the Orange Free State in 1854. Tokugawa Ieyoshi becomes shogun in Japan. Frenchman Jules Dumont d'Urville attempts to chart the coast of Antarctica.

1838 Lieutenant Charles Wilkes leads a US expedition to Antarctica. The Trail of Tears in the United States; thousands of eastern Native Americans are forced to move west, many dying on the way. Nakayama Miki founds the faith-healing Tenri sect in Japan.

1839 Ottoman sultan Abdul Majid starts the Tanzimat, a programme of modernization. Turkey invades Syria but loses the Battle of Nesib. Rebellions take place in Upper and Lower Canada. Britain occupies Aden. The beginning of the First Afghan War with the British; a British force is annihilated. The Opium War begins between Britain and China, lasting until 1842. The term 'OK' is invented by Boston newspapers, standing for 'oll korrect'. French Impressionist painter Paul Cézanne is born.

1840 Bosnian rabbi Judah Alkalai proposes the idea of a Jewish homeland. Upper and Lower Canada are united in a self-governing union. Imam Sayyid Said, ruler of Oman (1806–56), makes Zanzibar, a small island off the East African coast, his capital. The Treaty of Waitangi makes New Zealand a crown colony. Kamehameha III launches a system of constitutional monarchy in Hawaii. The first postage stamp, the Penny Black, is introduced in Britain. French Impressionist artist Claude Monet is born. French sculptor Auguste Rodin is born.

1841 The Straits Convention: the Dardanelles and the Bosphorus are to be closed to foreign warships. Mohammed Ali becomes hereditary ruler of Egypt. French Impressionist artist Auguste Renoir is born. The Ottomans establish a postal service.

1842 Britain withdraws from Kabul, Afghanistan. The Treaty of Nanking between Britain and China gives Britain Hong Kong. France annexes the Marquesas Islands and makes Tahiti a protectorate. Women are forbidden to work underground in British mines. Austrian physicist, Christian Doppler discovers the Doppler Effect.

1843
Britain takes Natal from the Boers as a British colony. The first advertising agency is established in Philadelphia by Volney Palmer. Charles Dickens publishes *A Christmas Carol*. Sir Henry Cole prints the world's first Christmas cards in London. The first edition of the British magazine *The Economist* is published.

1844 The Dominican Republic declares independence from the state of Haiti. Cambodia becomes a Thai protectorate. The first effective Factory Act is passed in Britain. The first electrical telegram is sent by Samuel F. B. Morse from the US Capitol in Washington, DC to Baltimore, Maryland; it says, 'What hath God wrought'. A patent for vulcanization, a process to strengthen rubber, is gained by Charles Goodyear. The safety match is invented by Swedish chemistry professor Gustaf Erik Pasch. Locksmith Alexander Fichet invents the first safe.

1845 The Irish potato famine begins. The Sikh Wars with Britain last until 1849; Britain annexes the Punjab. Britain defeats the Bantu in South Africa. The first act of segregation in South Africa; Zulu reserves are established. Texas joins the United States. The rubber band is invented in England by Stephen Perry.

1846 The potato famine is at its height in Ireland. The Corn Laws are repealed in Britain. The Mexican War between the United States and Mexico begins; California and New Mexico are ceded to the United States. The first baseball game is played in Hoboken in the United States. German astronomer Johann Galle discovers the planet Neptune.

1847 The Istanbul slave market is closed. Liberia declares independence.

1848 A year of revolution in Europe: In France, Louis Philippe abdicates and Napoleon's nephew, Louis Napoleon, becomes president; revolutions in Milan, Naples, Venice and Rome, Berlin, Vienna, Prague and Budapest; in Austria, Prince Metternich resigns. The Frankfurt National Assembly meets to discuss the unification of Germany. Switzerland becomes a federal state. Karl Marx and Friedrich Engels publish the *Communist Manifesto*. Algeria is declared part of France. The accession of Nasir ud-din, of the Kajar dynasty of Persia. The United States gains New Mexico and California. Hawaiian King Kamehameha III gives his people shares in the islands. The First Convention for Women's Rights in New York. Richard Wagner begins writing *Der Ring des Nibelungen*. French Impressionist artist Paul Gauguin is born.

1849 The revolutions in Italy and Hungary are crushed. Britain completes the conquest of India. The start of the California Gold Rush. Harriet Tubman escapes slavery in the United States, starting the Underground Railroad to free slaves. A cholera epidemic kills 16,000 in London.

1850 The population of the world is 1¼ billion. Britain transfers powers to the four major Australian colonies; they achieve self-government by 1856. Ethiopia is unified by King Kassa. National progress begins in Brazil under Pedro II. In South America, slavery is abolished in Spanish-speaking republics. The US Congress compromises over the expansion of slavery. The Taiping rebellion against the Manchus begins in China; millions die until 1864. The Krupp metalworks in Germany produces the first all-steel guns. Jeans are invented in California, United States. Rama IV becomes king of Thailand, opening the country to foreign trade. Romantic music composed by Berlioz, Liszt, Wagner, Brahms and Verdi is at its most popular. Around this time, painter and printmaker Hiroshige, famed for the 53 Stations of the Tokaido, is working. The discovery of gold in southern Africa brings a flood of immigrants to the continent. The Taiping Rebellion begins in China. Isaac Singer patents the sewing machine. Gold is found in south-eastern Australia. French physicist Léon Foucault uses a pendulum to prove the Earth rotates.

1851 The Great Exhibition, the world's first industrial fair, opens in London. America wins the first America's Cup race. The *New York Times* is founded. Reuters News Service is founded. Herman Melville publishes *Moby Dick*. Verdi's *Rigoletto* is premiered in Venice.

1852 The French Republic falls; Louis Napoleon becomes Emperor Napoleon III. Nasir-ud-Din takes personal power in Persia; major reforms are implemented. Tukolor leader al-Hajj 'Umar launches jihad along Senegal and upper Niger rivers to establish an Islamic state. The modern safety elevator is invented by Elisha Otis. Harriet Beecher Stowe publishes *Uncle Tom's Cabin*. In South Africa, Britain recognizes the Transvaal's independence. The brown paper bag is invented.

1853 Turkey declares war on Russia; Russia takes control of the Black Sea. France annexes New Caledonia. Commander Matthew Perry sails into Edo Bay in Japan, seeking a trade treaty. Britain wins the Second Burmese War. Mindon Min becomes king of Burma. Baron Hausmann begins the reconstruction of Paris. Scottish explorer David Livingstone begins his exploration of Africa. India's first railway and telegraph lines are opened. The potato chip is invented by George Crum in New York. Dutch Impressionist artist Vincent van Gogh is born.

1854 The Crimean War begins, until 1856; Britain, France and Turkey oppose Russia; the Russians lose the battles of Balaclava and Inkerman and are besieged at Sevastopol for a year. Liberal revolution in Spain overthrows the government. The Orange Free State is established in

South Africa. Eureka stockade: a brief miners' revolt at Ballarat. The United States and Japan agree a trade treaty.

1855   English nurse Florence Nightingale reforms nursing methods during the Crimean War. Ottowa becomes capital of Canada.

1856   The Treaty of Paris ends the Crimean War. Britain goes to war with Persia. The anti-slavery Republican Party is formed in the United States. New Zealand and Tasmania gain self-government from Britain. Britain and France fight the Second Opium War against China, until 1860. David Livingstone completes his eastward crossing of Africa.

1857   The Indian Mutiny: a rebellion of native soldiers in the Bengal army against British rule; Lucknow is besieged. An earthquake in Tokyo kills 100,000. Sheffield FC, the oldest football club in the world, is founded in England.

1858   Lucknow is relieved and the Indian Mutiny comes to an end. Reformer Benito Juarez becomes Mexican president. The French occupy Saigon. The Virgin Mary is said to appear to St Bernadette of Lourdes. The first Australian Rules football match is played. The British explorers, Sir Richard Burton and John Speke discover Lake Tanganyika.

1859

France and Piedmont go to war with Austria; Austria loses and Piedmont gains Lombardy. John Brown's attempt to start a slave revolt alarms whites in the southern United States. Charles Darwin publishes *The Origin of Species*.

1860   Parma, Modena, Tuscany and Romagna unite with Piedmont; the Italian parliament meets in Turin; Garibaldi takes southern Italy; most of Italy is unified. Spain invades Morocco. In the United States, South Carolina withdraws from the Union. Britain and France occupy Beijing, ending the Second Opium War. The Second Maori War is fought in New Zealand. Robert O'Hare Burke and William John Wills cross Australia from south to north; both die on the return journey. Around this time, novels are being written by Dickens, Dumas, Flaubert, Turgenev, Dostoevsky and Tolstoy. The Pony Express begins cross-country mail delivery in the United States. The neo-Gothic British Houses of Parliament, designed by Barry and Pugin, are completed. Composer Gustav Mahler is born.

1861   Prince Albert, husband of Queen Victoria, dies. Victor Emmanuel, king of Piedmont, becomes king of the united Italy (all except Rome and Venice). Tsar Alexander II abolishes serfdom in Russia. Abraham Lincoln becomes president of the United States. The outbreak of Civil war in the United States; an attempt by southern states to secede is defeated. Gold is discovered in Otago, New Zealand. Louis Pasteur develops the theory that germs are the cause of disease.

1862   Otto von Bismarck becomes prime minister of Prussia, until 1890. US land is given to European immigrants to farm. Richard Jordan Gatling patents the Gatling gun. Victor Hugo publishes *Les Misérables*.

1863   The Poles rebel unsuccessfully against Russian rule. Al-Hajj 'Umar takes Timbuktu. Lincoln announces the abolition of slavery in the United States. The Confederates lose the Battle of Gettysburg. France invades Mexico and sets up the Austrian archduke Maximilian as emperor. France begins to establish protectorates in Indochina. The first underground railway is built in London. Cartoonist Thomas Nast creates the modern Santa Claus in a drawing for *Harper's Weekly*. Norwegian painter Edvard Munch is born. Edouard Manet paints *Déjeuner sur L'Herbe*, creating a scandal.

1864 Austria and Prussia capture Schleswig-Holstein from Denmark. In the United States, the Union army controls Georgia. The first French convicts are sent to New Caledonia. Karl Marx founds the First International in London. Henri Dunant founds the Red Cross in Switzerland. Henri Toulouse-Lautrec, French Impressionist painter, is born.

1865 President Lincoln is assassinated. Confederate General Lee surrenders and the American Civil War ends; the Thirteenth Amendment to US Constitution outlaws slavery. The War of the Triple Alliance: Argentina, Brazil and Uruguay against Paraguay. The first Chinese labourers arrive in Hawaii. The New Zealand seat of government is transferred from Auckland to Wellington. King Kojong persecutes Christians in Korea. The Salvation Army is founded in London by William and Catherine Booth. Lewis Carroll publishes *Alice's Adventures in Wonderland*. In Britain, the first speed limit is introduced; 2 mph in town and 4 mph in the country.

1866 Prussia and Italy form an alliance; Prussia defeats Austria at Sadowa in the Seven Weeks War over Schleswig-Holstein; Italy gains Venice; the Treaty of Prague ends the Austro-Prussian War and Austria agrees to withdraw from German affairs. Northern US Republicans force through radical reconstruction of the southern states. Diamonds are discovered at Kimberley in South Africa. Russian painter Wassily Kandinsky is born.

1867 The Second Reform Bill is passed in Britain. Britain makes Canada a dominion. Johann Strauss's 'The Blue Danube' is first performed. The United States buys Alaska from Russia for $7.2 million.

1868 William Gladstone becomes British prime minister for the first time. The North German Confederation is constituted under Prussian leadership. The beginning of the Austro-Hungarian monarchy; Franz Josef of Austria also becomes king of Hungary. An uprising in Spain forces Queen Isabella to abdicate. France is forced out of Mexico. Rama V, founder of modern Thailand, comes to power. The beginning of the Meiji period in Japan (until 1912) bringing a great leap forwards in industrialization; the capital is moved to Edo (renamed Tokyo), the shogunate is abolished and a civil legal code drawn up. Louisa May Alcott writes *Little Women*.

1869 The Disestablishment Act is passed in Britain; the Irish Church ceases to exist. The Suez Canal is opened. Japan colonizes Hokkaido. The transcontinental railroad is completed in the United States. Leo Tolstoy publishes *War and Peace*. French artist Henri Matisse is born.

1870 The Franco-Prussian War; the Prussians besiege Paris; Napoleon III abdicates and the Third Republic is established in France (to 1940). The kingdom of Italy annexes the Papal States and Rome becomes the Italian capital. The infallibility of the pope is proclaimed by the Roman Catholic Church. The transatlantic slave trade between Africa and the Americas ends. A Gold Rush occurs in New Caledonia. Antonio Guzman rules Venezuela, introducing major reforms. The War of the Triple Alliance ends in defeat for Paraguay. Charles Dickens dies of a stroke.

1871 Trade unions are legalized in Britain. Unification of Germany: Prussian King William I becomes emperor. Paris surrenders and the Paris Commune is set up in opposition to the government and to the peace terms; Alsace-Lorraine is ceded to Germany. Henry Stanley finds David

Livingstone in Africa with the words: 'Doctor Livingstone, I presume'. The Albert Hall is opened in London by Queen Victoria. The FA Cup is created in England. Verdi's *Aïda* premieres in Cairo.

1872 The League of Three Emperors – William I, Franz Joseph I and Tsar Alexander II. Cape colony in South Africa is granted self-government by Britain. The first Japanese railway opens between Tokyo and Yokohama. Military conscription is introduced in Japan. Dutch abstract artist Piet Mondrian is born. English artist Aubrey Beardsley is born.

1873 The first republic in Spain. Britain wins the second war with the Ashanti kingdom in West Africa. The Heineken brewery is founded in Amsterdam. DDT is first synthesized. Central Park in New York is completed.

1874

Disraeli becomes prime minister in Britain for a second time. The Spanish monarchy is restored. The beginnings of the Mande state in old Mali under Samori Turé. Prince David Kalakaua becomes ruler of Hawaii. The first Impressionist exhibition is held in Paris; among Impressionist painters are Monet, Renoir and Degas. Henry Stanley discovers the source of the White Nile in Burundi. Verdi's *Requiem* premieres in Milan.

1876 Queen Victoria of Britain is proclaimed empress of India. The Turks put down a Bulgarian uprising with great cruelty. Serbia and Montenegro are defeated by Turkey. Famine in the Deccan, southern India kills more than five million. General George Custer is defeated and killed at the Battle of Little Big Horn. Mark Twain publishes *Tom Sawyer*. Japan recognizes Korean independence. In the United States, Alexander Graham Bell invents the telephone. Pierre-Auguste Renoir paints *Le Bal au Moulin de la Galette*. Tchaikovsky writes *Swan Lake*. Wagner's *The Ring Cycle* is performed in full at the Bayreuth Festival. Johannes Brahms writes his First Symphony.

1877 The Satsuma rebellion in Japan; the last stand of the traditional samurai class is defeated. US inventor Thomas Edison invents the record-player.

1878 The Congress of Berlin ends the Russo-Turkish War; independence for Romania, Serbia and Montenegro. The Second Afghan War: the British invade Afghanistan to counter Russian influence. The New Caledonians rebel against the French. Edison invents the incandescent lightbulb. The first electric street lighting appears in London.

1879 The French complete the conquest of Algeria. The War of the Pacific between Chile, Peru and Bolivia lasts until 1894. The Zulus go to war with the British; the British are defeated at Isandlwana but victorious at Ulundi. F.W. Woolworth opens his first '5 and dime' store.

1880 The beginning of the European Scramble for Africa. France annexes Tahiti as a colony. Australia's most famous bushranger, Ned Kelly, is hanged and becomes a folk hero. Tchaikovsky writes the 1812 Overture.

1881 Tsar Alexander II of Russia is assassinated; his son, Alexander III, takes the throne. Tunisia becomes a French protectorate. The first migration of Jews to Palestine. Wyatt Earp takes part in the gunfight at the OK Corral in Arizona. Spanish artist Pablo Picasso is born.

1882 The Triple Alliance is formed between Germany, Austria and Italy. British forces bombard and occupy Alexandria. Belgium acquires the Congo. US outlaw Jesse James is killed. Antoni Gaudi's Church of La Sagrida Familia is begun; it is still unfinished.

1883 Bolivia loses its coastline to Chile in the War of the Pacific. German engineer Gottfried Daimler creates a portable engine that leads to the automobile. The Brooklyn Bridge is completed. The Boys Brigade is founded in Glasgow. The Orient Express makes its first journey.

1884 A conference in Berlin divides Africa between the European powers. The siege of Khartoum in the Sudan begins. Germany takes control of Cameroon. Dowager Empress Cixi sacks the grand council of China. The first edition of the *Oxford English Dictionary* (OED) is published. Mark Twain writes *The Adventures of Huckleberry Finn*. The prime meridian (0° longitude), running through Greenwich in London, is established.

1885 Serbia goes to war with Bulgaria and is defeated. In Sudan, Muslim leader the Mahdi takes Khartoum from Egypt; General Gordon is killed. The foundation of the Indian Congress Party; the campaign for home rule begins. Gold is discovered in the Transvaal in southern Africa. Goldfields are opened up in Papua New Guinea. The Third Burmese War; Britain annexes Burma. The Statue of Liberty, a gift from France, arrives in New York. The world's first skyscraper is built in Chicago. The Canadian Pacific railway opens. Gilbert and Sullivan write *The Mikado*.

1886 Apache war chief Geronimo surrenders to the US army after being on the run for years. Coca-Cola is invented by pharmacist Dr John Stith Pemberton.

1887 Bulgaria elects Ferdinand of Coburg as king; it becomes the leading Balkan state. France invades Tunisia. Gottfried Daimler unveils his first automobile.

1888 William II becomes Kaiser (emperor) of Germany. Slaves are freed in Brazil. Scottish vet John Boyd Dunlop patents the pneumatic tyre. In England, the Football League is formed. Jack the Ripper kills five women in London. Vincent van Gogh cuts off a piece of his ear. The gramophone is patented by Emil Berliner. Strauss writes the symphonic poem, *Don Juan*.

1889

The revolutionary Young Turk organization is founded in Istanbul; Pedro II is deposed by army revolt; Brazil becomes a republic. Italy takes control of Eritrea. Malietoa Laupepa becomes king of Samoa. The Meiji constitution is adopted in Japan; the first general election takes place in 1890. The Eiffel Tower opens in Paris. Russian painter Marc Chagall is born.

1890 Otto von Bismarck is dismissed as German chancellor. The Arab slave trade in East Africa is disappearing. Native American resistance in America comes to an end when 200 are massacred at Wounded Knee, South Dakota. The United States becomes the world's leading industrial power. Around this time, Strindberg, Chechov and Shaw are writing realistic dramas. The Forth Bridge is opened. Vincent van Gogh shoots himself and dies a few days later.

1891 The Portuguese Republican Revolution breaks out. In Russia, thousands of Jews are forced into ghettos. Civil war breaks out in Chile. Construction begins on the Trans-Siberian railroad. Basketball is invented by James Naismith. The radio is patented by Thomas Edison. Carnegie Hall opens in New York.

1892
Arthur Conan Doyle publishes *The Adventures of Sherlock Holmes*.

1893 France conquers Laos. New Zealand becomes the first country to give women the vote. The first car number plates are used in Paris. Edvard Munch paints *The Scream*. Dvořák composes 'From the New World'.

1894 Nicholas II, the last Tsar of Russia, takes the throne. The French set up a protectorate in Dahomey (Benin), West Africa. The First Sino-Japanese War; the Japanese win and occupy Korea. The Dreyfus Affair begins in France. London's Tower Bridge opens.

1895 The Jameson Raid into the Transvaal in South Africa is carried out. In France, the Lumière brothers invent the film projector. John Harvey Kellog invents cornflakes. Guglielmo Marconi invents wireless telegraphy. Olscar Wilde's play, *The Importance of Being Earnest*, is first performed; later this year, Wilde is sentenced to two years in prison for 'sodomy and gross indecency'. Wilhelm Conrad Röntgen discovers the x-ray. Hungarian Jew Theodor Herzl calls for a Jewish homeland in The Jewish State. Russian scientist Konstantin Tsiolkovsky develops a theory of space flight, including a multi-stage rocket.

1896 Emperor Menelik of Ethiopia defeats the Italians in the Battle of Adowa, securing an independent Ethiopia. The British persuade the Malay states to form a federation. The shortest war in history takes place, the Anglo-Zanzibar War; it lasts 45 minutes. Miners rush to the gold fields of the Klondike in the Yukon area of Canada. Alfred Nobel's will establishes the Nobel Prizes for peace, science and literature. The first modern Olympic Games are held in Athens.

1897 The Egyptian National Party is formed by Mustafa Kamil to rid the country of the British. New Zealand introduces an eight-hour working day and old age pensions. Bram Stoker publishes *Dracula*. Queen Victoria celebrates her Diamond Jubilee.

1898 The United States annexes Hawaii. The Spanish–American War; Spain gives Cuba independence; the United States takes Puerto Rico, Guam and the Philippines as colonies. In China, Dowager Empress Cixi crushes attempts at reform. In France, Marie and Pierre Curie discover radium. In England, Henry Lindfield becomes the world's first fatality from an automobile accident. English sculptor Henry Moore is born.

1899   Lord Curzon becomes viceroy of India. The Boer War breaks out between the Afrikaners and the British in southern Africa; the Siege of Mafeking begins. France proclaims a protectorate in Laos, south-east Asia. Samoa is divided between the United States and Germany. The first Hague Convention is signed. Felix Hoffmann patents Aspirin. In France, Alfred Dreyfus is pardoned.

the Modern World

1900 – 2007

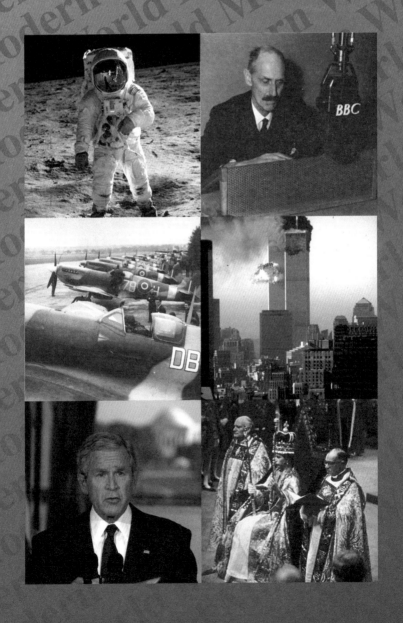

1900 The population of the world is more than 1½ billion. The Labour Party is founded in Britain; Ramsay MacDonald is appointed secretary. German naval law introduces a 20-year building programme for a high seas fleet to compete with the British Navy. In the Boer War, Mafeking is relieved after 217 days; Britain annexes the Transvaal and the Orange Free State and captures Pretoria and Johannesburg. Buganda, East Africa, is ruled by the Kabaka, or king, with British advice. An Ashanti rising occurs in West Africa; Britain annexes Ashanti. Russia annexes Manchuria. The Boxer Rebellion in China against the Qing emperor is put down. New Zealand annexes the Cook Islands. Britain takes control of Tonga's external relations. The international court of arbitration is created at The Hague. Sigmund Freud's *Interpretation of Dreams* signals the birth of psychoanalysis. Giacomo Puccini's opera *Tosca* is performed for the first time. In the United States, the Brownie camera is widely available. Jean Sibelius's *Finlandia* premieres in Helsinki.

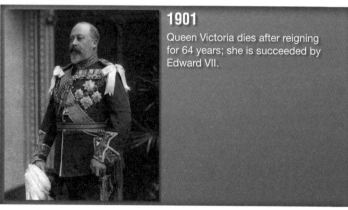

1901
Queen Victoria dies after reigning for 64 years; she is succeeded by Edward VII.

1901 Church and State begin to separate in France. The Russian Social Revolutionary Party (Bolsheviks) is founded. US President William Mackinlay is assassinated; Theodore Roosevelt becomes president. Cuba becomes a US protectorate. The Commonwealth of Australia is founded. The Metro subway opens in Paris. Britain launches its first submarine. Rudyard Kipling publishes *Kim*. Pablo Picasso enters his Blue Period. The adrenalin hormone is isolated. Ragtime jazz gains popularity. Marconi transmits the first transatlantic radio signal.

1902 The Triple Alliance between Germany, Italy and Austria-Hungary is renewed. The first Aswan Dam is built in Egypt. Ibn Saud captures Riyadh, beginning the creation of Saudi Arabia. The Treaty of Verceniging ends the second Boer War in South Africa; Britain defeats the Boers. Women are allowed to vote in Australia. The Anglo-Japanese Alliance is formed. A series of commercial treaties are entered into by China and Britain, United States and Japan.

1903 Alexander, king of Serbia is assassinated. The Sokoto caliphate in Hausaland is taken over by Britain. Panama secedes from Colombia. Orville and Wilbur Wright make a powered flight at Kitty Hawk, North Carolina. In Britain, Emmeline Pankhurst founds the National Women's Social and Political Union. The first motor taxis appear in London. Henry James publishes *The Ambassadors*. Richard Steiff designs the first teddy bears, named for President Teddy Roosevelt. The first transatlantic radio broadcast is made. The first Tour de France cycle race is held.

1904 The Entente Cordiale is signed between Britain and France. The Russo-Japanese War begins and involves trench warfare for the first time.

The French create the federation of French West Africa. The United States ends its occupation of Cuba. Work begins on the Panama Canal. A final settlement is agreed between Bolivia and Chile after the War of the Pacific. Ismael Montes becomes president of Bolivia, introducing social and political reforms. The British explorer Sir Francis Younghusband explores Tibet and captures Lhasa. Licensing laws for pubs and bars are introduced in Britain. The Rolls-Royce Company is founded in Britain. Anton Chechov writes *The Cherry Orchard*. Beatrix Potter publishes *Peter Rabbit*. The film *The Great Train Robbery* is the longest moving picture to-date at 12 minutes. J.M. Barrie's *Peter Pan* is performed for the first time in London. Edward Elgar composes 'Pomp and Circumstance'.

1905 Sinn Féin is founded in Dublin. General strike and a failed revolution in Russia; limited reforms are granted in the October Manifesto. Kaiser William II of Germany visits Tangier and provokes a crisis with France. Norway breaks away from Sweden and elects King Haakon VII. In Crete, the Greeks revolt against Turkish rule. In the Russo-Japanese War, the Russian army surrenders at Port Arthur; the Treaty of Portsmouth ends the war in which 100,000 die; Russia cedes Manchuria to Japan. There is severe famine in Russia; 20 million are starving by 1908. The partitioning of Bengal increases nationalist feelings. British New Guinea becomes a possession of Australia, and is named Papua. The 1,300-year-old civil service exam system in China is abolished. The first buses operate in London. Pablo Picasso arrives in Paris from Spain and begins his Pink Period. Franz Lehar writes his operetta, *The Merry Widow*. Albert Einstein formulates the special theory of relativity. Neon signs begin to appear. A total of 20,000 die in an earthquake in India. Las Vegas is founded.

1906
Mount Vesuvius erupts causing widespread damage to Naples.

1906 A Liberal government comes to power in Britain. The first Russian Duma (representative body) meets. A liberal revolution takes place in Persia. Cuba is occupied by US forces following a liberal revolt. The first French Grand Prix motor race is held. Clemens von Pirquet introduces the term 'allergy'. The first modern battleship, HMS *Dreadnought*, is launched in Britain. An earthquake kills around 3,000 in San Francisco, and 10,000 die in a tsunami in Hong Kong. SOS becomes the international signal for distress.

1907 Germany opposes arms limitation at the Second Hague Peace Conference. Entente Cordiale between Russia and Britain and Triple Entente between Britain, France and Russia opposes the Triple Alliance formed by Germany, Austro-Hungary and Italy. The Second and Third Dumas are held in Russia. Britain and Russia partition Iran. Nairobi becomes capital of British East Africa (now Kenya). A run on American banks is checked by financier J.P. Morgan. New Zealand becomes a dominion of the British Empire. The Philippines holds its first elections. In Britain, Robert Baden-Powell founds the Boy Scout movement. Henri Matisse invents the term 'Cubism' and the first Cubist exhibition is staged in Paris. E.M. Forster writes *A Room with a View*. Kenneth Graeme publishes *The Wind in the Willows*. Bela Bartok composes his String Quartet No. 1. The Hoover vacuum cleaner is invented.

1908 Crete unifies with Greece. Austria annexes Bosnia and Herzegovina. Bulgaria declares independence from Turkey and declares Ferdinand I emperor. Carlos I of Portugal is assassinated. The Young Turk revolution takes place in Turkey. A successful counter-revolution in Persia is supported by Russia. Mahatma Gandhi, leader of the Indian protest movement in the Transvaal, is released from prison. Congo Free State becomes the Belgian Congo. The powerful Chinese Empress Dowager Tz'u His dies. The General Motors Corporation is founded. Isadora Duncan becomes a popular interpreter of dance. Jack Johnson becomes boxing's first black heavyweight world champion. The Union of South Africa is created. An earthquake in Calabria and Sicily kills 150,000; the most violent earthquake ever in Europe.

1909
Henry Ford starts to produce cheap cars using assembly line technology; 15 million Model T Fords are eventually produced.

1909 The Sultan of Turkey is overthrown and replaced by his brother, Muhammad V. Bakelite is manufactured commercially. US explorer Robert Peary reaches the North Pole. British explorer Ernest Shackleton finds the magnetic South Pole. Old age pensions are introduced in Britain. Tel Aviv is founded. Louis Bleriot flies across the English Channel.

1910 George V becomes king of Britain. Portugal becomes a republic. Montenegro becomes an independent kingdom. South Africa becomes a dominion of the British Empire. Japan annexes Korea. The tango becomes popular in Europe and the United States. Halley's Comet is observed. Thomas Edison demonstrates talking motion pictures. The first Zeppelin airship flight takes place. Igor Stravinsky's ballet, *The Firebird*, is danced for the first time by Diaghilev's Ballets Russes in Paris. Wassily Kandinsky invents abstract painting.

1911 The Agadir crisis, when the German gunship *Panther* enters the port of Agadir in Morocco, heightens tension between Germany and Britain. Italy goes to war with Turkey after occupying Tripoli. The Mexican Revolution; President Porfirio Diaz is overthrown. Universal military training is established in New Zealand. Sun Yat-sen leads a rebellion against the Manchus and forms a Chinese republic. Norwegian Roald Amundsen, becomes the first person to reach the South Pole. Ernest Rutherford develops his atomic structure theory. The *Mona Lisa* is stolen; it is returned in 1913. Strauss's *Der Rosenkavalier* premieres in Dresden.

1912 The Fourth Russian Duma. The First Balkan War: Bulgaria, Greece, Montenegro and Serbia fight Turkey. Albania declares independence from Turkey. A French protectorate is established in Morocco. Arizona and New Mexico become US states. Universal suffrage is introduced in Argentina. The founding of the African National Congress in South Africa. The end of the Qing dynasty in China; the Republic of China is established; the Kuomintang, the Chinese Nationalist Party, is founded. The beginning of the Taisho period in Japan. Edwin Bradenberger invents a process to manufacture cellophane. Jim Thorpe is the outstanding participant in the Stockholm Olympics. Grand Central station opens in New York. The Royal Flying Corps (later the Royal Air Force) is founded in Britain. Albert Schweizer, a German medical missionary, opens a hospital in Lambarene in the French Congo. Carl Jung publishes *Psychology of the Unconscious*. The British liner *Titanic* sinks with the loss of 1,513 people. Captain Robert Falcon Scott's expedition to the South Pole fails; all of the party die. American artist Jackson Pollock is born. Marcel Duchamp paints *Nude Descending a Staircase*. Georges Braque invents collage in painting.

1913 The threat of civil war rises in Ireland. The Young Turks stage a coup in Turkey. The Balkan states win the First Balkan War; the Second Balkan War sets Serbia, Greece, Romania and Turkey against Bulgaria. Woodrow Wilson becomes president of the United States. The South African government introduces laws to reserve 87 per cent of land for whites; Mohandas Gandhi is arrested while protesting. China recognizes Outer Mongolia. D.H. Lawrence writes *Sons and Lovers*. Thomas Mann publishes *Death in Venice*. Niels Bohr formulates the theory of atomic structure. Bela Schick discovers the diphtheria immunity test. The zip fastener becomes popular. The Indian poet, Rabindranath Tagore is awarded the Nobel Prize for Literature. The Armory Show in New York introduces post-Impressionism and Cubism to America. Stravinsky's *The Rite of Spring*, choreographed by Vaslav Nijinsky, causes a riot in Paris. Emily Davison, a suffragette, dies after throwing herself under the king's horse at the Epsom Derby. The first crossword puzzle is published in the *New York World*.

1914
World War I
Archduke Franz Ferdinand of Austria is assassinated by Bosnian student, Gavrilo Princip (left), triggering the outbreak of World War I in which Britain, France, Russia, Italy and the United States face the Central Powers, Germany, Austria-Hungary and Turkey.

1914 **28 July**, Austria invades Serbia.
4 August, Germany invades Belgium.
26 August, the Russians are defeated by Germany at the Battle of Tannenburg.
5 to 9 September, the Battle of the Marne; the German advance on Paris is halted.
6 to 15 September, the Battle of the Masurian Lakes; Russia retreats from east Prussia.

30 October to 24 November, the Battle of Ypres; Germany fails in its attempts to reach the Channel ports.

The Irish Home Rule Act allows for a separate Parliament in Ireland. Northern and southern Nigeria are united. The Panama Canal is opened. The Grand Trunk Pacific Railway is completed in Canada. New Zealand occupies Western Samoa. Ralph Vaughan Williams composes 'The Lark Ascending'.

1915   **5 January**, Britain begins a naval blockade of Germany.

April, The Gallipoli Campaign begins, lasting until 22 March 1916; Allied forces fail to gain control of the Dardanelles.

18 February, Germany begins a submarine blockade of Britain.

22 April to 25 May, The Second Battle of Ypres; the first use of poison gas by Germany.

7 May, the sinking of the British liner *Lusitania*, with many civilian deaths.

22 May, Italy joins the Allied powers.

15 October, Bulgaria joins the Central Powers.

The Swiss physicist Albert Einstein publishes the General Theory of Relativity. Alexander Graham Bell makes the first transatlantic telephone call. Japan makes a number of demands threatening China's sovereignty. Marcel Duchamp paints the first works in a Dada style. The first all-metal fighter aircraft is built in Germany by Hugo Junkers.

1916   **21 February to July**, the Battle of Verdun – appalling losses and resulting stalemate.

31 May, the Battle of Jutland, a naval battle between Britain and Germany.

4 June, the Brusilov Offensive, a failed Russian attack.

1916

1 July to 18 November, the Battle of the Somme; more than one million killed and tanks used in battle for the first time by Britain.

The Easter Rising is suppressed in Ireland. Daylight-saving time is introduced in Britain. The beginning of Arab revolt against the Ottoman Turks in Hijaz; Hussein proclaims himself king of the Arabs. The Boer leader Jan Smuts leads an anti-German drive from Kenya into Tanzania (German East Africa). Margaret Sanger opens the first birth control clinic in the United States. The United States purchases the Dutch East Indies (the Virgin Islands) for $25 million. The jazz craze sweeps across the United States. Hipolito Irigoyen is elected president of Argentina, bringing extensive reforms.

1917   **11 March**, Britain takes Baghdad from Turkey.

6 April, the United States declares war on Germany.

6 July, T.E. Lawrence ('Lawrence of Arabia') takes command of the Arab revolt against Turkey.

31 July, the Third Battle of Ypres, also known as Passchendaele, ends in virtual stalemate.

24 **October**, the Battle of Caporetto; the Italians lose.

9 **December**, Britain takes Jerusalem.

In the October Revolution, the Bolsheviks, led by Vladimir Lenin, seize power in Russia. The Balfour Declaration; Britain announces support for a Jewish state in Palestine. Ras Tafari (later, Haile Selassie) becomes regent of Ethiopia. Puerto Rico becomes a US territory. Mexico adopts a new constitution. Brazil declares war on Germany. Sun Yat-sen establishes a military government in Guangzhou in opposition to the Beijing government. China declares war on Germany and Austria. Amadeo Modigliani paints *Crouching Female Nude*. Sigmund Freud publishes *Introductory Lectures to Psychoanalysis*.

1918   3 **March**, Russia withdraws from the war.

15 **July to 2 August**, the Second Battle of the Marne.

8 **August**, the beginning of the Allied offensive; the Germans retreat.

24 **October**, Italy wins the Battle of Vittorio Veneto; Austria-Hungary surrenders.

7 November, revolution in Germany; William II abdicates and a republic is declared.

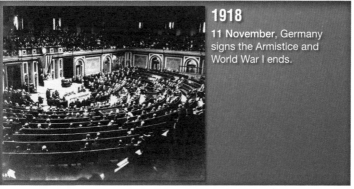

1918
11 November, Germany signs the Armistice and World War I ends.

The Russian Tsar Nicholas II and his family are murdered. Russia adopts the Gregorian calendar. Emir Faisal proclaims the Syrian state and becomes king in 1920. The Venezuelan oilfields are opened. Queen Salote becomes queen of Tonga. A worldwide influenza epidemic lasting several years, kills millions. Women over 30 are given the vote in Britain.The first exhibition of the work of Spanish painter Joan Miro. The first airmail postage is introduced in the United States.

1919   Sinn Féin lead a rebellion in Ireland. The Peace Conference begins in Paris; the founding of the League of Nations. The Treaty of Versailles means Germany loses Alsace-Lorraine and its colonies and has to pay reparations. The Treaty of St Germain ends the Habsburg monarchy, and Czechoslovakia, Poland, Yugoslavia and Hungary gain independence. Germany adopts the Weimar Constitution; socialist leader Rosa Luxemburg is murdered. Benito Mussolini founds the Fascist movement in Italy. Amanullah becomes the Amir of Afghanistan. Ernest Rutherford splits the atom for the first time. In Britain, Lady Astor becomes the first female MP. Walter Gropius founds the Bauhaus movement in Germany. Max Planck wins the Nobel Prize for Physics for introducing quantum theory.

1920   Civil war breaks out in Ireland; Northern Ireland accepts the Home Rule Act. The Treaty of Rapallo is signed by Italy and Yugoslavia. The Bolsheviks win the Russian civil war. Russia and Poland go to war. Turkey is forced to dissolve the Ottoman Empire as a result of its support of Germany in World War I. The first meeting of the League of Nations takes place. Palestine is established as a Jewish state under British supervision. Mohandas Gandhi becomes leader of India's struggle for independence. Prohibition against the sale of alcohol begins in the United States and lasts until 1933. Women are given the vote in the United States. Pancho Villa surrenders to the Mexican authorities. New Zealand is given a mandate over Samoa. An earthquake in China kills 200,000 people. John T. Thompson patents the sub-machine gun, the 'Tommy gun'. Herman Rorsach develops the inkblot test. Writer Gertrude Stein coins the phrase 'the lost generation' to describe the disillusioned expatriot writers Hemingway, Fitzgerald, Sherwood Anderson and others living and working in Paris after the war. Oxford University enrols female students. The Hague becomes the home of the International Court of Justice.

1921 Greece attacks Turkey but is defeated. A Turkish National Government is established in Ankara. The Treaty of Riga ends the Russo-Polish war. Lenin introduces the New Economic Policy in Russia. Abd-el-Krim leads the Berbers and Arabs against Europeans in North Africa. The meeting of the first Indian parliament takes place. Britain, France, Japan and the United States sign the Pacific Treaty. Australia is given a mandate over German New Guinea. President Juan Bautista Saavedra begins a period of progressive government in Bolivia. Sun Yat-sen is elected president of China. Mongolia becomes the world's second communist state. Rudolf Valentino stars in the film *The Sheik*. Albert Camlette and Camille Guerin introduce the BCG tuberculosis vaccine. Marie Stopes opens Britain's first birth control clinic.

1921
The British Broadcasting Company (BBC) is founded.

1922 The Irish Free State is founded. Mussolini marches on Rome and forms a Fascist government. The Union of Socialist Soviet Republics (USSR) is established in Russia. The sultan of Turkey is deposed by Mustafa Kemal who is elected president the following year. Egypt becomes independent from Britain under King Fuad. In India, Gandhi is sentenced to six years' imprisonment for civil disobedience. The first portable radio and first car radio are made in the United States. James Joyce's *Ulysses* and T.S. Eliot's *The Waste Land* are published, two examples of the new literary movement, modernism. A.E. Housman publishes *Last Poems*. P.G. Wodehouse writes *The Inimitable Jeeves*. Picasso begins his Abstract Period. Canadian doctors Banting, Best and MacLoed administer the first insulin to diabetes sufferers. Tutankhamun's tomb is discovered near Luxor by Howard Carter and the Earl of Carnarvon.

1923 The first victory for the British Labour Party at a general election; Ramsay MacDonald becomes prime minister. French and Belgian troops occupy the Ruhr Valley in Germany after the latter's failure at reparations. Adolf Hitler, founder of the National Socialist Party in Germany, fails to overthrow the Bavarian government and is imprisoned. General Primo de Rivera becomes dictator in Spain, until 1930. Turkey is declared a republic under President Mustafa Kemal; Ankara replaces Istanbul as capital. Transjordan gains independence under the leadership of Amir Abdullah. Rhodesia (modern-day Zimbabwe) becomes a self-governing British colony. Mexican bandit and revolutionary Pancho Villa is killed by gunmen. The Argentinian Enrique Triboschi becomes the first person to swim the English Channel from France to England. A total of 120,000 die in an earthquake in Japan that destroys the centres of Tokyo and Yokohama. Bessie Smith records her first song, 'Down-Hearted Blues'.

1924 The death of Vladimir Lenin; Joseph Stalin succeeds him. Greece and Albania become republics. The shah of Persia is deposed; he is replaced by Reza Shah. Gandhi is released from prison on medical grounds. The United States grants independence to Cuba. A government led by Sun Yat-sen, and including Communists, is installed in China. Insecticides are used for the first time. Up to 25,000 die in a plague epidemic in India. The first Winter Olympic Games are held in Chamonix in France; the Summer Olympics are held in Paris. George Gerschwin composes 'Rhapsody in Blue'. Franz Kafka dies of starvation brought on by tuberculosis. George Mallory and Andrew Irvine disappear on Mount Everest. Maurice Ravel's *Bolero* opens in Paris.

1925 The Locarno Agreements between the major European powers aim to maintain peace and stability. The modernization of Turkey by President Kemal Attaturk; Islam is abolished as the state religion; the wearing of the fez is banned. Abd-el-Krim's Arab uprising in Morocco is quashed by the French and Spanish. Ibn Saud creates Saudi Arabia. Blacks, Indians and people of mixed race are prevented from taking skilled jobs in South Africa; Afrikaans becomes the official language. F. Scott Fitzgerald publishes *The Great Gatsby*. *The Trial* by Franz Kafka is published posthumously. The first Surrealist exhibition takes place in Paris. The Pasteur Institute in Paris discovers anti-tetanus serum. America's first motel opens in California. Adolf Hitler publishes *Mein Kampf*. The *Exposition des Arts Decoratifs* in Paris demonstrates the popularity of the Art Deco movement. Norway's capital Christiana is renamed Oslo.

1926
John Logie Baird invents television.

1926 The General Strike in Britain; an unsuccessful attempt to force the government to act against wage reduction and poor conditions for coal miners. Mussolini takes complete control of Italy. In Portugal, the army overthrows the government. Germany is admitted to the League of Nations. The republic of Lebanon is proclaimed. Panama and the United States agree to protect the Panama Canal in wartime. Canberra becomes the Australian capital. Hirohito becomes emperor of Japan.

The Seven Pillars of Wisdom is published by T.E. Lawrence (Lawrence of Arabia). A.A. Milne publishes *Winnie the Pooh*. Indian women are allowed to stand for public office. Robert Goddard launches the first liquid-fuelled rocket from Aubuurn, Massachusetts.

1927 Leon Trotsky is expelled from the Soviet Communist Party. Iraq discovers oil. Saudi Arabia gains independence. Kuomintang leader Chiang Kai-shek purges the communists and establishes a government at Nanking; civil war breaks out in China. Virginia Woolf publishes *To the Lighthouse*. *In Search of Lost Time* (*A la Recherche du Temps Perdu*) by Marcel Proust, is published posthumously. The iron lung is invented. Ivan Petrovich Pavlov publishes *Conditioned Reflexes*. A flu epidemic in Britain kills 1,000 people a week. The Academy of Motion Picture Arts and Sciences is founded. Charles Lindbergh makes the first solo transatlantic flight. A total of 200,000 die in an earthquake in China. The talking picture *The Jazz Singer*, marks the end of the silent film. Belgian astronomer Georges Le Maitre proposes the Big Bang theory for the creation of the universe.

1928 The French begin to build the defensive Maginot Line on the German border. Malta becomes a British dominion. Alexander Fleming discovers penicillin. King Fuad becomes dictator of Egypt. Japanese troops murder the military ruler of Manchuria. Hirohito becomes emperor of Japan. Chinese nationalists capture Beijing. In Australia, the Royal Flying Doctor Service is inaugurated. George Eastman shows the first colour motion pictures in New York. The Olympic Games take place in Amsterdam. Mickey Mouse appears in *Steamboat Willie*, the first cartoon to have sound.

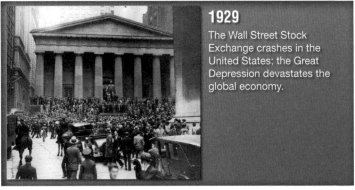

1929

The Wall Street Stock Exchange crashes in the United States; the Great Depression devastates the global economy.

1929 The Vatican State is created. Stalin launches his first Five Year Plan. Trotsky is expelled from the USSR. The first major conflict between Arabs and Jews takes place in Palestine. The Partido Revolucionario Institucional (PRI) begins one party rule in Mexico which lasts until the late 1990s. Richard Byrd makes the first flight over the South Pole. Chiang Kai-shek drives the communists into rural China. William Faulkner publishes *The Sound and the Fury*. Ernest Hemingway publishes *A Farewell to Arms*. The Museum of Modern Art (MOMA) opens in New York. Construction starts on the Empire State Building. The Graf Zeppelin airship circumnavigates the globe in 20 days, 4 hours and 14 minutes. The first Academy Awards are presented.

1930 The Nazis win 107 seats in the German elections. The Treaty of Ankara is signed between Greece and Turkey. Ras Tafari is crowned emperor of Ethiopia, taking the name Haile Selassie. White women are given the vote in South Africa. The first Round Table Conference between the British government and Indian parties is held; Gandhi demands Indian independence. Getulio Vargas becomes Brazilian president, assuming dictatorial powers in 1937. Dashiel Hammett publishes *The Maltese Falcon*. Grant Wood paints *American Gothic*. The planet Pluto is discovered by amateur astronomer Clyde Tombaugh. The Empire State Building opens. The two halves of the Sydney harbour bridge are joined. The first World Cup football tournament is played in Uruguay.

1931

Chicago gangster Al Capone is jailed for income tax evasion.

1931 Britain abandons the gold standard. The Statute of Westminster makes dominions of the British Empire self-governing. Spain is declared a republic after King Alfonso XIII abdicates. The first trans-African railway is completed, from Angola to Mozambique. The Japanese occupy the Chinese province of Manchuria. Mao Zedong becomes chairman of the central executive committee of the Chinese Socialist Republic. Toni and Franz Schmid make the first ascent of the Matterhorn in Switzerland. The Jehovah's Witnesses are founded. Salvador Dali paints *Persistence of Memory*. American engineer Karl Jansky discovers radio waves.

1932 Britain gives trading preference to the Commonwealth nations. Antonio de Oliveira Salazar becomes dictator of Portugal. Stalin launches the second Five Year Plan in the USSR; there is a devastating famine. The untouchables gain voting rights in India. Democrat Franklin D. Roosevelt becomes US president. Paraguay and Bolivia go to war (until 1935) over the Chaco region. Absolute monarchy ends in Siam (Thailand). Aldous Huxley writes *Brave New World*. Work begins on the Golden Gate Bridge in San Francisco. The Zuider Zee drainage project, begun in 1906 in Holland, is completed.

1933 Nazi leader Adolf Hitler is appointed German chancellor; Germany withdraws from the League of Nations; all books by Jewish and non-Nazi authors are burned; the first concentration camps are built. In Russia, Stalin purges the Communist Party. Britain recognizes Iraqi independence; King Ghazi takes the throne. Zahir Shah becomes king in Afghanistan after the assassination of his father. Prohibition ends in the United States. Roosevelt introduces the New Deal. In Cuba, Fulgencio Batista y Zaldivar becomes dictator. The Peruvian president Sanchez Cherro is assassinated. Australia takes control of a large area of Antarctica. Carl Jung publishes *Psychology and Religion*. Leon Trotsky publishes the *History of the Russian Revolution*. The Loch Ness Monster is sighted.

1934 Hitler becomes Führer; he purges the Nazi Party in 'the night of the long knives'; he meets Mussolini in Venice. The Austrian chancellor is killed by Nazis. The British oil pipeline from Kirkuk (Iraq) to Tripoli (Syria) is opened. In Turkey, women get the vote. The British colonial government of Ghana suppresses radical African critics. The communists, led by Mao Zedong and Zhu De, begin the Long March through China. Hosts Italy win the second World Cup.

1935 Hitler renounces the Treaty of Versailles and starts to rearm. The persecution of the Jews begins in Germany with the Nuremberg Laws; compulsory military service is introduced. The monarchy is restored in Greece. Persia changes its name to Iran. The provinces of British India are granted autonomy and self-government from 1937. The first Labour government is elected in New Zealand. *Porgy and Bess*, an opera by George Gershwin, opens in New York. Robert Watson-Watt builds radar equipment to detect aircraft. The Moscow subway opens. Alcoholics Anonymous is founded in New York. German boxer Max Schmelling wins the world heavyweight title from the American Joe Louis.

1936 Edward VIII, king of Britain, abdicates to marry double divorcee, Wallis Simpson; George VI becomes king. Germany invades the Rhineland region on the French–Belgian border and starts construction of the defensive Siegfried Line. The Spanish Civil War begins (until 1939). The Rome–Berlin Axis is established. Italy invades and annexes Ethiopia. Prince Faisal takes power in Egypt. The French grant Syria home rule. Palestinians begin the Great Revolt against Zionist settlement. The first fascist regime in the Americas comes to power in Paraguay. The Representation of Natives Act denies black South Africans political equality. Chiang Ki-shek declares war on Japan. The Long March of the Chinese Red Army ends in Yanan. The Hoover Dam is completed in the United States. Dale Carnegie publishes *How to Win Friends and Influence People*. Margaret Mitchell publishes *Gone with the Wind*. John Steinbeck publishes *The Grapes of Wrath*. The BBC launches a television service. To Hitler's chagrin, the black American athlete Jesse Owens wins four gold medals at the Berlin Olympics.

1937
American architect Frank Lloyd Wright designs Falling Water, a masterpiece of 20th-century architecture.

1937 A coalition government headed by Neville Chamberlain is formed in Britain; Britain adopts a policy of appeasement towards Germany. Eamonn de Valera becomes prime minister of the Republic of Ireland. German planes bomb Guernica in Spain. Jews and Arabs fight in Palestine; a Royal Commission on Palestine advocates the formation of Arab and Jewish states. The Iraqi dictator General Bakr Sidki Pasha is assassinated. Japan invades China; undeclared war is waged until 1945; more than 300,000 Chinese civilians are slaughtered; around 80,000 women are raped; the Japanese seize Peking, Tientsin, Nanjing, Shanghai and Hangchow; the Kuomintang (Nationalist People's Party) government in Nanjing flees to south-west China. Pablo Picasso paints *Guernica*. William Faulkner publishes *The Sound and the Fury*. Wallace

H. Carothers patents nylon for the Dupont Company in Delaware. Frank Whittle builds the first jet engine. The airship *Hindenberg* bursts into flames while trying to dock at New Jersey. Amelia Earhart disappears on a solo flight across the Pacific. The Duke of Windsor (formerly Edward VIII of Britain) marries Mrs Wallis Simpson.

1938 Hitler invades and annexes Austria. The Munich crisis: France and Britain agree to let Germany partition Czechoslovakia; Kristallnacht, a pogrom against the Jews in which the Nazis attack Jewish homes and businesses, takes place across Germany during the night of 9 November. The Japanese set up a puppet regime in Nanking in China and withdraw from the League of Nations. Oil is discovered in Saudi Arabia. Italy win the 1938 World Cup in France. Orson Welles's *War of the Worlds* radio broadcast causes mass panic. László Bíró patents the ballpoint pen.

1939

Germany annexes Czechoslovakia; Italy invades Albania; Germany invades Poland; Britain and France declare war on Germany. Russia invades Poland; Poland is partitioned between Germany and Russia.

1939 In Spain, the nationalists under General Franco take Barcelona; the surrender of Madrid ends the Spanish Civil War. The Russo-Finnish War is being fought (Russia wins in 1940). Robert Menzies becomes Australian prime minister. An earthquake in Turkey kills 45,000. The first helicopter is built by Igor Sikorsky in the United States. The Rh factor in human blood is discovered. The first nylon stockings appear in the United States. Trotsky is assassinated on the orders of Stalin.

1940 **27 March**, Heinrich Himmler starts the construction of the Auschwitz concentration camp.

9 April, Germany invades Denmark and Norway.

30 April, Japan joins the Axis powers.

10 May, Germany invades Belgium, The Netherlands and Luxemborg.

17 May, Germany invades France.

27 May, The British army is evacuated from Dunkirk, France.

10 June, Italy declares war on Britain and France.

14 June, The Germans occupy Paris and France surrenders.

3 July, The Royal Navy destroys the French fleet to stop it falling into German hands.

10 July, Britain wins the Battle of Britain, an air victory preventing invasion by Germany.

7 September, Hitler's bombing blitz of London starts.

28 October, Italy invades Greece.

15 November, in Warsaw, 350,000 Jews are confined to a ghetto.

9 December, Britain launches an attack on Italian forces in the Western Desert.

British scientists develop radar. President Roosevelt declares US neutrality in World War II. Syria becomes part of Vichy France. Italy bombs Palestine. Japan, Germany and Italy sign a military and economic pact.

The Lascaux Caves are discovered in France. The five-year-old Dalai Lama is enthroned in Tibet. Books published: *For Whom the Bell Tolls* by Ernest Hemingway; *Farewell, My Lovely* by Raymond Chandler; *You Can't Go Home Again* by Thomas Wolfe; *To the Finland Station* by Edmund Wilson; *The Interpretation of Personality* by Carl Jung; *Darkness at Noon* by Arthur Koestler. The first electron microscope is demonstrated in the United States.

1941 **14 February**, Erwin Rommel's Afrika Korps land in Tripoli.

13 April, Stalin signs a neutrality pact with Japan.

26 April, German troops march into Athens.

22 June, Germany invades the USSR.

20 May, Italian East Africa surrenders to the British at Addis Ababa.

13 July, Britain signs a pact with the USSR.

27 July, Japanese troops move into Cambodia, Thailand and Vietnam and occupy Bataan in the Philippines.

1 September, Italy and Germany invade Egypt.

8 September, the Siege of Leningrad begins; it is relieved in January 1944.

19 September, British and Soviet forces take Teheran in Iran.

17 October, General Tojo takes over government of Japan.

1941

7 December, Japan bombs the US fleet in Pearl Harbour, Hawaii.

8 December, The United States declares war on the Axis powers. Britain declares war on Finland, Hungary and Romania.

11 December, Hitler and Mussolini declare war on the United States.

25 December, Hong Kong surrenders to Japan.

Reza Shah of Iran is deposed. Edward Hopper paints *Nighthawks*. Orson Welles's *Citizen Kane* is among the biggest films of the year. Noel Coward writes the play *Blithe Spirit*. Atomic research begins on the Manhattan Project. Plutonium is discovered. Hans Haas develops underwater photography. British aviator Amy Johnson dies when her plane crashes.

1942 **2 January**, Japan captures Manila and goes on to take Singapore, Rangoon, Mandelay, and the Philippines.

20 January, Reinhard Heydrich unveils his plan to eliminate 11 million Jews in Europe, the 'final solution'.

1 February, Vidkun Quisling is appointed puppet prime minister in Norway.

26 March, the first deportation of Jews to Auschwitz.

28 March, the RAF begins bombing German munitions factories.

18 April, United States aircraft bomb Tokyo.

8 May, the Americans win the Battle of the Coral Sea.

27 May, Tobruk falls to Rommel's troops.

31 May, Gestapo leader Heydrich is assassinated by Czech partisans.

7 June, the Japanese withdraw from Midway Island after heavy fighting.

29 June, German forces advance on Stalingrad.

30 August, Rommel launches an offensive in Egypt.

6 September, the Germans are defeated in the Battle of Stalingrad.

30 October, the Battle of El Alamein; the Germans under Rommel are defeated in Egypt.

7 November, the Germans retreat into Libya.

In India, Gandhi appoints Jawaharlal Nehru as his successor. The Mildenhall Treasure, a hoard of Roman silverware, is found in Suffolk, England. Films of the year include Disney's *Bambi*. Books – *Les Mouches* by Jean-Paul Sartre; *L'Étranger* by Albert Camus; *The Four Quartets* by T.S. Eliot; *English Social History* by G.M. Trevelyan. Benjamin Britten composes *Sinfonia da Requiem*. Enrico Fermi splits the atom. The first automatic computer is developed in the United States. The turboprop engine is developed by Max Müller of Junkers in Germany. Oxfam is founded. Bing Crosby records 'White Christmas'.

1943
14 January, Churchill and Roosevelt meet at Casablanca.

1943   **18 January**, the Soviets break the siege of Leningrad after 16 months.

23 January, the Allies take Tripoli, the last Axis stronghold in North Africa.

28 January, Hitler orders the mobilization of the entire German population, from 16 to 65.

31 January, The Germans surrender at Stalingrad.

9 February, Japanese resistance ends on Guadalcanal in the Solomon Islands.

14 April, the Allies take Tunis.

1 June, French resistance leader Jean Moulin is arrested by Gestapo chief, Klaus Barbie.

1 July, the US begins to recapture Japanese-held islands in the Pacific.

13 July, the Germans lose the Battle of Kursk to the Russians.

25 July, Mussolini falls from power.

17 August, Sicily falls to the Allies.

3 September, the Italian government surrenders.

13 October, Italy declares war on Germany.

11 November, the Axis forces launch an invasion of Vichy France.

26 November, the Soviets break through German lines at Stalingrad.

The Keynes plan for postwar economic recovery is published. A military junta, under Arturo Rawson, takes power in Argentina. American painter Jackson Pollock stages his first exhibition. Piet Mondrian paints *Broadway Boogie-Woogie*. Marc Chagall paints *The Juggler*.

1944   **4 January**, Hitler orders the mobilization of children over the age of ten.
19 January, the Soviets defeat the German siege of Leningrad.
3 February, US warships shell the Japanese island of Paramishu.
24 April, the Japanese evacuate New Guinea.
4 June, the Allies enter Rome.
6 June, the Allies land in Normandy, beginning the invasion of Europe and the Germans are forced to retreat.
15 June, American planes bomb the Japanese mainland.
25 June, Major General Dwight Eisenhower is put in command of US forces in Europe.
3 July, Minsk, the last German base in the USSR, falls.
20 July, a plot to blow up Hitler fails.
31 July, the Germans are driven into Normandy.
2 September, the Allies liberate Paris and Brussels.
8 September, the first V-2 missile hits England.
11 September, the Allies arrive on German soil.
3 October, resistance in Warsaw is crushed by the Germans.
25 October, the Japanese navy is defeated at the Battle of Leyte Gulf.
16 December, in Belgium, the start of the Battle of the Bulge, Germany's final counter-attack.
Lebanon gains independence. The Jewish organization Irgun, under Menachem Begin, proclaims a revolt against British rule in Palestine. Tennessee Williams writes *The Glass Menagerie*. Aaron Copeland composes *Appalachian Spring*. Jean Giradoux publishes *The Mad Woman of Chaillot*. Henri Matisse paints *The White Dress*. DNA is discovered by American, Oswald Avery.

1945   **17 January**, Russia captures Warsaw.
7 Febuary, Churchill, Stalin and Roosevelt meet at Yalta to discuss post-war settlements.
7 March, the Allies invade Germany. The bombing of Dresden.
April, Allied troops liberate the concentration camps at Bergen-Belsen, Buchenwald and Dachau.
12 April, President Roosevelt dies; Harry S. Truman becomes president.
28 April, Mussolini is executed by Italian partisans.

1945
30 April, Adolf Hitler commits suicide.

7 May, Germany surrenders.
8 May, VE (Victory in Europe) Day.
16 July, the first atomic bomb is detonated at Alamogordo, New Mexico.

July/August, the Potsdam Conference is held to discuss postwar settlements.

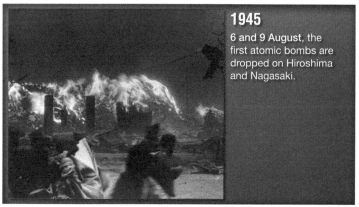

1945
6 and 9 August, the first atomic bombs are dropped on Hiroshima and Nagasaki.

14 August, Japan surrenders. The end of World War II.
8 September, the United States and USSR divide Korea.
14 September, VJ (Victory in Japan) Day.
The United Nations Charter is signed. The Arab League is founded to fight the creation of a Jewish state. The Jewish Brigade raises the Jewish flag. The Indian Congress Party calls for freedom from colonial rule. The republic of Indonesia is proclaimed. Frank Lloyd Wright designs the Guggenheim Museum in New York. *Animal Farm* by George Orwell and *Brideshead Revisited* by Evelyn Waugh are published. Prokoviev's ballet *Cinderella* opens in Moscow. Benjamin Britten's *Peter Grimes* premieres in London. The long-playing record is introduced.

1946 The League of Nations is ended. Norwegian Trygve Lie becomes the first Secretary-General of the United Nations. The peace conference opens in Paris. The Nuremberg Trials of Nazi war criminals take place. A republic is declared in Italy; women get the vote. The Republic of Hungary is founded. Britain and America agree to the economic merger of their zones in Berlin. Churchill warns of an 'Iron Curtain' between communist and non-communist Europe. The kingdom of Jordan gains independence. The Baath Party is established in Iraq. India and Pakistan become separate British dominions. The United States tests an atomic bomb; continuing US and French nuclear testing on Pacific islands causes anger. Juan Peron is elected president of Argentina. The Vietnamese nationalists, led by Ho Chi Minh, fight the French in Indo-China. Buckminster Fuller designs the Dymaxion House.

1947 The Allies sign peace treaties with Italy, Romania, Hungary, Bulgaria and Finland. A conference on Germany fails to reach agreement. US Secretary of State George Marshall introduces the Marshall Plan, an aid programme for Europe. Palestine is partitioned into Arab and Jewish states; Arabs reject the partition. India gains independence; Hindu India and Muslim Pakistan become two separate dominions. Burma gains independence. In the Truman Doctrine, the US government promises aid to any government resisting communism. Tennessee Williams writes *A Streetcar Named Desire*. *The Diary of Ann Frank* is published. Winston Churchill publishes *The Gathering Storm*. Alfred Kinsey publishes *Sexual Behaviour in the Human Male*. The Dead Sea Scrolls are discovered in Wadi Qumran. The American X-1 aircraft, piloted by Chuck Yeager, breaks the sound barrier. Bell Laboratories invent the transistor.

1948 The National Health Service is introduced in Britain. The Soviet Union establishes a blockade of West Berlin; the Berlin airlift supplies the zone until 1949. A communist coup creates the People's Republic of Czechoslovakia. The state of Israel is declared; war breaks out between Israel and the Arab League. Mahatma Gandhi is assassinated. India becomes a republic. Ceylon becomes a self-governing dominion. South Africa becomes independent. Communists and nationalists fight in China. Korea is divided into the Republic of Korea, in the south and the People's Republic in the north. Mao Zedong establishes a Communist government in China; nationalist leaders flee to Taiwan (Formosa). The Union of Burma becomes an independent republic. Norman Mailer publishes *The Naked and the Dead*. George Orwell publishes *Nineteen Eighty-Four*. Jackson Pollock paints *Composition No. 1*. The World Council of Churches is founded.

1949 Britain recognizes the independence of the Republic of Ireland; bread and clothes rationing ends. The Berlin airlift ends; Germany is split in two, the Federal Republic (West) and the German Democratic Republic (East). Comecon (the Council for Mutual Economic Assistance) is created by the Soviet Union and other communist countries. Twelve German war criminals are hung. The North Atlantic Treaty Organization (NATO) is formed by Western nations. David Ben-Gurion becomes prime minister of the new state of Israel; war between the Arab League and Israel ends in a truce; Jerusalem is partitioned. Apartheid becomes official government policy in South Africa. France recognizes Vietnam and Cambodia. Russia recognizes the People's Republic of China. Arthur Miller writes *Death of a Salesman*. Soviet scientists develop an atom bomb.

1950 The population of the world is 2½ billion. Britain and Egypt argue over Sudan and the Suez Canal. Joseph McCarthy leads an inquiry into 'un-American (communist) activities' in the United States. The Philippines gain independence. China occupies Tibet. The Korean War begins between North Korea, with China's support, and South Korea, supported by the forces of the United Nations. Ten million die in droughts and floods in China. The first credit card is introduced.

1951 Winston Churchill forms his first peacetime government in Britain. West Germany is admitted to the Council of Europe. Egypt withdraws from the agreement on Suez; British troops occupy the Canal Zone. King Abdullah of Jordan is assassinated. Libya gains independence from Italy. The Marshall Plan ends. Japan signs a peace treaty at San Francisco. China occupies Tibet. Electric power is produced from atomic energy for the first time in Idaho. Disc jockey Alan Freed coins the term 'rock 'n' roll'. William Morgan, an American astronomer, announces that the Milky Way is spiral-shaped.

1952
Elizabeth II becomes queen of the United Kingdom.

1952 The occupation of West Germany ends. Turkey and Greece join NATO. The Mau Mau (a secret organization of Kikuyu tribesmen) begin terrorist activities against the British in Kenya. In India, Jawaharlal Nehru is elected prime minister. The Allied occupation of Japan ends. Jonas Salk discovers polio vaccine. Mother Theresa opens her Home for Dying Destitutes in Calcutta. The British De Havilland Comet becomes the first turbojet passenger plane. Albert Schweizer wins the Nobel Peace Prize.

1953
Scientists, molecular biologists, American James Watson and Englishman Francis Crick, demonstrate their double helix DNA model.

1953 Dag Hammarskjöld becomes United Nations Secretary-General. Joseph Stalin dies; Georgi Malenkov becomes Soviet premier. In Yugoslavia, communist leader, Marsahal Tito becomes president. Kenyan politician Jomo Kenyatta is accused of Mau Mau involvement and imprisoned. Dwight D. Eisenhower becomes president of the United States. A military coup ends the monarchy in Egypt; a republic is created. In Iran, the CIA helps in the restoration of the Shah to power. The Treaty of Panmunjon ends the Korean War. France occupies Dien Bien Phu in North Vietnam; Viet Minh forces invade Laos. Cambodia gains independence from France. The Redstone missile, the first intermediate range ballistic missile, is developed in the United States by Werner von Braun and other former Nazi scientists. The USSR tests its first hydrogen bomb. New Zealander Edmund Hillary and Sherpa Tensing become the first to climb Mount Everest. Flooding kills 2,000 in Holland. Simone de Beauvoir publishes the landmark feminist book, *The Second Sex*. Ian Fleming publishes his first James Bond novel, *Casino Royale*. Cigarette smoking is reported to cause cancer.

1954 Trouble flares up in Cyprus and Greece over their union. War for independence from France begins in Algeria. Colonel Gamal Abdul Nasser is elected Egyptian president. The US Supreme Court rules that segregation in public schools is unconstitutional. France is defeated by the Viet Minh at Dien Bien Phu. The Geneva Conference divides Vietnam into North (communist) and South (supported by Britain and the United States). The South East Asia Treaty Organization (SEATO) is created to prevent the spread of communism in the area. The first colour televisions are introduced in the United States. British athlete, Roger Bannister is the first person to run a mile in under four minutes. China's Yangtze River floods, killing 40,000 and forcing 10 million to evacuate. The United States launches the *Nautilus*, the first nuclear-powered submarine. Ernest Hemingway is awarded the Nobel Prize for Literature.

1955 Winston Churchill resigns as prime minister in Britain. The Warsaw Pact is signed by the communist states. West Germany is admitted to NATO. The Greek Cypriot terrorist organization, EOKA, begins activities in Cyprus. Israel raids the borders of Egypt and Syria. The first Sudanese civil war begins. A conference at Geneva discusses the peaceful exploitation of atomic energy. The arrest of Rosa Parks in Montgomery, Alabama, launches the American Civil Rights movement. In Argentina, there is an armed rebellion and general strike; President Juan Peron goes into exile. Commercial television is launched in Britain. The British develop an atomic clock. Sony develops the first pocket-size transistor radio.

1956 Soviet premier Nikita Kruschev denounces Joseph Stalin. An anti-Russian uprising in Hungary is quashed by the Russians. Britain withdraws its troops from the Suez Canal Zone; President Nasser nationalizes the canal; Israel invades Egypt; Britain and France reoccupy the Canal Zone; the United Nations sends in forces to police a ceasefire. France recognizes the independence of Morocco and Tunisia. Pakistan becomes an Islamic republic. President Eisenhower is re-elected in the United States. Elvis Presley releases *Heartbreak Hotel*, the first of more than 170 hit records. sixteen-year-old Pelé signs for the Santos football club in Brazil. American film star Grace Kelly marries Prince Rainier of Monaco. FORTRAN, the first computer language, is developed.

1957

The Soviet Union launches Sputnik I, the first artificial satellite; Laika, a dog, becomes the first living creature to travel into space.

1957 The Treaty of Rome is signed by a number of European nations, establishing the European Economic Community, the 'Common Market'. Ghana becomes the first sub-Saharan African nation to obtain independence. The Suez Canal is reopened. Fidel Castro leads guerrilla activity in Cuba against the dictator Fulgencio Batista. 'Papa Doc' Duvalier becomes president of Haiti. The natural proteins, interferons, are discovered. Leonard Bernstein completes the musical *West Side Story*.

1958 Charles de Gaule is elected first president of the French Fifth Republic. Pope John XXIII becomes pope until 1963. Egypt and Syria form the United Arab Republic (UAR); joined by Yemen, it becomes the United Arab States. Abdul Kassem leads a military revolt in Iraq; King Faisal II is assassinated and a republic is declared. Fidel Castro launches a revolution in Cuba. China begins the Great Leap Forward, a move towards rapid industrialization. The United States launches Explorer I and the space race begins. Smallpox and cholera kill more than 75,000 in East Pakistan. The US government creates the National Aeronautics and Space Administration (NASA) and initiates the Mercury manned space programme. US engineer Jack Kilby invents the integrated circuit, revolutionizing the electronics industry. Brazil win the World Cup in Sweden. Elvis Presley is inducted into the US Army.

1959 Riots against European rule erupt in Leopoldville, in the Belgian Congo. The militant Arab organization al-Fatah is founded in Kuwait by Yasser Ararfat. The Batista dictatorship in Cuba is overthrown; communist guerrilla Fidel Castro becomes prime minister. Tibet revolts against Chinese rule; the Dalai Lama escapes to India as the revolt is crushed. Alaska and Hawaii become the 49th and 50th American states. The first commercial copier is sold. Crown Prince Akihito of Japan marries a commoner; the first time this has happened in 1,500 years. The Soviet spacecraft *Luna 3* photographs the far side of the Moon for the first time.

1960 The population of the world is more than three billion. The Irish Republican Army (IRA) begins a guerrilla campaign against the British. The European Free Trade Association (EFTA) and the Central American Common Market are formed. Cyprus becomes an independent republic under President Archbishop Makarios. Leonid Brezhnev becomes president of the Soviet Union. In Turkey, a military coup restores secularism. OPEC (Organization of Petrol Exporting Countries) is founded. Sixteen African colonies become independent. Civil war rages in the Congo. John Fitzgerald Kennedy becomes the youngest president of the United States. A United States reconnaissance plane is shot down over Soviet territory, initiating the U-2 crisis. All territorial claims on Antarctica are waived; it is reserved for scientific research. The St Lawrence Seaway, linking the Great Lakes and the Atlantic, is completed. Former Gestapo chief Adolf Eichmann is tracked down in South America; he is hanged in Israel in 1962. American scientists develop the laser. The heart pacemaker is developed. British scientists invent a vertical take-off jet. At the Rome Olympics, Ethiopian marathon runner Abebe Bikila is the first African to win an Olympic track and field gold medal.

1961 East Germany builds the Berlin Wall. Britain begins an unsuccessful application to join the European Economic Community. The Bay of Pigs exiles' invasion of Cuba, aimed at overthrowing Castro's government, fails. U Thant becomes secretary-general of the UN after Dag Hammarskjöld dies in a plane crash. Syria withdraws from the United Arab Republic. South Africa becomes a republic and withdraws from the Commonwealth. The female oral contraceptive pill comes onto the market. Soviet cosmonaut Yuri Gagarin becomes the first man in space. The morning sickness drug Thalidomide is discovered to cause birth defects. Ray Kroc buys the MacDonalds fast food chain from the MacDonald brothers.

1962
US artist Andy Warhol paints *Campbell's Soup Tins*.

1962 The Cuban Missile Crisis: a confrontation between the United States and Russia over Russian missiles and bombers based in Cuba; the Soviet Union backs down. The Second Vatican Council introduces reforms to the Catholic Church. Malta becomes independent. Algeria gains independence from France. Yemen splits in two after a coup; the north is a monarchy, the south a republic. Jamaica becomes independent. Nelson Mandela is imprisoned for treason in South Africa. There are border clashes between India and China. Tens of thousands march on Washington DC to press for civil rights for black Americans. Western Samoa becomes independent. John Glen is the first American to orbit the Earth. The Telstar communications satellite is launched, providing the first live TV broadcasts between the United States and Europe. The first Wal-Mart store is opened.

1963

US president John F. Kennedy is assassinated by Lee Harvey Oswald; Lyndon Johnson becomes president.

1963 The British government is shaken by the Profumo scandal. France vetoes British membership of the EEC. France detonates its first atomic bomb. Paul VI becomes pope. Britain, the United States and Russia sign a nuclear test ban treaty. A hotline is set up between the USSR and the United States. Malaysia is created from the federations of Malaya, Singapore, North Borneo and Sarawak (Singapore later withdraws). A military coup overthrows the government of South Vietnam. African states form the Organization of African Unity (OAU). The measles vaccine is developed. The Beatles release their first records, taking Britain and then the world by storm. An exhibition of pop art in New York features painters Andy Warhol and Jasper Johns; American pop artist Roy Lichtenstein paints *Whaam*. Cassette tapes are developed in the Netherlands. Valentina Tereshkova is the first woman in space. Dutch astronomer Maarten Schmidt discovers the first quasar. Arno Penzias and Robert Wilson discover faint radiation which turns out to be the remnants of the Big Bang. Martin Luther King delivers his 'I have a dream' speech in Washington DC.

1964 Nikita Kruschev loses power in the Soviet Union; Leonid Brezhnev succeeds him. Greeks and Turks fight in Cyprus; United Nations troops are sent in to maintain peace. The Palestine Liberation Organization is formed to unite Palestinian refugees. The Civil Rights Act bans racial discrimination in federal funding and employment in the United States. The United States declares support for the South Vietnamese against the Viet Cong. Military leaders seize power in Brazil. Indonesia and Malaysia go to war. China tests its first atomic bomb. The Tokyo Olympic Games: the first Olympics staged in Asia and the first event to be relayed to the world by satellite. The Beatles make their US debut on the *Ed Sullivan Show*. The first home videotape player is introduced.

Cassius Clay (Muhammad Ali) becomes heavyweight champion of the world. Bob Dylan makes folk music popular with social protest songs.

1965
The United States initiates bombing of North Vietnam and the first US marines land in South Vietnam.

1965 India and Pakistan go to war over Kashmir. Under premier Ian Smith, Rhodesia makes a unilateral declaration of independence from Britain; Britain places economic sanctions on Rhodesia. Ghanaian president Kwame Nkrumah is toppled by the army. Colonel Joseph Mobutu seizes power in the Congo. Singapore breaks away from Malaysia and declares independence. The American Gemini space missions send two-man crews into orbit. Russian Alexei Leonov is the first man to 'walk' in space. *Mariner 4* takes the first close-up pictures of Mars. Bob Dylan goes electric.

1966 Indira Gandhi becomes prime minister of India. Gambia gains independence from France. Bothswana and Lesotho gain independence from Britain. Black American Muslim leader Malcolm X is assassinated. South African premier Dr Hendrik Verwoerd is assassinated and succeeded by John Vorster. The United Nations imposes sanctions on Rhodesia. Jean-Bedel Bokassa takes over the Central African Republic, declaring himself president-for-life in 1972 and Emperor in 1977. The Cultural Revolution begins in China (until 1968); the Red Guards are formed; intellectuals are purged. The war between Indonesia and Malaysia ends. Ferdinand Marcos is elected president of the Philippines. The Soviet Union lands the unmanned *Luna 9* spacecraft on the Moon. Floods damage art treasures in northern Italy. Temples and statues of Abu Simbel in Egypt are moved to protect them from the rising waters of the Aswan High Dam. Hosts, England win the World Cup.

1967 France vetoes a British application to join the EEC for a second time. Colonel George Papadopoulos leads a successful military coup in Greece. In the Six Day War between Arabs and Israelis, Israel occupies the Sinai Desert, Jerusalem and the west bank of the Jordan; the United Nations brokers a ceasefire; the Suez Canal is closed until 1975. Biafra breaks away from the Nigerian Federation, leading to civil war. Che Guevara is killed in Bolivia. China detonates its first hydrogen bomb. Dr Christian Barnard performs the world's first heart transplant operation in South Africa. In the United States, Green Bay win American football's first Superbowl. Space flights are suspended after a disastrous fire on the new Apollo spacecraft kills three astronauts. The first ATM is launched at a Barclays bank in North London. Irish astronomer Jocelyn Bell discovers pulsars the remnants of supernova explosions. The Beatles release *Sergeant Pepper's Lonely Hearts Club Band*. The summer of love; hippies listen to psychedelic music and are encouraged to 'turn on, tune in and drop out'.

1968 Civil rights riots result in crisis in Northern Ireland. Student demonstrations lead to riots in Paris; universities and factories are taken over by workers and students. Soviet forces invade Czechoslovakia to bring to an end the liberal reforms of the government of Alexander Dubcek. The Baath Party comes to power in Iraq. The Ethiopian civil war begins; 500,000 die in the North African Sahel region in a drought lasting six years. An earthquake in Iran kills 12,000. In America, civil rights leader Martin Luther King is assassinated. As he campaigns for the presidency, Robert Kennedy, brother of assassinated US president, John Kennedy, is assassinated. Richard Nixon becomes American president. The Viet Cong launch the Tet Offensive in Vietnam; major protests break out in the United States against the war; there are 480,000 US troops in Vietnam. The pope issues an encyclical against artificial contraception. Soviet nuclear scientist Andrei Sarkhov criticizes Soviet totalitarianism. Soviet writer Alexander Solzhenitsyn is expelled from the Soviet Writers' Union for political heresy; next year he is awarded the Nobel Prize for Literature. Frank Borman, James Lovell and William Anders orbit the Moon in *Apollo 8*.

1969

The American astronaut Neil Armstrong becomes the first man to set foot on the Moon. The Soviet Union achieves the first docking of two manned spacecraft.

1969 Britain sends troops into Northern Ireland. French president Charles de Gaule resigns. President Nixon engages in the SALT (Strategic Arms Limitation Talks) with the USSR. Golda Meir is elected Israel's fourth prime minister. Muammar al-Qadaffi seizes power in Libya. Bermuda is granted self-government by Britain. Concorde, the world's first supersonic aircraft, makes its maiden flight. More than 500,000 rock fans attend the Woodstock music festival in the United States.

1970 The population of the world is more than 3½ billion. Civil war breaks out in Jordan. Anwar Sadat becomes president of Egypt. Biafra surrenders, ending the Nigerian civil war. Up to 500,000 die in cyclones and floods in East Pakistan. Communist Khmer Rouge forces take power in Cambodia; the United States invades. Tonga and Fiji gain independence from Britain. Four students protesting against the Vietnam War are shot dead by National Guardsmen at Kent State University, Ohio. The development of micro-computers begins in the United States. The Advanced Research Projects Agency Network (ARPANET) system goes online, forerunner of the Internet. Between 50,000 and 70,000 die in floods, earthquakes and landslides in Peru. Pelé leads Brazil to their third World Cup victory, in Mexico. The Beatles break up.

1971 The Shah of Iran celebrates 2,500 years of continuous Iranian monarchy with a lavish event. Mobutu renames the Republic of the Congo 'Zaire'. Idi Amin takes control of Uganda and rules brutally. East Pakistan gains independence as Bangladesh after civil war and Indian intervention. Former president Juan Peron returns to Argentina from exile. Communist China joins the United Nations; Taiwan is expelled. British scientists develop the CT scan and MRI. Greenpeace is founded. Chilean poet Pablo Neruda wins the Nobel Prize for Literature. The pocket calculator is introduced. The USSR launches *Salyut 1*, the first manned space station. China launches its first satellite.

1972
'Bloody Sunday' in Londonderry, Northern Ireland; troops fire on civil rights marchers, killing 14; Britain takes over direct rule.

1972 At the Munich Olympics, 11 Israeli athletes are killed by the Arab Black September organization. The first Sudanese civil war ends and southern Sudan is granted autonomy. Ceylon becomes the Republic of Sri Lanka. US planes secretly bomb Cambodia. The United States returns Okinawa to Japan. The US Congress passes the Equal Opportunity Act in response to the growing women's movement. Washington DC police arrest five men inside the Democratic headquarters at the Watergate Hotel, beginning the Watergate scandal. The Star of Sierra Leone, the largest diamond ever found at 969.8 carats, is unearthed. In a politically charged match, American, Bobby Fischer wins the world chess title from Soviet Boris Spassky in Iceland. The World Trade Center twin towers in New York, the tallest structures in the world, are completed. The Liquid Crystal Display (LCD) is developed in Switzerland. American swimmer Mark Spitz wins a record seven gold medals at the Munich Olympics.

1973 Britain, Ireland and Denmark are admitted to the EEC. Arab oil-producing countries restrict oil supplies, leading to a world economic crisis. The Yom Kippur War a coalition of Arab states, led by Egypt and Syria, attacks Israel; a ceasefire is imposed after five weeks. The United States withdraws from Vietnam and a peace settlement is signed in Paris. A military coup in Chile overthrows the Marxist president, Salvador Allende. Juan Peron again becomes president of Argentina. Abortion becomes a US constitutional right. Secretariat wins horseracing's Triple Crown in America. The United States launches *Skylab*, an orbiting space station.

1974 The IRA bombs the Tower of London and Houses of Parliament. A coup in Portugal ends the dictatorship of President Caetano. The Greek military junta resigns; elections are held. The Turks occupy Nicosia on Cyprus; the island is partitioned into Greek and Turkish sections. Syria and Israel agree a ceasefire in the Golan Heights. Former

Portuguese colonies Guinea-Bisseau, Angola and Mozambique gain independence. Nigeria becomes the leading oil producer in Africa. A revolutionary Marxist regime deposes Haile Selassie and takes power in Ethiopia; civil war spreads. The Bahamas are given independence from Britain. Grenada proclaims independence from Britain. President Richard Nixon is forced to resign because of the Watergate scandal; he is succeeded by Gerald Ford. Drought in Africa threatens the lives and livelihoods of millions; 30,000 die of smallpox in India. The Sears Tower in Chicago becomes the world's tallest building. India detonates a nuclear device, the sixth nation to do so.

1975 King Juan Carlos I becomes king of Spain after 44 years of Franco's dictatorship. Civil war breaks out in Lebanon between Muslims and Christians. South Vietnam surrenders to North Vietnam, ending the Vietnam War. Pol pot's Khmer Rouge seize power in Cambodia; more than two million Cambodians die in the 'killing fields'. Political crisis mounts in Australia as the governor-general, appointed by the British monarch, dismisses the elected government. Papua New Guinea gains independence from Australia. The first US–Soviet link-up in space takes place. The MITS Altair is the first desktop micro-computer. Bill Gates founds Microsoft in the United States.

1976 The Helsinki convention on human rights is adopted. Jimmy Carter becomes president of the United States. Between 1976 and 1984, thousands disappear in Argentina's 'dirty war'. African schoolchildren spark uprisings in Soweto in South Africa; hundreds are shot dead. The Angolan civil war begins, until 1989. In China, Zhou Enlai and Mao Zedong die; the fall of the 'Gang of Four'; Hua Kuo-feng becomes Chinese premier. North and South Vietnam are united. The first warnings are issued that fluorocarbons (CFCs) used in aerosol sprays can damage the ozone layer. Britain suffers its worst-ever drought. Earthquakes in Italy, Turkey, China, the Philippines, Bali and Guatemala kill around 780,000 people. The Episcopal Church approves the ordination of women priests and bishops. *Viking I* and *II* transmit the first pictures from the surface of Mars. The first incidence of Legionnaire's Disease occurs at a convention in Philadelphia. Philip Glass completes *Einstein on the Beach*.

1977

The film *Star Wars* causes a sensation.

1977 Italy announces that Catholicism is no longer the state religion. Two hundred and forty Czech intellectuals sign Charter 77 stating that democratic freedoms are still being denied. Peace negotiations take place between Israel and Egypt. In Pakistan, General Mohammed Zia ul-Haq overthrows Zulfiqar Ali Bhutto, the country's first elected prime minister. The Panama Canal is returned to Panama by the United

States. Elvis Presley dies. Punk Rock scandalizes England. The first Apple II computers go on sale. The last ever smallpox case is isolated in Somalia. The Pompidou Centre in Paris is built.

1978 A year of three popes: Pope John Paul I succeeds Paul VI and is replaced by Pope John Paul II when he dies two months later; John Paul II is Polish, the first non-Italian pope for over 450 years. Afghanistan president Daoud Khan is killed during a military coup; he is succeeded by Nur Mohammed Taraki. Ethiopia launches an offensive in Eritrea. The United States hosts the Camp David summit between Egypt and Israel. The United States agrees to diplomatic relations with China, ending those with Taiwan. Vietnam invades Cambodia and forces out the Khmer Rouge. The first 'test tube baby' is born, in England. Hosts Argentina win the World Cup.

1979
Britain elects its first female prime minister, Margaret Thatcher; she begins privatizing state-owned companies.

1979 Lord Mountbatten is killed by an IRA bomb. The first direct elections to the European Parliament are held. The shah of Iran goes into exile after riots and political pressure; the exiled religious leader, Ayatollah Khomeini, returns and adopts an Islamic constitution for Iran. The ten-year Iran–Iraq war begins. Russian forces move into Afghanistan. A peace treaty is signed in Washington between Israel and Egypt. Sadam Hussein becomes president of Iraq and wins US support. Idi Amin flees from Uganda. Emperor Bokassa of the Central African Empire is overthrown in a French-backed coup. Elections are held in Rhodesia under an internal settlement; guerrilla warfare continues; Britain takes control of the country. The communist Sandinistas seize power in Nicaragua. China invades Vietnam. Nuclear catastrophe is narrowly averted at the Three Mile Island nuclear plant in Pennsylvania. The Sony Walkman is introduced. Mother Theresa is awarded the Nobel Peace Prize. The Sugar Hill Gang record the first commercial rap hit, *Rapper's Delight*.

1980 The population of the world is almost 4½ billion. The socialist François Mitterand becomes president of France. President Tito of Yugoslavia dies. The independent trade union Solidarity is formed in Poland. Indira Gandhi returns to power after being imprisoned. Rhodesia becomes independent as Zimbabwe, under Robert Mugabe. Former film star Ronald Reagan is elected president of the United States. Civil war breaks out in El Salvador. In China, Deng Xiaoping consolidates his position as leader of the Communist Party, improving relations with the West and developing the concept of a socialist market economy. CNN becomes the first 24-hour news television station. The Mount St Helens volcano erupts in the United States. Scientists identify the AIDS virus. Japan becomes the world's largest car manufacturer. The

Moscow Olympics are boycotted by 50 countries, protesting at the Soviet invasion of Afghanistan. The *Voyager I* space probe transmits spectacular pictures of Saturn. Former Beatle, John Lennon is shot to death by an obsessed fan.

1981 Charles, Prince of Wales, marries Lady Diana Spencer. Pope John Paul II is shot by a Turk, Mehmet Ali Agca, but survives. The Polish prime minister Józef Pinkowski resigns; he is replaced by General Wojciech Jaruzelski. Egyptian president Sadat is assassinated. The Sikhs begin fighting for Punjabi independence. Israel annexes the Golan Heights. John Hinckley tries to assassinate President Reagan in Washington. Jiang Qin, 'Madam Mao', Mao Zedong's fourth wife, is sentenced to death in China; the sentence is later commuted, but she commits suicide. MTV is launched. The US space shuttle *Columbia* makes its maiden flight. The world's fastest train, the TGV, begins to run in France. Bill Gates devises MS-DOS for IBM.

1982

Michael Jackson records *Thriller*, the biggest-selling album ever.

1982 The Falklands War; Argentina occupies the Falkland Islands; a British task force recaptures them. The Red Brigade carries out terrorist activities in Italy. Helmut Kohl replaces Helmut Schmidt as chancellor of Germany. In the Soviet Union, former KGB head Yuri Andropov becomes general secretary of the Communist Party's Central Committee, succeeding the late Leonid Brezhnev. Israeli forces invade Lebanon to drive out the PLO; Lebanese Christian Militia kill hundreds of Palestinians in the Sabra and Chatila refugee camps in West Beirut. Hezbollah, a political and military organization, is founded in Lebanon. Mexico fails to repay foreign loans, provoking an international financial crisis. Colombian author Gabriel Garcia Marquez is awarded the Nobel Prize for Literature. Italy win the World Cup in Spain.

1983 Margaret Thatcher wins by a landslide in a general election in Britain. The IRA continues terrorist activities in Britain. More than 200 marines die when a bomb is detonated at the US embassy in Beirut; America withdraws from Lebanon. Israel signs an agreement to withdraw from Lebanon. African countries adopt IMF (International Monetary Fund) plans for managing their economies. More than 1½ million people die in the second Sudanese civil war between Muslims and non-Muslims. Tamil Tiger rebels begin their fight for a separate state for the minority Tamils. Democratic elections take place in Argentina after seven years of military rule. Maurice Bishop, the prime minister of Grenada, and 40 others are executed in a military coup. Benigno Aquino Jr., Philippine opposition leader, is assassinated in Manila as he returns from exile. The population of China reaches a billion. Nazi war criminal Klaus Barbie is arrested in Bolivia. Bjorn Borg wins his fifth consecutive

Wimbledon championship and retires from tennis. Seatbelts become compulsory in Britain. Microsoft Word is first released. *Pioneer 10*, an American spacecraft, becomes the first man-made object to travel beyond the solar system.

1984   The Provisional Irish Republican Army (PIRA) tries to assassinate the British Cabinet with a bomb in the Grand Hotel in Brighton. The year-long miners' strike begins in Britain. Konstantin Chernenko becomes general secretary of the Communist Party of the Soviet Union. Indian troops attack the Sikh Golden Temple at Amritsar; Indian prime minister, Indira Gandhi is assassinated by Sikhs; Rajiv Gandhi becomes prime minister of India. The sultanate of Brunei gains independence. Upper Volta becomes Burkina Faso. Famine begins in Ethiopia. New Zealand is declared a nuclear-free zone. The first commercial CD players are introduced. A leak of toxic gas from a Union Carbide plant in Bhopal in India kills 2,500 and leaves lasting effects on countless others. Ronald Reagan is re-elected president of the United States. Half a million people in Manila demonstrate against the government of Ferdinand Marcos. The Soviet Union and other communist countries boycott the Los Angeles Olympics. Apple introduces the Macintosh, the first PC with a graphical interface. The first commercial CD players are introduced. Bishop Desmund Tutu, general secretary of the South African Council of Churches, wins the Nobel Peace Prize.

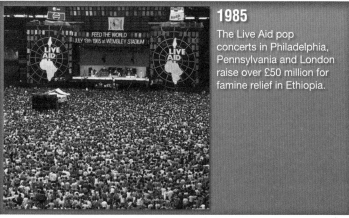

1985
The Live Aid pop concerts in Philadelphia, Pennsylvania and London raise over £50 million for famine relief in Ethiopia.

1985   Mikhail Gorbachev is elected Soviet party leader and introduces reforms. South Africa ends its ban on interracial marriages. In Japan, the CD-ROM (Compact Disk Read-Only Memory) is introduced. In Australia, the first child is born from a frozen embryo. The first British cellphone call is made (by comedian Ernie Wise, to Vodafone). A total of 10,000 die in tropical storms in Bangladesh; 9,000 die in an earthquake in Mexico City; 23,000 die when the Nevada del Ruiz volcano erupts in Colombia. Microsoft releases the first version of its Windows operating system. British scientist Alec Jeffreys develops genetic fingerprinting.

1986   Spain and Portugal join the European Community. A state of emergency is declared in South Africa after a general strike by 1.5 million blacks. US warplanes bomb Libya in retaliation for Libyan terrorist activity. Yoweri Museveni becomes president of Uganda after a five-year liberation struggle. President Jean-Claude Duvalier flees Haiti; his family have ruled for 28 years. President Marcos of the Philippines flees after doubts about his election victory; Corazon Aquino becomes president. The Treaty of Rarotonga sets up a South Pacific Nuclear-Free Zone. Toxic gas from the volcanic Lake Nyos in Cameroon kills

2,000. The final supplement of the *Oxford English Dictionary* (Se to Z) is published, more than a century after the first edition. The space shuttle *Challenger* explodes not long after take-off, killing all seven crew members, including the first civilian spaceship passenger. The Soviet Union launches the *Mir* space station. The Chernobyl power station in Kiev is the source of the world's worst nuclear accident with fallout affecting almost all of Europe. British journalist John McCarthy is kidnapped in Beirut; he is released in 1991. Argentina win the World Cup in Mexico.

1987 The population of the earth is five billion. Margaret Thatcher wins her third general election in the United Kingdom. On Black Monday, 19 October, stockmarkets around the world plummet. Soviet leader Gorbachev announces his policies of glasnost (openness) and perestroika (reconstruction). Soviet forces begin a withdrawal from Afghanistan. The Palestinian Intifada uprising against Israel begins. Vincent Van Gogh's *Irises* becomes the world's most expensive painting at $49 million. Terry Waite, special envoy of the Archbishop of Canterbury, is kidnapped in Beirut; he is released in 1991. *The Simpsons* debuts on television. The first heart–lung transplant takes place in the United States. Nazi war criminal Rudolf Hess is found dead in his cell in Spandau Prison where he had been incarcerated since the World War II. Work begins on the Channel Tunnel linking France and England.

1988

A Pan Am Boeing 747 is blown up over Lockerbie, Scotland, killing 270 people; Syrian-backed terrorists are thought responsible.

1988 Ethnic Albanians in Kosovo demonstrate for independence from Serbia. A ceasefire comes into being in the Iran–Iraq War; an estimated one million lives have been lost. The Iraqi government forces carry out a poison gas attack on the Kurdish town of Halabja. Benazir Bhutto becomes the first woman to lead an Islamic nation. George H.W. Bush becomes president of the United States. Prozac becomes available. The drug Crack cocaine gains popularity. A total of 80,000 die in an earthquake in Armenia. The original Globe Theatre is uncovered in London. The Olympic Games are held in Seoul, South Korea. Brazilian union and environmental activist Chico Mendes is assassinated by ranchers opposed to him.

1989 Anti-communist revolutions take place all over Central and Eastern Europe. East Germany's communist government resigns; the Berlin Wall is dismantled. The Communist Party in Poland legalizes the Solidarity union; Solidarity wins the election. Protesters in Romania overthrow President Nicolae Ceauçescu and execute him and his wife. Playwright Vaclav Havel becomes president of the newly non-communist Czechoslovakia. Pakistan rejoins the British

Commonwealth from which it withdrew in 1972. Zambia and other countries see changes of government by democratic election. The United States invades Panama and deposes its ruler, General Noriega. A military coup in Paraguay overthrows Alfredo Stroessner who has been in power since 1954. Chile holds its first free election in 16 years. F.W. de Klerk succeeds P.W. Botha as president in South Africa. Mass demonstrations for democracy take place in Tiananmen Square in Beijing, China; they end in massacre. The Showa period in Japan ends with the death of Emperor Hirohito; Akihito becomes Emperor. Vietnamese troops withdraw from Cambodia. Burma is renamed Myanmar after a military coup; opposition leader Aung San Suu Kyi is placed under house arrest. The tanker *Exxon Valdez* causes the world's biggest oil spill (11 million gallons). Sky Television is launched in Europe. A Fatwah is announced on Anglo-Indian author Salman Rushdie, for writing *The Satanic Verses*.

1990
Nelson Mandela is freed from prison in South Africa; the process of dismantling apartheid begins.

1990   The population of the world is 5¼ billion. Riots break out in London against Margaret Thatcher's poll tax. East and West Germany are unified as one nation; Helmut Kohl becomes chancellor. Slobodan Milošović becomes president of Serbia. Solidarity's leader Lech Walesa is elected president of Poland. In the Lebanese Civil War, Syrian military forces invade Lebanon and oust General Michel Aoun's government. Iraq invades Kuwait; the United States and allies send forces to the Gulf region and the Gulf War begins. The Sandinistas are defeated in elections in Nicaragua. Namibia gains independence. The Hubble Space Telescope comes into operation. Vincent Van Gogh's *Portrait of Dr Gachet* becomes the world's most expensive painting at $82.5 million. West Germany win the World Cup in Italy.

1991   John Major replaces Margaret Thatcher as prime minister in Britain. The break-up of the Soviet Union; the resignation of Gorbachev; Boris Yeltsin takes power in Russia; the Baltic states declare independence from the Soviet Union; the Warsaw Pact is dissolved; the USSR ceases to exist on 9 December. Allied forces liberate Kuwait. Rajiv Gandhi is assassinated in India. A cyclone in Bangladesh kills 200,000; a later storm surge in the Chittagong Delta kills another 150,000. The decade-long civil war in El Salvador comes to an end. Apartheid is dismantled in South Africa; Nelson Mandela becomes its first black president. Tim Berners-Lee launches the World Wide Web. Northern Irish writer Brian Keenan, held hostage for nearly five years in Lebanon, is released.

1992   John Major unexpectedly wins the general election in Britain. Black Wednesday; the pound and the Italian lira are forced out of the European Exchange Rate Mechanism; the British Treasury estimates the cost to be £3.4 billion. The Maastricht Treaty, creating the European Union, is signed. Yugoslavia breaks up and erupts into bloody civil war; a UN peacekeeping force is sent in; Slovenia and Croatia gain independence. A bodyguard assassinates President Muhammad Boudiaf of Algeria; the country experiences turmoil until 2002. Bill Clinton defeats the incumbent, George Bush, and independent, Ross Perot, to become president of the United States. The civil war in El Salvador ends after 12 years. Taiwan suspends the ban on trade and social links with China. Boutros Boutros Ghali becomes Secretary-General of the United Nations. The Olympic Games are held in Barcelona. Prince Charles and Princess Diana of Britain announce they are to separate; the British Queen describes 1992 as an *Annus Horribilis*.

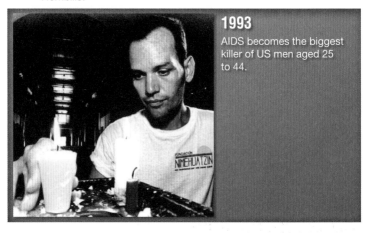

1993
AIDS becomes the biggest killer of US men aged 25 to 44.

1993 Two children die when an IRA bomb explodes in Warrington, England. Czechoslovakia splits into the Czech and Slovak Rebublics. Palestinian leader, Yasser Arafat, and Israeli prime minister, Rabin, sign a peace agreement in the United States; Arafat forms the Palestine National Authority to govern Gaza and Jericho. Eritrea (in north Ethiopia) breaks away from Ethiopia. Nineteen American soldiers die in a major battle with local militia in Mogadishu in Somalia. President Ranasinghe Premadasa of Sri Lanka is assassinated by a Tamil Tiger suicide bomber. America launches a cruise missile attack on Iraqi intelligence headquarters in the Al-Mansur District of Baghdad, in response to the attempted assassination of former US president George Bush during a visit to Kuwait. North Korea refuses access to nuclear sites and withdraws from the Nuclear Non-proliferation Treaty. A terrorist bomb goes off in the World Trade Center in New York, killing six. 10,000 die in an earthquake in India.

1994 In Ireland, the Provisional IRA announces a cessation of military operations. A Bosnian Serb army mortar shell kills 68 civilians in a Sarajevo market. A Chechnyan revolt is crushed by Russia. US president Bill Clinton and Russian president Boris Yeltsin sign the Kremlin Accords, stopping the preprogrammed aiming of nuclear missiles towards each country's targets. Jordan and Israel sign a treaty ending conflict between the two countries. The African National Congress (ANC) wins the first multi-racial election ever held in South Africa. A total of 500,000 Tutsi are killed by Hutu gangs in civil war in Rwanda. Itzhak Rabin, prime minister of Israel, is assassinated; Benjamin Netanyahu becomes prime minister and brings the Israeli–Palestinian accord to an end. Vietnam restores diplomatic relations with the United States. Kim Jong II replaces his father as leader in North Korea. The World Trade Organization is created to promote global economic development. The Channel Tunnel, linking Britain and France, is opened. Britain creates the world's first DNA-based crime database. Online auction site eBay is founded. Sports legend, O.J. Simpson, is tried for murder and is acquitted in 1995. Racing driver Ayrton Senna is killed in an accident at the San Marino Grand Prix. Brazil win the World Cup in the United States.

1995 Jacques Chirac becomes president of France. NATO bombs Serbian troop positions in Bosnia. Twenty-one Bosnian Serb commanders are charged with genocide and crimes against humanity; a peace agreement for Bosnia is reached. In Iraq, Saddam Hussein continues to hinder searches for weapons of mass destruction. Barings Bank collapses after broker Nick Leeson loses $1.4 billion on the Tokyo Stock Exchange. A bomb is exploded in a federal building in Oklahoma City, United States, killing 168 people. The Bosman Ruling is introduced in football, allowing footballers to move freely at the end of their contracts.

1996
Internet seach engine Google is launched.

1996 The IRA ceasefire is ended by a bomb in Canary Wharf in London; peace talks with Sinn Féin begin in June. Boris Yeltsin negotiates a ceasefire with the Chechnyans. The Taliban seize power in Afghanistan and impose strict Islamic law. Osama Bin Laden is expelled from Sudan and moves to Afghanistan. Al-Hakam, Iraq's main production facility of biological warfare agents, is destroyed under the supervision of the United Nations Special Commission (UNSCOM). Yasser Arafat is voted president in the first Palestinian elections. Israel launches a major offensive against Hezbollah. Bill Clinton is re-elected as president of the United States. The US launches Operation Desert Strike against Iraq. An outbreak of mad cow disease leads to a ban on exports of beef from the UK. In Japan, the first DVD players are released. The Petronas Towers in Kuala Lumpur become the world's tallest buildings. The first version of Java programming language is released. Sixteen children are killed by Thomas Hamilton in a school at Dunblane in Scotland. The Olympic Games take place in Atlanta in the United States. Charles and Diana divorce. Jazz singer Ella Fitzgerald dies.

1997

Diana, Princess of Wales dies in a car crash in Paris; more than a billion people watch her funeral.

1997 Labour's Tony Blair becomes British prime minister. Wales and Scotland vote in favour of having their own parliaments. Russia and Chechnya sign a peace treaty. Israel hands Hebron back to the Palestinians, the last West Bank city it controlled. Iraq says it will begin shooting down UNSCOM surveillance. Zaire becomes the Democratic Republic of the Congo; President Mobutu flees. Hong Kong reverts to Chinese rule. Deng Xiaoping, the last of the People's Republic of China's major revolutionaries, dies. Hun Sen of the Cambodian People's Party overthrows Norodom Ranariddh in a coup. British scientists clone an adult sheep; they name her Dolly. The comet Hale-Bopp makes its closest approach to Earth, inspiring 39 Heaven's Gate cult members to commit suicide. J.K. Rowling publishes the first of her Harry Potter books, launching a publishing phenomenon. Che Guevara's remains are returned to Cuba for burial. Designer Gianni Versace is shot to death in Florida. Mother Theresa dies. Hong Kong kills all chickens in an attempt to stop the spread of a deadly influenza strain. Viagra becomes the fastest-selling drug of all time in the United States. Tiger Woods becomes the youngest person to win the Masters golf tournament.

1998 The Belfast Agreement is signed between the British and Irish governments and most Northern Irish political parties; the Omagh bombing in Northern Ireland kills 29. NATO launches air strikes against Yugoslavia; President Milošović is ordered to withdraw troops from Kosovo. Iraq stops UN weapons inspectors from conducting searches; Kofi Annan, UN secretary-general brokers a deal that prevents war. India and Pakistan begin testing nuclear weapons. Impeachment proceedings begin against US president Bill Clinton for the Monica Lewinsky affair. Hugo Chavez becomes Venezuelan president. In South Africa, the Truth and Reconciliation Commission condemns both sides for committing atrocities. An economic crisis strikes South East Asia. President Suharto resigns after 32 years as president of Indonesia. The ocean-atmospheric phenomenon, El Niño, is blamed for droughts and scorching temperatures. Hosts France win the World Cup. Former Chilean president, General Augusto Pinochet, is placed under house arrest during medical treatment in the UK. The European Court of Human Rights is instituted in Strasbourg. Construction of the International Space Station begins. Singer Frank Sinatra, dies of a heart attack, aged 82.

1999 The first meetings take place of the Scottish and Welsh parliaments. The Euro currency is introduced. War breaks out between Yugoslavia and NATO until June. Hungary, Poland and the Czech Republic join NATO. Russia invades Chechnya. Mohammed VI becomes king of

Morocco. King Hussein of Jordan dies; his son Abdullah II ascends the throne. Ehud Barak becomes prime minister of Israel. Military rule ends in Nigeria. General Pervez Musharraf seizes power in Pakistan in a bloodless military coup. The impeachment of US President Clinton fails. The Panama Canal comes under Panamanian control. Australia votes to keep the Queen as head of state. Portugal hands Macau over to China. East Timor votes for independence from Indonesia. MySpace. com is launched. The Columbine massacre takes place in Colorado. BBC presenter Jill Dando is shot dead. A total solar eclipse is viewed in Europe and Asia. An earthquake kills 17,000 in Turkey. The world worries unduly about Y2K date-handling problems on computers as the millennium approaches.

2000   As the world celebrates the millennium, its population has risen to six billion. There are fuel protests in Britain. Vladimir Putin is elected president of Russia. Yugoslav president Slobodan Milošović is forced from office. In Croatia, Stjepan Mesic is elected president. After years of killing and terror, the Islamic Salvation Front disbands in Algeria. Terrorist organization al-Qaeda holds a summit. Bashar al-Assad becomes Syria's leader in a national referendum. India and Pakistan come close to war after the Indian parliament is attacked by terrorists. In Aden the USS *Cole* is damaged by suicide bombers, killing 17. Around this time, AIDS becomes an epidemic in Africa; in some countries, almost 40 per cent of the population is HIV-positive. George W Bush becomes president of the United States in the closest election ever; the result is delayed for a month because of disputed votes. Vincente Fox becomes Mexican president, the first president from a party other than the PRI since 1929. Alberto Fujimori is sacked as president of Peru. Yoshiro Mori becomes prime minister of Japan. The 'dotcom boom' goes bust and many businesses go under. British doctor Harold Shipman is sentenced to life in prison, suspected of having killed 365 people. Hans Blix becomes president of the United Nations Monitoring, Verification and Inspection Commission (UNMOVIC). The Olympics are held in Sydney. A Concorde supersonic jet crashes in Paris, killing all 100 passengers.

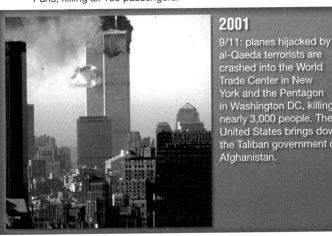

2001
9/11: planes hijacked by al-Qaeda terrorists are crashed into the World Trade Center in New York and the Pentagon in Washington DC, killing nearly 3,000 people. The United States brings down the Taliban government of Afghanistan.

2001   In Britain, Tony Blair's Labour Party win the general election. Foot and Mouth breaks out in Britain. Media magnate Silvio Berlusconi becomes prime minister of Italy for the second time. Slobodan Milošović surrenders to be tried for war crimes. Ariel Sharon is elected prime minister of Israel; violence with Palestinians worsens. Britain and the United States make bombing raids on the Iraqi defence network. Pervez

Musharraf becomes president of Pakistan. In Gujurat in India, more than 20,000 die in an earthquake. Junichiro Koizumi becomes prime minister of Japan. Gloria Macapagal-Arroyo becomes president of the Philippines. John Howard is re-elected prime minister in Australia. Apple releases the iPod. Enron files for bankruptcy. India becomes the second country, after China, to have one billion inhabitants.

2002   The European Union launches the Euro, the new currency of many of its member states. Jacqes Chirac retains the French presidency. Switzerland joins the United Nations. The trial of former Yugoslav President Slobodan Milošović opens in The Hague. Israel invades the Gaza Strip and West Bank; it builds a huge wall around its West Bank settlements. India and Pakistan continue their dispute over Kashmir and nuclear war is threatened. A ceasefire begins in Sri Lanka. 400,000 people are displaced by the eruption of Mount Nyiragongo in the Democratic Republic of the Congo. The United States Congress authorizes the president to use the United States Armed Forces as he deems necessary and appropriate, against Iraq. The United Nations Security Council approves Resolution 1441, forcing Saddam Hussein to disarm or face 'serious consequences'; Iraq agrees to its terms. North Korea admits to have been pursuing nuclear capability. Terrorists blow up two nightclubs in Bali, killing 202. East Timor becomes independent. The Millau Viaduct, the world's tallest bridge, is opened. The huge Larsen Ice Shelf in Antarctica begins to disintegrate. Queen Elizabeth the Queen Mother dies aged 101. Brazil win the World Cup in South Korea and Japan. Floods cause widespread damage in central Europe.

2003

A coalition led by the United States invades Iraq; Saddam Hussein is captured and his sons are killed, but the weapons of mass destruction thought to be there are not found.

2003   The Georgian Rose Revolution succeeds; Eduard Shevadnardze resigns. Israel bombs Syria. A UN peacekeeping force is sent to Liberia. Ethnic and religious turmoil erupts in Sudan's Darfur region. The Human Genome Project, identifying and mapping all the genes in human DNA, is completed. The *Columbia* space shuttle blows up, killing all seven of its crew. Hu Jintao becomes president of China. China launches its first manned space mission. The SARS virus spreads from China; Doctor Carlo Urbani, who first identified it, dies of the disease. The CIA leak scandal begins in the United States when agent Valerie Plame's name is released in the *Washington Post*. David Kelly, former UN weapons inspector, commits suicide; his death leads to the Hutton enquiry. There is a heatwave in Europe; 475 people die in Paris. Actor Arnold Schwarzenegger becomes governor of California. China launches its first manned space mission. Concorde makes its last commercial flight. Michael Jackson is arrested for child molestation. England win the Rugby World Cup. Libyan Al Ali Mohmed Al Megrahi, is convicted of bombing Pan Am Flight 103 over Lockerbie in Scotland in 1988. More than 40,000 die in an earthquake in Bam in the south-east of Iran.

2004 The Treaty and Final Act establishing the first European Constitution is signed in Rome. Explosions on rush-hour trains in Madrid kill 190 people. Vladimir Putin is re-elected Russian president. The Ukrainian election result is annulled; a new election is held and won by opposition candidate, Viktor Yuschenko. Chechnyan rebels seize a school in Russia; more than 300 adults and children are killed. It emerges that POWs in the Abu Ghraib prison in Iraq have been tortured by their US captors. In Iraq, sovereignty is transferred by the US-led coalition to an Interim government. The UN Security Council calls for the removal of all foreign troops from Lebanon. Hamid Karzai is elected president in Afghanistan. George W. Bush is re-elected president in the United States; Condoleeza Rice becomes secretary of state. A rebellion in Haiti replaces Jean-Bertrand Aristide as president. Prince Norodom Sihamoni becomes king of Cambodia. In one of the worst natural disasters in history, a tsunami kills 300,000 in Indonesia and South Asia. Taipei 101 becomes the world's tallest building. Drought and locusts threaten the lives of millions in West Africa's Sahel region. Harold Shipman is found hanged in his cell. The Hutton enquiry exonerates the British government, but criticizes the part played by the BBC in the death of David Kelly. NATO membership is increased with the addition of Bulgaria, Estonia, Latvia, Lithuania, Romania, Slovakia and Slovenia. Former film star and US president, Ronald Reagan dies, aged 93. The Olympic Games take place in Athens. Edvard Munch's *The Scream* is stolen in Oslo. Formula One driver Michael Schumacher,wins a record seventh world championship. The new Scottish parliament building is opened. In Northern Ireland, armed robbers steal over £22 million from the headquarters of the Northern Bank.

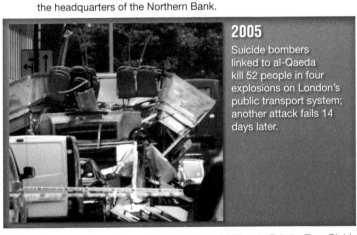

2005
Suicide bombers linked to al-Qaeda kill 52 people in four explosions on London's public transport system; another attack fails 14 days later.

2005 The population of the world is almost 6½ billion. In Britain, Tony Blair's Labour Party is re-elected with a reduced majority. The Provisional IRA formally orders an end to its armed campaign, ongoing since 1969. Widespread rioting breaks out among disaffected youths in Paris; President Chirac declares a state of emergency after 12 days. Dutch and French referendums reject the European Constitution. Christian Democrat Angela Merkel becomes chancellor of Germany. Pope John Paul II dies; four million mourners travel to the Vatican; German Cardinal Joseph Ratzinger becomes Benedict XVI. Prince Rainier III of Monaco dies; Albert II succeeds him. Mahmoud Abbas becomes president of the Palestinian Authority following the death of Yasser Arafat. Rafik Hariri, the prime minister of Lebanon, is killed by a suicide bomber. Syria withdraws the last of its troops from Lebanon after 29 years. Iraq holds its first free elections in more than 50 years; bombings and protests continue; Saddam Hussein's trial begins. King Fahd of Saudi Arabia is succeeded by his half-brother Abdullah. Chad declares war on Sudan. Hurricane Katrina strikes the US Gulf Coast creating one of the worst national disasters in American history. A state of emergency is declared in Ecuador; the president flees. North Korea announces that it possesses nuclear weapons. US cyclist Lance Armstrong wins an unprecedented seventh consecutive Tour de France cycle race. An al-Qaeda-linked organization kills 26 people in explosions on Bali. The Kyoto Protocol on climate change comes into effect without the support of the United States or Australia. In Britain, Prince Charles marries Camilla Parker Bowles. Michael Jackson is acquitted of all child molestation charges. Live 8 concerts in support of Make Poverty History take place across the world; violent demonstrations take place at the G8 conference in Gleneagles in Scotland. England wins the Ashes. 80,000 die in an earthquake in Kashmir; 6,000 die in an earthquake in Java. In Thailand, the army announces the removal of Prime Minister Thaksin Shinawatra from power. North Korea tests a nuclear device. The first human face transplant is carried out in France.

2006

Alexander Litvinenko, a former Russian KGB agent, dies from being poisoned with Polonium-210 in a London sushi bar.

2006 Romano Prodi narrowly defeats Silvio Berlusconi in the Italian general election. ETA declares a permanent ceasefire in its campaign for Basque independence from Spain. Former Yugoslav president Slobodan Milošović is found dead in his cell in The Hague. Montenegro declares independence; Serbia and Montenegro is dissolved. Israeli premier Ariel Sharon suffers a massive stroke; Ehud Olmert takes power. Israel invades Lebanon; Hezbollah declares war against Israel. Hamas wins a majority in elections to the Palestinian Legislative Council. Saddam Hussein is executed in Baghdad; bombings and protests against occupations continue in Iraq. Ethiopia invades Somalia. President Yoweri Museveni wins his second re-election in Uganda, leading to riots in Kampala. US Defence Secretary Donald Rumsfeld, resigns. Fidel Castro temporarily passes power in Cuba to his brother, Raul, prior to surgery. North Korea tests at least seven missiles. South Korean Ban Ki-moon becomes secretary-general of the United Nations. The world prepares for an avian flu epidemic as more human cases occur. Italy wins the World Cup in Germany. American cyclist Floyd Landis win the Tour de France, but fails a drugs test.

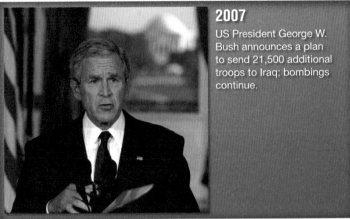

2007
US President George W. Bush announces a plan to send 21,500 additional troops to Iraq; bombings continue.

2007 British prime minister Tony Blair is questioned in the Cash for Honours investigation. Ulster Democratic Unionist leader, Ian Paisley, exchanges a historic handshake with Sinn Féin president, Gerry Adams. Bulgaria and Romania join the European Union. Russian oil supplies to Poland, Germany, and Ukraine are cut as the Russia–Belarus energy dispute escalates; they are restored after three days. Al-Qaeda kills 33 people with two bombs in the Algerian capital, Algiers. Barzan Ibrahim al-Tikriti, former Iraqi intelligence chief and half-brother of Saddam Hussein, and Awad Hamed al-Bandar, former chief judge of the Revolutionary Court, are executed in Iraq. Iran's Revolutionary Guard hold Royal Navy personnel for 12 days after capturing them in disputed Iran–Iraq waters. In Somalia, fighters of the Islamic Courts Union flee to Kenya. North Korea agrees to give up its nuclear programme in exchange for oil. Student Cho Seung-hui shoots 32 dead at Virginia Polytechnic Institute and State University in the United States. Former Russian president Boris Yeltsin dies of heart failure, aged 76. Gordon Brown succeeds Tony Blair as British prime minister.